SUDOKU

Published by

ISBN: 978-1-906068-09-7

CONTENTS

How to Play Sudoku

Sudoku is a game of logic, based on a grid of 9 columns and 9 rows. This is subdivided into nine 3 x 3 squares, which are known as boxes.

A completed Sudoku puzzle comprises this grid completely filled with the numbers 1 - 9 appearing exactly once in each row, column and square, as in the example grid below:

8	7	5	3	1	6	2	9	4
6	2	3	9	7	4	1	5	8
4	1	9	5	8	2	6	7	3
5	8	2	7	3	1	9	4	6
3	9	4	6	2	8	7	1	5
7	6	1	4	5	9	3	8	2
1	3	7	2	4	5	8	6	9
9	5	8	1	6	3	4	2	7
2	4	6	8	9	7	5	3	1

In order to solve a sudoku puzzle, there are various strategies that you can employ. These strategies are given different names in different books, however the techniques remain the same.

Region Elimination

The technique you will find yourself using the most throughout the process of solving a puzzle is called region elimination. First an explanation of what a region is: it is simply an individual row, column or box. In the sudoku puzzles in this book, there are 27 regions: 9 rows, 9 columns and 9 boxes.

Region elimination is the process of checking where each number from 1 - 9 can go in each region, and using this to either reduce the options for each cell or to actively place a number.

In order to see how to apply this technique, we need to remember that each number from 1 - 9 must be placed exactly once in each row, column and box.

Therefore by going through each region and seeing where a number can be placed, we can often make good progress with solving the puzzle.

Let's have a look at a concrete example of this technique to see how we can use it to place numbers in a region:

	7	5	3	1				
						1		8
4			5		2	6		3
			7	3			4	6
		4		2		7		
7	6			5	9			
1		7	2		5			9
9		8						
				9	7	5	3	

Look at the top three rows of this puzzle. We can use the numbers in these three rows to instantly place the '5' in the second row.

Now, we know that '5' must be placed once in the second row, and it is not currently there. We also know that a number can only be placed once in each box. Now, in the first three cells of the row, there is a '5' in the same box, so the '5' cannot go here. The same applies for cells 4,5,6 of this row.

This just leaves the last three cells of the row as possible locations for the '5'.

Now, of these the first contains a '1' and the third contains an '8': therefore this only leaves cell 8 in this row, and thus we place the '5' here. Row 2 now contains these numbers:
\- - - - - - 1 5 8

You will find that you can use this technique often during the course of solving a sudoku puzzle to help you get nearer the solution.

Cell Elimination

Another common and useful technique in sudoku is called cell elimination. Here we don't concentrate on where a number can go within a region, but rather we look at the puzzle on an individual cell by cell basis and work out which numbers can be placed in that cell. As there are 81 cells, this is often a time consuming technique and it is wisest at the start of a puzzle to use region elimination first.

Let's look at this technique in action, and also use it to illustrate another essential element to solving sudoku puzzles:

	7	5	3	1				
						1		8
4			5		2	6		3
			7	3			4	6
		4		2		7		
7	6			5	9			
1		7	2		5			9
9		8						
				9	7	5	3	

This time, look at the third row, and the cell between the '5' and '2' – this is the fifth cell in the row, right in the middle.

Now, we want to know what number is placed here. Well, we can use the rule that a number can only go once in each row, column and box to narrow down the options. So, let's look at the other numbers in the same region, column and box:
In the box: 3, 1, 5, 2
In the row: 4, 5, 2, 6, 3
In the column: 1, 3, 2, 5, 9

Now we simply go through the numbers from 1 – 9 to see what numbers are missing. By going through the list we find that only 7 and 8 are missing. This means that the middle cell of the third row must contain either 7 or 8.

How do we mark this on the grid for future reference? We use a simple method, called pencil marks. This is simply the process of using our pencil to write a small '7' and a small '8' within the cell so as when we come back to examine this cell again later on, we remember that it can only contain one of these two values and saves us repeating our thought processes again later.

Pairs Elimination

Pairs elimination is another technique that can be useful to help you solve a sudoku puzzle. This tells us that if there are two cells within a region that both contain exactly the same two pencilmarks, then we can eliminate those values from other cells in the region.

This is a slightly trickier method to use as it is harder to spot and a little trickier to understand, but you will find it can help you to solve harder puzzles in less time, and sometimes you may have to use this technique to make progress.

To keep it simple, let's just examine one row of a puzzle and see how this can help us solve the puzzle. Imagine we have the following pencilmarks in a particular row of the puzzle half way through the solving process, with a '/' denoting the different pencilmarks left in a cell.

1/2 | 1/2 | 1/2/3 | 456789 | 346789 | 345789 | 45679 | 345678 | 3456789

Perhaps at first glance things don't look too encouraging - most cells have many possible values in them.

However, we can use the new rule - pairs elimination to place exactly the number in the third cell, which has these options: 1/2/3.

Here's why: We know that each number has to be placed once in the region.

Now, the first two cells in the region both have the same pencilmarks: 1/2 and 1/2.

We know that there are therefore two possible options for these cells: the solution is either 1 in the first cell and 2 in the second cell, or 2 in the first cell and 1 in the second cell.

The crucial point is this:

Whatever the actual solution, the first two cells of this region must contain the '1' and the '2'.

Knowing this, we can now go through all the other cells in the region and eliminate '1' and '2' wherever they occur. We see that the third cell in the region contains both '1' and '2', so we take these out. This enables us to place precisely the number in this cell: it must be '3', and we update our puzzle accordingly.

This rule can be extrapolated for three cells in a region that each contain the same three numbers, four cells that contain the same four numbers and so on.

By using these three rules you will be able to have a methodical and sensible approach to solving sudoku puzzles, and need not tear your hair out anymore!

There are many other rules that you can also use when solving sudoku puzzles,some of them separate to those above and others hybrids.

Part of the fun and charm of sudoku is discovering some of the more obscure rules for yourself - or if you are impatient or curious, searching on the internet and finding about weird sounding patterns like swordfish and X-wings!

Good luck, and remember - with patience, and the correct application of solving techniques, you will be able to tackle even the toughest sudoku puzzle.

PUZZLES

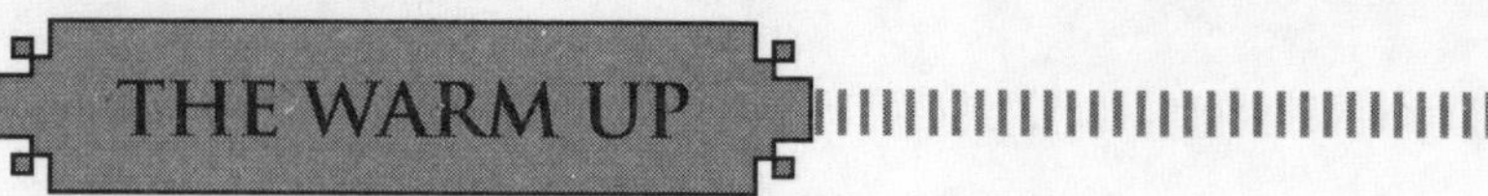

Puzzle 1

START TIME

2		7	9			3		6
	6	8		7	2	5		4
9	1			5				
		2				6		1
1		3		6		2		5
6		5				4		
	3			1			4	7
7		9	4	3		1	6	
4		1			6	9		3

FINISH TIME

DIFFICULTY

Puzzle 2

START TIME

5	6				2		3	7
4		7				9	8	
	2		9		4	5	6	1
3	4		2		8			
			1	9	6			
			7		3		5	8
	8	6	4		9		1	
	3	4				8		6
9	7		6				2	4

FINISH TIME

DIFFICULTY

Puzzle 3

START TIME

	3	4				2	8	
9	2		3		1		5	
1			5	8	2			
6		5	7	2			9	
		3		6		5		
	8			5	4	1		3
			4	1	6			7
	4		8		5		1	9
	6	1		3		8	4	

FINISH TIME

DIFFICULTY

Puzzle 4

START TIME

5					2	3	7	9
	7		5	6	4	8	2	1
	2		7			4		
	5				8			
1	8						4	2
			4	5			3	
		5			7		6	
4	3	2	6	1	9		8	
7	6	8	2				9	4

FINISH TIME

DIFFICULTY

Puzzle 5

START TIME

			4		8		6	2
			3	2	7	5	1	
			1	5		4		
	4	8		6			2	1
5	2	9				6	7	4
7	1			4		3	5	
		5		8	4	1		
	3	1	6	7	9			
4	8				3			

FINISH TIME

DIFFICULTY

Puzzle 6

START TIME

6		5						4
	8			6	5			
	3	4	2		8	1	6	
8		3	6			5		
	5	6	7	8	1	4	3	
		2			9	8	7	6
	4	7	8		2	6	1	
			9	7			4	
2						3		7

FINISH TIME

DIFFICULTY

Puzzle 7

START TIME

	3		2	8			7	
		4	3		5	8	2	
8	2		7				9	5
6		9		4		1	3	2
				5				
1	8	7				4		9
3	9				2		8	7
	1	8	9		6	2		
	7			3	8		1	

FINISH TIME

DIFFICULTY

Puzzle 8

START TIME

9	4	7			3			5
	6	2		9		1		
3	1		7				9	4
7	9			3		4		8
			9	4	6			
1				8			5	6
4	7				9		8	2
		1		2		7	3	
6			3			5	4	1

FINISH TIME

DIFFICULTY

Puzzle 9

START TIME

1	8	6				7		
4		9		7	5	3	1	6
3				1		2	9	
			6			4	7	
		3		8		5		
5	4	2			7			
	3	5		6				4
8	6	4	2	3		1		7
		1				6	3	2

FINISH TIME

DIFFICULTY

Puzzle 10

		2	9				5	7
			5					
3				2	7			
1	3	8	7	9	4	5	6	
	2	7	3	8	6	4	9	
	4	9	1	5	2	3	7	8
			8	3				5
					5			9
9	8				1	2		

Puzzle 11

START TIME

	4		3					7
		6			7	5		3
2		3	8	5	1	4		
			4		3		2	1
4	1			7			5	9
3	6		9		5			
		4	7	2	6	9		5
6		5	1			8		2
7					8		6	

FINISH TIME

DIFFICULTY

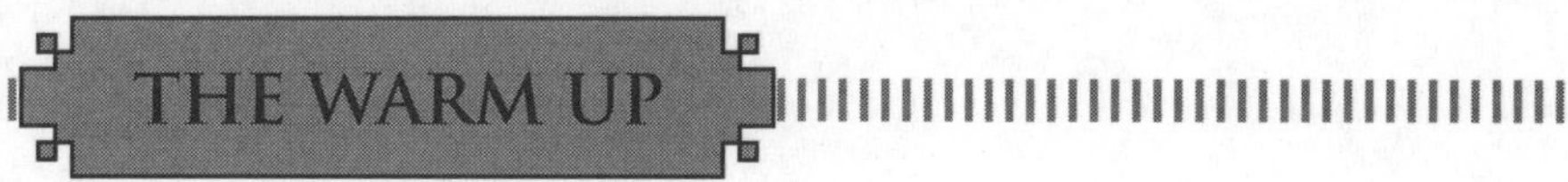

Puzzle 12

START TIME

	8				2	1		9
					9	7		6
3			1	6	7	5	8	
	9			2		6	5	7
	2	4	6		1	3	9	
8	6	5		9			1	
	7	6	9	3	5			
5			8					
9		8	2				7	

FINISH TIME

DIFFICULTY

Puzzle 13

START TIME

			1	8	5	9		
7	5			3	9		8	1
	8					3		
5			3				7	
1	4	8	9	2	7	5	6	3
	2				6			9
		5		9			3	
2	1		5	7			9	6
		4	6	1	3			

FINISH TIME

DIFFICULTY

Puzzle 14

START TIME

		8	1	4	9		5	
	4		5				8	7
	5	2			6	3		
		1				4	3	
5	2			9			6	1
	6	9				7		
2		7	6			9	1	
8	1				2		4	
	9		8	3	1	5		

FINISH TIME

DIFFICULTY

Puzzle 15

START TIME

					6	9	7	3
		3		8	7		1	4
1			3		5		2	
	6			2			5	1
	4			5			8	
9	3			6			4	
	1		6		2			8
4	8		5	3		2		
3	7	2	8				6	

FINISH TIME

DIFFICULTY

Puzzle 16

START TIME

8		2		9				3
	7		3	6			1	2
	3		5					8
	6	4	8			3	2	
3	5			1			4	9
		1			9	6	7	
7					4		5	
6	2			7	3		8	
4				2		9		7

FINISH TIME

DIFFICULTY

Puzzle 17

START TIME

9	1		5	3			8	
5			9	7		1	4	
4			6	2	1			5
7		6			2	3		
				5				
		4	1			2		7
3			2	6	5			4
		5		4	9			6
	4			1	3		2	9

FINISH TIME

DIFFICULTY

Puzzle 18

START TIME

		8	6					
2	6		3	1	5	9		
3				8			6	1
	9	5		4				7
	8	2		5		4	3	
7				9	1	6	2	
4	2			6				3
		9	1	3	2		4	6
					8	1		

FINISH TIME

DIFFICULTY

Puzzle 19

START TIME

5		3	8		4	7	9	
						2	8	
8	9				7	3		4
				3				5
2		5	1	8	9	4		7
9			4	2				
3		2	5				7	8
	8	1						
	5	9	3		8	1		2

FINISH TIME

DIFFICULTY

Puzzle 20

START TIME

			1		3	9		4
4					6	8		
	1	6	7		9		3	
	6	8		2		1	9	
1	7						2	6
	4			1		3	7	
6	8		9		4	2	5	
		9	8					1
2		4	5		1			

FINISH TIME

DIFFICULTY

Puzzle 21

START TIME

			7		5	2	4	8
				9	8	7	3	
5					3	1	6	9
		4	3			8	5	2
		5				3		
3	8	9			2	6		
	9	7	2					
	5	3	1	8				
6	1	2	9		4			

FINISH TIME

DIFFICULTY

Puzzle 22

START TIME

2	5		6	9	3		4	
	4					6	7	
6		1			4		9	5
5	8					1		
	1			8			6	
		6					8	4
9	7		5			4		6
	6	5				3	1	
	2		9	4	6		5	8

FINISH TIME

DIFFICULTY

Puzzle 23

START TIME

			5	9				2
5	1		6	8	3	7		
9					2	6		
6	2	7		4				8
1	3		2		8			9
4				6		2	3	7
			4					5
		4	9	5	1		2	6
3				2	7			

FINISH TIME

DIFFICULTY

Puzzle 24

START TIME

	5				1	3		
1			7	3			9	
	3	7	5	2				
	8		9	7		2	4	
2	1	4				9	7	3
	9	3		1	2		6	
		9		5	7	6	1	
				4	6			9
		2	1				5	

FINISH TIME

DIFFICULTY

Puzzle 25

START TIME

			4		5	2		
		1		2	9			6
2	4	9		6		5	1	
		4		5	2		3	
8				4		9		5
	2		1	9		6		
	7	2		3		1	9	8
6			2	7		3		
		3	9		4			

FINISH TIME

DIFFICULTY

Puzzle 26

START TIME

	8	2		3	9			1
7	3	6	1	4			8	
	1		6			4		
5		9						
		1	7	5	4	8		
						3		7
		4	9		5		2	
	5			8	7	1	6	9
1			3	2		5	4	

FINISH TIME

DIFFICULTY

Puzzle 27

START TIME

		1	5				4	6
8			1			5		
6	5	3	4				8	9
	3			8	7			
2		9				7		1
7			9	1			5	
3	1				6	4	2	5
		7			4			8
	9				1	3		

FINISH TIME

DIFFICULTY

Puzzle 28

START TIME

	3	2	7		4			9
	8							4
7	5		8		9		2	
2	6	3		4		1		
4								7
		7		1		2	4	3
	4		5	8	3		7	2
3							1	
5			2			4	3	

FINISH TIME

DIFFICULTY

Puzzle 29

		4				3	2	7
7			6	5			8	
			4	7	3	9		5
		7		6				9
	4	9	8		7	5	3	
5				9		7		
9		1	2	8				
	3			4	1			8
	8	6				2		

Puzzle 30

START TIME

7				8	9		6	4
8	6		2					
	1		7	4		8		
3	4	6				1		
	7		3	1	4		2	
		1				7	4	3
		3		2	7		9	
					1		5	8
	8		6	3				1

FINISH TIME

DIFFICULTY

Puzzle 31

			5	8	1			
	2			3				5
	1				7		9	3
3	8			2	9		1	6
4	6			5			3	2
	5		3	1			7	8
2	7		6				8	
8				7			4	
			8	9	3			

Puzzle 32

START TIME

3	1		5			6		8
				9		2		5
	7	2	8	6	1		3	4
								7
9			6	2	4			1
4	9		2	8	7	5	6	
2		5		1				
7		8			5		4	2

FINISH TIME

DIFFICULTY

Puzzle 33

START TIME

9	6		1	3				8
	8		4				9	2
		4			9			
			9		3		8	
4	9	1		6		2	5	3
	3		5		4			
6			3			4		
2	5				7		1	
1				5	2		6	7

FINISH TIME

DIFFICULTY

Puzzle 34

	1			3		4		8
8						3	7	9
9	4							
2	9	5	8					
3	7		6	9	5		4	2
					3	9	5	1
							8	4
1	2	8			4			6
7		4		2			1	

Puzzle 35

START TIME

	5	9	8			4		2
7					3	5		
		8	6	5				
6		2	3	7			5	
8				2				7
	9			8	4	2		6
				4	8	6		
	8	5	7					9
4		1			5	7	2	

FINISH TIME

DIFFICULTY

Puzzle 36

START TIME

3	9	7	5	2		8		1
	2				3			
		4	7			3		
	3		4	5	8			2
				1				
7			3	6	2		8	
		9			1	4		3
			6				9	
6		3		9	4	1	5	7

FINISH TIME

DIFFICULTY

Puzzle 37

START TIME

		2			3			6
	6			2	7			1
			8	6	4		7	9
5		4					2	
3		6		5		4		7
	9					6		5
9	5		6	1	2			
4			3	8	5		6	
6			7			1		

FINISH TIME

DIFFICULTY

Puzzle 38

START TIME

9	5			4			6	
8		3	1	6		5		
4		6		8	5			
2	3					9		
1		9		2		4		6
		4					1	5
			7			6		1
		1		3	4	7		9
	9			5			4	3

FINISH TIME

DIFFICULTY

Puzzle 39

START TIME

6	7	1	2		4		5	
		8	9			1		
5	3	9			6			
8				5		6	9	2
2	4	5		9				8
			1			2	6	3
					3	9		
			7		9	5	8	1

FINISH TIME

DIFFICULTY

Puzzle 40

START TIME

4					2		6	
		7	4					1
	9			3	5			
3	5	8		4				
7		6	9	5	3	1		2
				6		4	3	5
			3	1			2	7
5					6	3		
	2		5					8

FINISH TIME

DIFFICULTY

Puzzle 41

START TIME

				4		6		5
5		8	7				1	2
				3	5	8	9	
				5			8	6
		2		1		5		
3	6			7				
	3	4	6	2				
2	9				3	1		7
8		7		9				3

FINISH TIME

DIFFICULTY

Puzzle 42

7	4			1				6
				6	3	4		1
	5			9		7	2	
5					6			
	7		5	2	1		9	
			9					2
	2	8		4			1	
4		7	1	5				9
1				3			4	7

Puzzle 43

START TIME

	7	9				5		4
2	4	8			9		6	
		5			7	1		
	1	6		4	2		3	
			9		8			
	9		3	6		7	5	
		3				2		
			2			8	9	5
9		1				6	4	

FINISH TIME

DIFFICULTY

Puzzle 44

START TIME

7					3		1	
6			7	2		3		5
	5	8	1	4	6	2		
			9					
	1		4	7	8		6	
					5			
		9	2	3	1	4	5	
4		5		8	7			1
	3							7

FINISH TIME

DIFFICULTY

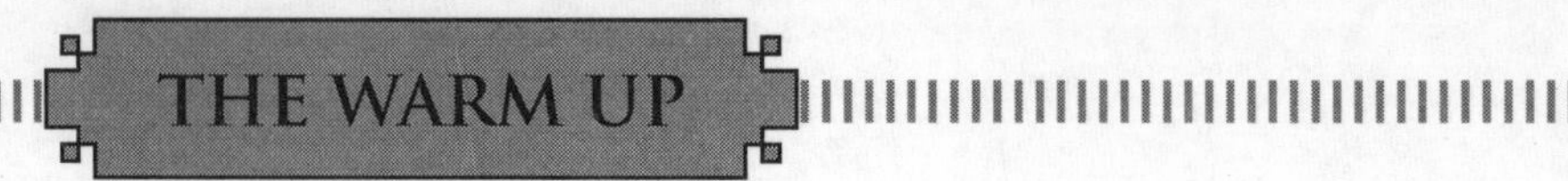

Puzzle 45

	8	3		2	7	9	1	
	2		9				8	7
	6			7	5			
4		9	3		6	8		2
			8	9			6	
6	4	5			1	2	9	
	3	2	4	6		5	7	

Puzzle 46

START TIME

6		2					5	
	3		2		6			8
1		4		5	3	6		
			3		5		7	
			6	1	7			
	4		8		2			
		1	7	3		4		6
8			4		1		3	
	6					7	1	9

FINISH TIME

DIFFICULTY

Puzzle 47

START TIME

		7	4				8	
5			6	1	8	3		
	3	6		5				1
	1		7	8		5		
				6				
		8		9	2		6	4
4				7		9	3	
		2	8	3	1			6
	6				9	8		

FINISH TIME

DIFFICULTY

Puzzle 48

START TIME

			4	9				1
						7		
	9	2			5	6		8
9				5		8	7	2
8	7			4			3	5
2	5	1		8				4
3		7	5			4	1	6
		9						
4				3	7			

FINISH TIME

DIFFICULTY

Puzzle 49

1	6	5	8			9	4	
	7					6		
9	4				7			2
7				1			6	8
			4	9	8			
3	2			6				9
5			3				7	6
		6					9	
		7			6	3	5	1

Puzzle 50

START TIME

8	6	4		5		3		
	9	1			3	4		8
2					4		1	
		5	9		1			
7	1						5	3
			5		7	1		
	5		3					
4		9	7				3	
		3		8		6	9	2

FINISH TIME

DIFFICULTY

PUZZLES

Puzzle 1

START TIME

4			8	9		1		
		7		4			3	2
					6	9		
7	8							
5	1	3		2		6	8	9
		6					2	5
		8	4					
2	7			8		3		
		9		1	7			8

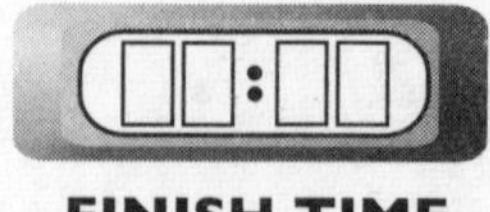
FINISH TIME

DIFFICULTY

Puzzle 2

4				2			9	
8	6		9			3	1	
3			8		1			
1	2		6	7				
				3				
				8	9		4	7
	8		2		6			3
	1	3			8		2	4
	9			1				8

DIFFICULTY

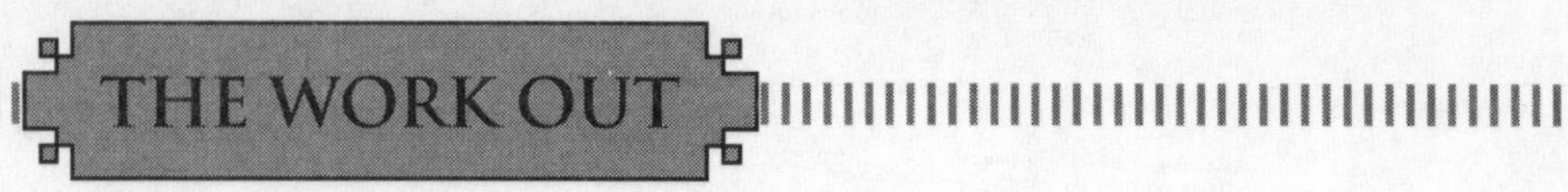

Puzzle 3

START TIME

	6	2	1		5	9		4
		3	6				5	
					3			1
7		6	3					
	5			6			1	
					2	6		7
3			5					
4	8				6	2		
6		5	4		1	3	8	

FINISH TIME

DIFFICULTY

Puzzle 4

START TIME

		9				7	5	8
2			1					4
				4	8	2		1
	2			3	9			
	7	1		8		4	9	
				6			7	
9		6	8	5				
4					7			5
8	5	7				3		

FINISH TIME

DIFFICULTY

Puzzle 5

START TIME

5			6		9			8
2		6						7
	9	1	2			5		
8		5				2	9	
	2			8			1	
	3	4				7		5
		7			3	8	5	
						3		9
3			5		7			2

FINISH TIME

DIFFICULTY

Puzzle 6

START TIME

9		8			1			6
5				3	9	8		4
						9	3	
		2	7		5			3
7				4				2
1			2		3	7		
	5	9						
4		7	9	2				
3			5			2		7

FINISH TIME

DIFFICULTY

Puzzle 7

START TIME

		2				8		
		3		2		1	9	5
	1			5	9			6
	5			1				3
2	3						1	9
9					4		5	
8			7	3			6	
3	6	4		9		2		
		5				9		

FINISH TIME

DIFFICULTY

Puzzle 8

		1			9			7
4	2				1	8		3
9		3		2				
2	7			6				1
		5				4		
8							2	6
				8		9		5
1		2	7		5		3	8
7			3			1		

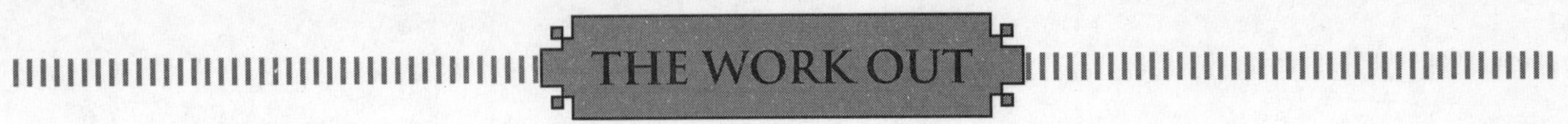

Puzzle 9

START TIME

		8	6	1	5	2		
		1		2				5
				3		9	8	
8					6	3	1	4
				7				
4	2	6	3					7
	8	4		6				
2				4		8		
			7	9	8	4		

FINISH TIME

DIFFICULTY

Puzzle 10

START TIME

	5	4	6		8		3	
9	8		3					
3								
	4	5			3	6		7
	6			7			4	
1		3	9			5	8	
								8
	3				6		2	4
	2		4		9	3	1	

FINISH TIME

DIFFICULTY

Puzzle 11

START TIME

	4	5					8	7
7	9			3	4			5
	1							4
		6		5			3	
			2		6			
	7			4		8		
2							4	
9			3	1			5	8
3	8					9	2	

FINISH TIME

DIFFICULTY

Puzzle 12

START TIME

	9							7
7			2	3			4	9
				9		5	6	
		1			6	4		8
		4		5		7		
9		5				2		
	2	9		1				
8	5			6	9			1
4							7	

FINISH TIME

DIFFICULTY

Puzzle 13

START TIME

		9	3	4	7	8		
3			2	5				
	4			1		7		
7		1	5			6		
		8				4		
		4			2	3		9
		5		8			4	
					9			8
		7		3	5	2		

FINISH TIME

DIFFICULTY

Puzzle 14

START TIME

	5		3			4		1
6	7	1		4	8			
		4	7					
2		6			3			
		7				1		
			1			5		7
					2	8		6
			6	3		7	4	5
1					7		9	

FINISH TIME

DIFFICULTY

Puzzle 15

4		7			6		5	2
						1		
	1		4		9		7	6
				9	2			5
	7						6	8
2			8					
6	5		2		1		8	
		2						
7	8		3			5		9

Puzzle 16

START TIME

			2				7	9
	3	5	9		7		1	
						8	2	
	9				3			7
	8	1				4	5	
7			4				8	
	5	7						
	2		5		1		3	
4	1			7	2			

FINISH TIME

DIFFICULTY

Puzzle 17

START TIME

		4		9			5	
		5						4
8					1	6		2
	9		7		8	4		3
			1	3	5			
7		3			9		1	
3		9	6					5
1						7		
	6			5		2		

FINISH TIME

DIFFICULTY

Puzzle 18

			8	7	4		9	
9					2	5		
	7					8		
7			5				6	1
		9		8	1	2		
1	2				6			9
		3					7	
		1	4					2
	5		9	1	3			

Puzzle 19

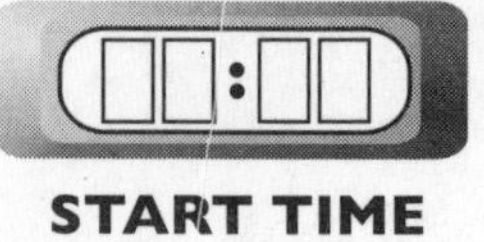
START TIME

						1		5
					8		6	
	1	6	7			2		
		2	3		6	7	8	
6			9	7	2			1
		7	4		1	9		
		4			9	3	1	
	7		8					
5		9						

FINISH TIME

DIFFICULTY

Puzzle 20

		6				1		
	5		1	9	7	6		
	4			5				2
	7		9					
6	1	2		7		3	4	9
					1		2	
9				2			8	
		4	7	1	6		9	
		3						

Puzzle 21

START TIME

1		2			8			7
	4			2	3		1	
		3			7	8		4
9	5	1						
	7						4	
						1	6	5
8		5	7			6		
	1		8	3			7	
4			1			3		8

FINISH TIME

DIFFICULTY

Puzzle 22

8						2		9
			5	2	7			
4		2			8	5		
	6	1	2		9		7	
	4						9	
	8		7		4	3	1	
		5	8			7		3
			6	5	2			
1		8						6

Puzzle 23

START TIME

9	5	4			7			
		8	4		2	5		
	7		5	1			9	8
		9		5				
	4						3	
				7		1		
1	8			6	5		7	
		5	7		1	3		
			9			6	5	1

FINISH TIME

DIFFICULTY

Puzzle 24

START TIME

6		8		7			9	2
5					2	4		
	2		9					8
	3			5		8		
8			4		7			3
		6		2			5	
1					5		4	
		4	2					5
2	9			8		6		7

FINISH TIME

DIFFICULTY

Puzzle 25

START TIME

5	3			7		2		
				6	3	4	7	
				9	5			1
	9		7				5	
	4	2				1	8	
	8				6		2	
9			6	1				
	5	6	9	2				
		4		3			9	2

FINISH TIME

DIFFICULTY

Puzzle 26

START TIME

7	4				5			8
5		9						2
						3	4	5
			1	9	7	5		
	5			4			9	
		2	5	8	3			
4	7	1						
2						1		7
8			6				5	4

FINISH TIME

DIFFICULTY

Puzzle 27

START TIME

	3		8			4		
	9		3		7		8	
	8	5						1
		7			4	8	5	
		3	1		2	7		
	2	9	5			1		
9						5	4	
	5		7		3		1	
		4			5		7	

FINISH TIME

DIFFICULTY

Puzzle 28

START TIME

	6		1	4	9			
	4					9	1	2
	1				7			
4		2		5				6
5			4		8			1
1				9		4		3
			9				4	
8	5	1					6	
			3	1	6		2	

FINISH TIME

DIFFICULTY

Puzzle 29

START TIME

4			8					5
	9			7		4	8	
	8			6	5			
		3	7		8			4
	7	6				2	9	
9			3		6	7		
			9	3			4	
	4	1		8			3	
5					1			2

FINISH TIME

DIFFICULTY

Puzzle 30

START TIME

2		4		5				7
	7	6		9			2	
			4				5	6
			5		9	4		
9	3						7	5
		1	7		2			
3	2				6			
	4			7		6	3	
6				4		7		9

FINISH TIME

DIFFICULTY

Puzzle 31

	9			6			4	7
	8	3			5			
	6				4			8
					7	1	2	
9		5	6		1	7		4
	3	1	4					
6			7				1	
			5			9	7	
3	7			2			8	

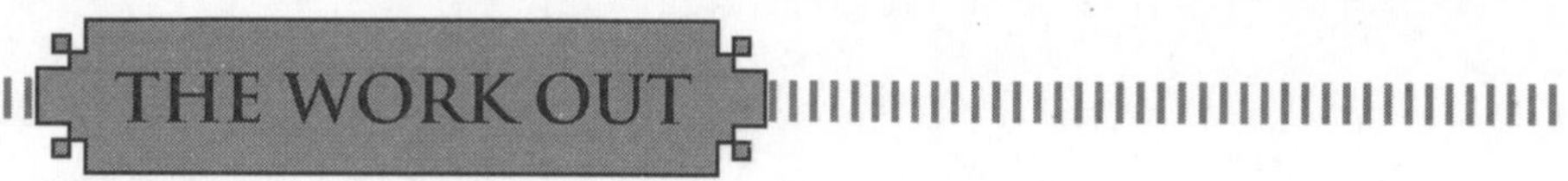

Puzzle 32

START TIME

2			8				5	7
7		8		5	1			
		6				4	9	
	2			9				5
	6		4		5		8	
3				2			4	
	3	1				5		
			5	1		8		4
8	5				4			9

FINISH TIME

DIFFICULTY

Puzzle 33

1	2				9		3	4
3						9		5
	9		6	1				
2			8		4	1		
		7				2		
		4	3		7			9
				8	5		2	
8		2						7
7	5		4				6	8

Puzzle 34

START TIME

5			7					
				9			6	5
	8	4		3			1	
		5	1	7		8		
6		7	5		4	9		1
		8		2	9	5		
	1			5		6	8	
4	3			6				
					1			3

FINISH TIME

DIFFICULTY

Puzzle 35

START TIME

				3	5			8
8	7				4		5	
5	9					7		4
1					8	5		
	6		1		9		8	
		9	4					2
4		7					2	9
	5		9				7	1
9			8	1				

FINISH TIME

DIFFICULTY

Puzzle 36

START TIME

5		6		7	3		2	9
			1				5	4
		4	5		2			7
	4		9					1
2					6		8	
4			7		8	3		
9	8				1			
1	2		6	5		9		8

FINISH TIME

DIFFICULTY

Puzzle 37

START TIME

				4	8			
		9		7		3		
	4	5	3			2	8	
9			4		6	5		
1	5						6	4
		4	1		3			2
	2	1			7	6	5	
		8		3		4		
			5	1				

FINISH TIME

DIFFICULTY

Puzzle 38

START TIME

6				8	3		7	
		1	6					3
		3		4			8	1
7			4	9				
4		8				1		9
				5	6			2
2	8			1		9		
1					7	8		
	4		5	2				6

FINISH TIME

DIFFICULTY

Puzzle 39

START TIME

		8	9				5	2
			1	7				
9	4	6				7		
2			8					5
	8	5	2		1	6	9	
6					9			1
		7				1	6	9
				9	7			
4	6				5	8		

FINISH TIME

DIFFICULTY

Puzzle 40

START TIME

		7		9				2
3	6	2						
9			3		4	5		
			8					3
4	8	6	7		2	9	1	5
1					5			
		4	9		1			6
						4	8	9
8				6		3		

FINISH TIME

DIFFICULTY

PUZZLES

Puzzle 1

		5		9	8	3		
4					3			
					1			8
	4			5	2	7		
7	5						1	2
		8	9	4			6	
1			6					
			7					4
		3	8	1		9		

Puzzle 2

START TIME

		9						3
			7	8			1	
	5	7			1			8
	1		6					4
		6	8	9	3	2		
3					4		6	
2			1			3	4	
	3			7	5			
5						7		

FINISH TIME

DIFFICULTY

Puzzle 3

START TIME

8		7			2			3
	5			1			9	
				5	4			7
2		3						
	9	1				5	2	
						3		1
5			8	3				
	4			9			3	
1			5			8		9

FINISH TIME

DIFFICULTY

Puzzle 4

START TIME

3	9	5			7			
					2		1	
	1				8	6		3
4	5				6			
		2	1		4	3		
			3				7	5
7		8	4				5	
	6		2					
			8			1	6	4

FINISH TIME

DIFFICULTY

Puzzle 5

START TIME

	2		4	3				
	1				5		4	7
		5	1			6		
	6					5		3
8								1
5		3					6	
		2			9	7		
3	9		5				2	
				8	4		3	

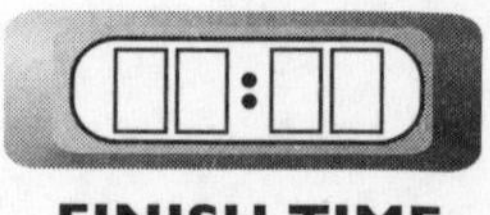
FINISH TIME

DIFFICULTY

Puzzle 6

START TIME

4		5						
	8			9		4	7	
2					7			8
			6	8			5	
	1		4		2		8	
	5			3	1			
6			9					5
	2	8		1			9	
						3		7

FINISH TIME

DIFFICULTY

Puzzle 7

START TIME

9			8				6	2
1			2	7		3		
	6		1					
						7	9	5
	7						3	
8	1	3						
					2		1	
		1		9	3			8
6	4				8			3

FINISH TIME

DIFFICULTY

Puzzle 8

START TIME

			6	9				
5		1		3			6	
9						3	1	
		7	8					6
1		8				9		7
3					7	1		
	8	4						1
	1			5		7		8
				8	2			

FINISH TIME

DIFFICULTY

Puzzle 9

START TIME

	7				2	6		
		6				3	1	
	1		6		3			2
				1			7	3
4		7				1		5
1	3			4				
2			8		5		6	
	8	5				2		
		1	7				9	

FINISH TIME

DIFFICULTY

Puzzle 10

START TIME

1	2							
8			6			1		4
		3	8		9	7		
4	3							
		7	4		1	9		
							3	6
		2	9		4	6		
9		6			2			1
							7	9

FINISH TIME

DIFFICULTY

Puzzle 11

START TIME

		8		4			9	
		2	6					4
		5		7	8			6
4	7				2			
		3				4		
			4				6	7
3			9	5		6		
1					3	2		
	9			2		5		

FINISH TIME

DIFFICULTY

Puzzle 12

START TIME

	4		5		2		9	
5			4					3
		2			6	4		
4		8					6	7
7	2					1		4
		1	3			9		
3					4			2
	9		7		1		8	

FINISH TIME

DIFFICULTY

Puzzle 13

START TIME

5			2				4	
					4		8	7
		8			3			2
4				3		5	9	
3								1
	6	5		4				3
8			6			2		
6	7		4					
	1				9			8

FINISH TIME

DIFFICULTY

Puzzle 14

START TIME

				3		8	2	
5					7	6		
2	6			1				
	9		7		2			
6		2				4		3
			3		1		9	
				9			7	8
		6	2					9
	1	9		5				

FINISH TIME

DIFFICULTY

Puzzle 15

START TIME

			9	5				
8				2			6	4
3	5	4						
4			8				7	
5	3			4			8	1
	8				3			5
						8	4	9
9	2			8				3
				3	9			

FINISH TIME

DIFFICULTY

Puzzle 16

9	4		7			3		5
7								1
			3			4		6
			9	7				
3		7				9		4
				1	2			
4		6			8			
2								7
8		9			7		4	3

Puzzle 17

START TIME

	7				9		8	
9				5	6			4
		6		4		7		
1	9							
	8	4				2	3	
							9	8
		3		8		9		
7			4	9				1
	1		2				4	

FINISH TIME

DIFFICULTY

Puzzle 18

START TIME

				5	2	1		
						2	3	
3		1						8
8			4			5		
1	6	5		8		4	2	3
		3			1			6
4						6		2
	5	9						
		8	7	3				

FINISH TIME

DIFFICULTY

Puzzle 19

START TIME

	4			8	2			
		6						
7					3	9		8
	7	5					8	4
	2						1	
8	9					3	6	
4		1	9					6
						1		
			6	1			5	

FINISH TIME

DIFFICULTY

Puzzle 20

START TIME

7	4		1					
				6			3	7
	1			8	2			
3					8	4		
5				2				6
		2	6					5
			8	7			4	
9	6			3				
					1		7	3

FINISH TIME

DIFFICULTY

Puzzle 21

START TIME

		5			1		2	6
							4	
				6	2	7	1	
4		2			5			
8								3
			8			4		7
	7	6	1	8				
	5							
3	8		6			1		

FINISH TIME

DIFFICULTY

Puzzle 22

START TIME

				1		2		
		1					7	
2	8		6					
		7					6	9
		8	7		3	1		
6	4					8		
					2		4	8
	1					3		
		5		7				

FINISH TIME

DIFFICULTY

Puzzle 23

START TIME

9	4			7		6		
			3			2		
			2				4	
2	9			3				6
		3				1		
1				6			3	5
	2				5			
		9			1			
		6		2			8	7

FINISH TIME

DIFFICULTY

Puzzle 24

START TIME

		1	3					4
3	8	6						
				5	2	1		
		3		9			4	
	5						6	
	4			6		2		
		8	5	1				
						5	7	9
7					3	4		

FINISH TIME

DIFFICULTY

Puzzle 25

START TIME

		3						1
	6	4		3	2			9
					9	4		
	1			9		7		
	9			6			1	
		5		4			8	
		2	3					
7			5	1		6	2	
5						1		

FINISH TIME

DIFFICULTY

Puzzle 26

START TIME

	5				1	2		
2			4			7		
				8		1		
7				1			4	
	9		7		5		2	
	6			2				9
		9		4				
		5			8			3
		2	6				8	

FINISH TIME

DIFFICULTY

Puzzle 27

START TIME

				6	9	8		
	8							2
		2	4					3
	6	9	8				2	
	5						6	
	2				6	7	3	
9					4	5		
3							7	
		8	9	7				

FINISH TIME

DIFFICULTY

Puzzle 28

START TIME

							5	
2				4	1			
	1	3	6					
5				6		3		1
	2	1				5	4	
3		4		7				9
					2	9	8	
			3	9				7
	4							

FINISH TIME

DIFFICULTY

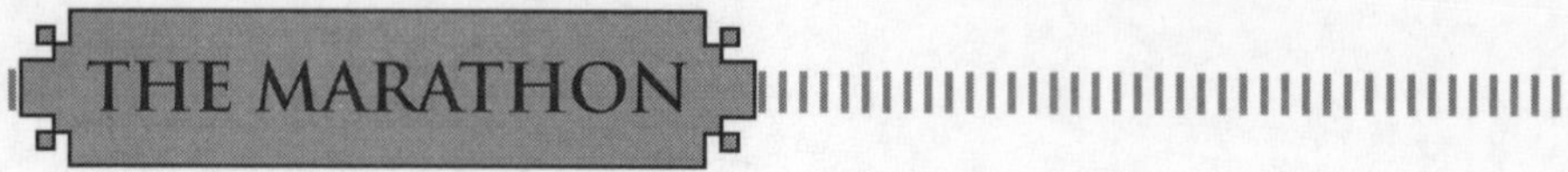

Puzzle 29

START TIME

2				1				3
			5			8		
7		3			4			
	4	7		6		1		
	3						8	
		1		8		5	9	
			4			3		6
		8			2			
9				5				8

FINISH TIME

DIFFICULTY

Puzzle 30

START TIME

						4	2	5
3					6			9
		2		9				
		9		2	1		4	
			7		3			
	7		4	8		2		
				1		3		
4			6					8
2	3	8						

FINISH TIME

DIFFICULTY

Puzzle 31

START TIME

							5	9
	1		2				4	3
		4	3	6				
				5		1	6	
		3		1		5		
	4	5		7				
				3	7	8		
5	6				8		1	
7	3							

FINISH TIME

DIFFICULTY

Puzzle 32

START TIME

					4			2
	4				5	6		1
			1		3	5	9	
	1						5	
9								6
	6						3	
	3	9	2		6			
6		8	3				4	
2			5					

FINISH TIME

DIFFICULTY

Puzzle 33

START TIME

				1		6		
	3		6	8		7		
	1				3			2
				7		1	4	5
4	8	3		6				
9			4				6	
		7		5	6		1	
		8		9				

FINISH TIME

DIFFICULTY

Puzzle 34

START TIME

			7	9		2		
2							6	1
6					2	5	4	
	2	9			1			
				3				
			2			4	7	
	7	2	8					6
8	4							3
		5		7	9			

FINISH TIME

DIFFICULTY

Puzzle 35

		6			2			
	5						4	6
		2	8		1	9		
					4		9	5
			6		3			
9	2		1					
		8	4		6	1		
2	6						7	
			9			8		

Puzzle 36

START TIME

	7						2	
		6	2		1			
1						9		5
				6		8		4
	2		1		8		5	
6		8		9				
4		1						9
			5		6	3		
	8						1	

FINISH TIME

DIFFICULTY

SOLUTIONS

Solution 1

2	5	7	9	4	8	3	1	6
3	6	8	1	7	2	5	9	4
9	1	4	6	5	3	7	2	8
8	4	2	5	9	7	6	3	1
1	9	3	8	6	4	2	7	5
6	7	5	3	2	1	4	8	9
5	3	6	2	1	9	8	4	7
7	8	9	4	3	5	1	6	2
4	2	1	7	8	6	9	5	3

Solution 2

5	6	9	8	1	2	4	3	7
4	1	7	3	6	5	9	8	2
8	2	3	9	7	4	5	6	1
3	4	1	2	5	8	6	7	9
7	5	8	1	9	6	2	4	3
6	9	2	7	4	3	1	5	8
2	8	6	4	3	9	7	1	5
1	3	4	5	2	7	8	9	6
9	7	5	6	8	1	3	2	4

Solution 3

5	3	4	6	9	7	2	8	1
9	2	8	3	4	1	7	5	6
1	7	6	5	8	2	9	3	4
6	1	5	7	2	3	4	9	8
4	9	3	1	6	8	5	7	2
2	8	7	9	5	4	1	6	3
8	5	9	4	1	6	3	2	7
3	4	2	8	7	5	6	1	9
7	6	1	2	3	9	8	4	5

Solution 4

5	4	6	1	8	2	3	7	9
3	7	9	5	6	4	8	2	1
8	2	1	7	9	3	4	5	6
6	5	4	3	2	8	9	1	7
1	8	3	9	7	6	5	4	2
2	9	7	4	5	1	6	3	8
9	1	5	8	4	7	2	6	3
4	3	2	6	1	9	7	8	5
7	6	8	2	3	5	1	9	4

Solution 5

1	5	3	4	9	8	7	6	2
8	6	4	3	2	7	5	1	9
9	7	2	1	5	6	4	8	3
3	4	8	7	6	5	9	2	1
5	2	9	8	3	1	6	7	4
7	1	6	9	4	2	3	5	8
6	9	5	2	8	4	1	3	7
2	3	1	6	7	9	8	4	5
4	8	7	5	1	3	2	9	6

Solution 6

6	2	5	3	1	7	9	8	4
1	8	9	4	6	5	7	2	3
7	3	4	2	9	8	1	6	5
8	7	3	6	2	4	5	9	1
9	5	6	7	8	1	4	3	2
4	1	2	5	3	9	8	7	6
3	4	7	8	5	2	6	1	9
5	6	1	9	7	3	2	4	8
2	9	8	1	4	6	3	5	7

Solution 7

9	3	5	2	8	1	6	7	4
7	6	4	3	9	5	8	2	1
8	2	1	7	6	4	3	9	5
6	5	9	8	4	7	1	3	2
2	4	3	1	5	9	7	6	8
1	8	7	6	2	3	4	5	9
3	9	6	4	1	2	5	8	7
5	1	8	9	7	6	2	4	3
4	7	2	5	3	8	9	1	6

Solution 8

9	4	7	8	1	3	2	6	5
8	6	2	4	9	5	1	7	3
3	1	5	7	6	2	8	9	4
7	9	6	5	3	1	4	2	8
2	5	8	9	4	6	3	1	7
1	3	4	2	8	7	9	5	6
4	7	3	1	5	9	6	8	2
5	8	1	6	2	4	7	3	9
6	2	9	3	7	8	5	4	1

Solution 9

1	8	6	9	2	3	7	4	5
4	2	9	8	7	5	3	1	6
3	5	7	4	1	6	2	9	8
9	1	8	6	5	2	4	7	3
6	7	3	1	8	4	5	2	9
5	4	2	3	9	7	8	6	1
2	3	5	7	6	1	9	8	4
8	6	4	2	3	9	1	5	7
7	9	1	5	4	8	6	3	2

Solution 10

8	6	2	9	4	3	1	5	7
7	9	4	5	1	8	6	2	3
3	5	1	6	2	7	9	8	4
1	3	8	7	9	4	5	6	2
5	2	7	3	8	6	4	9	1
6	4	9	1	5	2	3	7	8
2	1	6	8	3	9	7	4	5
4	7	3	2	6	5	8	1	9
9	8	5	4	7	1	2	3	6

Solution 11

5	4	1	3	6	9	2	8	7
8	9	6	2	4	7	5	1	3
2	7	3	8	5	1	4	9	6
9	5	7	4	8	3	6	2	1
4	1	8	6	7	2	3	5	9
3	6	2	9	1	5	7	4	8
1	8	4	7	2	6	9	3	5
6	3	5	1	9	4	8	7	2
7	2	9	5	3	8	1	6	4

Solution 12

6	8	7	5	4	2	1	3	9
2	5	1	3	8	9	7	4	6
3	4	9	1	6	7	5	8	2
1	9	3	4	2	8	6	5	7
7	2	4	6	5	1	3	9	8
8	6	5	7	9	3	2	1	4
4	7	6	9	3	5	8	2	1
5	1	2	8	7	4	9	6	3
9	3	8	2	1	6	4	7	5

Solution 13

4	3	6	1	8	5	9	2	7
7	5	2	4	3	9	6	8	1
9	8	1	7	6	2	3	4	5
5	6	9	3	4	1	2	7	8
1	4	8	9	2	7	5	6	3
3	2	7	8	5	6	4	1	9
6	7	5	2	9	8	1	3	4
2	1	3	5	7	4	8	9	6
8	9	4	6	1	3	7	5	2

Solution 14

3	7	8	1	4	9	2	5	6
9	4	6	5	2	3	1	8	7
1	5	2	7	8	6	3	9	4
7	8	1	2	6	5	4	3	9
5	2	3	4	9	7	8	6	1
4	6	9	3	1	8	7	2	5
2	3	7	6	5	4	9	1	8
8	1	5	9	7	2	6	4	3
6	9	4	8	3	1	5	7	2

Solution 15

8	5	4	2	1	6	9	7	3
6	2	3	9	8	7	5	1	4
1	9	7	3	4	5	8	2	6
7	6	8	4	2	9	3	5	1
2	4	1	7	5	3	6	8	9
9	3	5	1	6	8	7	4	2
5	1	9	6	7	2	4	3	8
4	8	6	5	3	1	2	9	7
3	7	2	8	9	4	1	6	5

Solution 16

8	4	2	7	9	1	5	6	3
5	7	9	3	6	8	4	1	2
1	3	6	5	4	2	7	9	8
9	6	4	8	5	7	3	2	1
3	5	7	2	1	6	8	4	9
2	8	1	4	3	9	6	7	5
7	9	3	1	8	4	2	5	6
6	2	5	9	7	3	1	8	4
4	1	8	6	2	5	9	3	7

Solution 17

9	1	7	5	3	4	6	8	2
5	6	2	9	7	8	1	4	3
4	8	3	6	2	1	9	7	5
7	5	6	4	8	2	3	9	1
2	9	1	3	5	7	4	6	8
8	3	4	1	9	6	2	5	7
3	7	9	2	6	5	8	1	4
1	2	5	8	4	9	7	3	6
6	4	8	7	1	3	5	2	9

Solution 18

9	1	8	6	2	7	3	5	4
2	6	4	3	1	5	9	7	8
3	5	7	9	8	4	2	6	1
6	9	5	2	4	3	8	1	7
1	8	2	7	5	6	4	3	9
7	4	3	8	9	1	6	2	5
4	2	1	5	6	9	7	8	3
8	7	9	1	3	2	5	4	6
5	3	6	4	7	8	1	9	2

Solution 19

5	2	3	8	6	4	7	9	1
1	7	4	9	5	3	2	8	6
8	9	6	2	1	7	3	5	4
4	1	8	7	3	6	9	2	5
2	3	5	1	8	9	4	6	7
9	6	7	4	2	5	8	1	3
3	4	2	5	9	1	6	7	8
7	8	1	6	4	2	5	3	9
6	5	9	3	7	8	1	4	2

Solution 20

5	2	7	1	8	3	9	6	4
4	9	3	2	5	6	8	1	7
8	1	6	7	4	9	5	3	2
3	6	8	4	2	7	1	9	5
1	7	5	3	9	8	4	2	6
9	4	2	6	1	5	3	7	8
6	8	1	9	7	4	2	5	3
7	5	9	8	3	2	6	4	1
2	3	4	5	6	1	7	8	9

Solution 21

9	3	6	7	1	5	2	4	8
2	4	1	6	9	8	7	3	5
5	7	8	4	2	3	1	6	9
1	6	4	3	7	9	8	5	2
7	2	5	8	6	1	3	9	4
3	8	9	5	4	2	6	7	1
8	9	7	2	5	6	4	1	3
4	5	3	1	8	7	9	2	6
6	1	2	9	3	4	5	8	7

Solution 22

2	5	7	6	9	3	8	4	1
8	4	9	1	5	2	6	7	3
6	3	1	8	7	4	2	9	5
5	8	2	4	6	9	1	3	7
7	1	4	3	8	5	9	6	2
3	9	6	2	1	7	5	8	4
9	7	8	5	3	1	4	2	6
4	6	5	7	2	8	3	1	9
1	2	3	9	4	6	7	5	8

Solution 23

7	6	3	5	9	4	1	8	2
5	1	2	6	8	3	7	9	4
9	4	8	7	1	2	6	5	3
6	2	7	3	4	9	5	1	8
1	3	5	2	7	8	4	6	9
4	8	9	1	6	5	2	3	7
2	9	1	4	3	6	8	7	5
8	7	4	9	5	1	3	2	6
3	5	6	8	2	7	9	4	1

Solution 24

4	5	8	6	9	1	3	2	7
1	2	6	7	3	8	4	9	5
9	3	7	5	2	4	1	8	6
6	8	5	9	7	3	2	4	1
2	1	4	8	6	5	9	7	3
7	9	3	4	1	2	5	6	8
8	4	9	3	5	7	6	1	2
5	7	1	2	4	6	8	3	9
3	6	2	1	8	9	7	5	4

Solution 25

7	3	6	4	1	5	2	8	9
5	8	1	3	2	9	4	7	6
2	4	9	8	6	7	5	1	3
9	6	4	7	5	2	8	3	1
8	1	7	6	4	3	9	2	5
3	2	5	1	9	8	6	4	7
4	7	2	5	3	6	1	9	8
6	9	8	2	7	1	3	5	4
1	5	3	9	8	4	7	6	2

Solution 26

4	8	2	5	3	9	6	7	1
7	3	6	1	4	2	9	8	5
9	1	5	6	7	8	4	3	2
5	7	9	8	6	3	2	1	4
3	2	1	7	5	4	8	9	6
6	4	8	2	9	1	3	5	7
8	6	4	9	1	5	7	2	3
2	5	3	4	8	7	1	6	9
1	9	7	3	2	6	5	4	8

Solution 27

9	7	1	5	3	8	2	4	6
8	2	4	1	6	9	5	7	3
6	5	3	4	7	2	1	8	9
1	3	5	2	8	7	6	9	4
2	8	9	6	4	5	7	3	1
7	4	6	9	1	3	8	5	2
3	1	8	7	9	6	4	2	5
5	6	7	3	2	4	9	1	8
4	9	2	8	5	1	3	6	7

Solution 28

1	3	2	7	5	4	8	6	9
9	8	6	1	3	2	7	5	4
7	5	4	8	6	9	3	2	1
2	6	3	9	4	7	1	8	5
4	1	5	3	2	8	6	9	7
8	9	7	6	1	5	2	4	3
6	4	1	5	8	3	9	7	2
3	2	9	4	7	6	5	1	8
5	7	8	2	9	1	4	3	6

Solution 29

6	5	4	9	1	8	3	2	7
7	9	3	6	5	2	1	8	4
8	1	2	4	7	3	9	6	5
3	2	7	1	6	5	8	4	9
1	4	9	8	2	7	5	3	6
5	6	8	3	9	4	7	1	2
9	7	1	2	8	6	4	5	3
2	3	5	7	4	1	6	9	8
4	8	6	5	3	9	2	7	1

Solution 30

7	3	2	1	8	9	5	6	4
8	6	4	2	5	3	9	1	7
9	1	5	7	4	6	8	3	2
3	4	6	9	7	2	1	8	5
5	7	8	3	1	4	6	2	9
2	9	1	5	6	8	7	4	3
1	5	3	8	2	7	4	9	6
6	2	7	4	9	1	3	5	8
4	8	9	6	3	5	2	7	1

Solution 31

6	9	3	5	8	1	7	2	4
7	2	8	9	3	4	1	6	5
5	1	4	2	6	7	8	9	3
3	8	7	4	2	9	5	1	6
4	6	1	7	5	8	9	3	2
9	5	2	3	1	6	4	7	8
2	7	9	6	4	5	3	8	1
8	3	5	1	7	2	6	4	9
1	4	6	8	9	3	2	5	7

Solution 32

3	1	9	5	4	2	6	7	8
8	4	6	7	9	3	2	1	5
5	7	2	8	6	1	9	3	4
6	2	3	1	5	8	4	9	7
9	8	7	6	2	4	3	5	1
1	5	4	3	7	9	8	2	6
4	9	1	2	8	7	5	6	3
2	3	5	4	1	6	7	8	9
7	6	8	9	3	5	1	4	2

Solution 33

9	6	2	1	3	5	7	4	8
3	8	5	4	7	6	1	9	2
7	1	4	2	8	9	5	3	6
5	2	7	9	1	3	6	8	4
4	9	1	7	6	8	2	5	3
8	3	6	5	2	4	9	7	1
6	7	8	3	9	1	4	2	5
2	5	3	6	4	7	8	1	9
1	4	9	8	5	2	3	6	7

Solution 34

6	1	7	5	3	9	4	2	8
8	5	2	4	1	6	3	7	9
9	4	3	7	8	2	1	6	5
2	9	5	8	4	1	6	3	7
3	7	1	6	9	5	8	4	2
4	8	6	2	7	3	9	5	1
5	3	9	1	6	7	2	8	4
1	2	8	3	5	4	7	9	6
7	6	4	9	2	8	5	1	3

Solution 35

3	5	9	8	1	7	4	6	2
7	2	6	4	9	3	5	8	1
1	4	8	6	5	2	9	7	3
6	1	2	3	7	9	8	5	4
8	3	4	5	2	6	1	9	7
5	9	7	1	8	4	2	3	6
9	7	3	2	4	8	6	1	5
2	8	5	7	6	1	3	4	9
4	6	1	9	3	5	7	2	8

Solution 36

3	9	7	5	2	6	8	4	1
5	2	8	1	4	3	6	7	9
1	6	4	7	8	9	3	2	5
9	3	6	4	5	8	7	1	2
8	4	2	9	1	7	5	3	6
7	1	5	3	6	2	9	8	4
2	5	9	8	7	1	4	6	3
4	7	1	6	3	5	2	9	8
6	8	3	2	9	4	1	5	7

Solution 37

7	4	2	1	9	3	5	8	6
8	6	9	5	2	7	3	4	1
1	3	5	8	6	4	2	7	9
5	1	4	9	7	6	8	2	3
3	8	6	2	5	1	4	9	7
2	9	7	4	3	8	6	1	5
9	5	8	6	1	2	7	3	4
4	7	1	3	8	5	9	6	2
6	2	3	7	4	9	1	5	8

Solution 38

9	5	7	2	4	3	1	6	8
8	2	3	1	6	7	5	9	4
4	1	6	9	8	5	3	7	2
2	3	5	4	1	6	9	8	7
1	7	9	5	2	8	4	3	6
6	8	4	3	7	9	2	1	5
3	4	8	7	9	2	6	5	1
5	6	1	8	3	4	7	2	9
7	9	2	6	5	1	8	4	3

Solution 39

6	7	1	2	3	4	8	5	9
4	2	8	9	7	5	1	3	6
5	3	9	8	1	6	7	2	4
8	1	3	4	5	7	6	9	2
7	9	6	3	8	2	4	1	5
2	4	5	6	9	1	3	7	8
9	5	7	1	4	8	2	6	3
1	8	2	5	6	3	9	4	7
3	6	4	7	2	9	5	8	1

Solution 40

4	8	5	1	7	2	9	6	3
6	3	7	4	8	9	2	5	1
2	9	1	6	3	5	8	7	4
3	5	8	2	4	1	7	9	6
7	4	6	9	5	3	1	8	2
9	1	2	7	6	8	4	3	5
8	6	9	3	1	4	5	2	7
5	7	4	8	2	6	3	1	9
1	2	3	5	9	7	6	4	8

Solution 41

9	2	3	8	4	1	6	7	5
5	4	8	7	6	9	3	1	2
6	7	1	2	3	5	8	9	4
4	1	9	3	5	2	7	8	6
7	8	2	4	1	6	5	3	9
3	6	5	9	7	8	4	2	1
1	3	4	6	2	7	9	5	8
2	9	6	5	8	3	1	4	7
8	5	7	1	9	4	2	6	3

Solution 42

7	4	3	2	1	5	9	8	6
2	8	9	7	6	3	4	5	1
6	5	1	4	9	8	7	2	3
5	9	2	3	8	6	1	7	4
3	7	4	5	2	1	6	9	8
8	1	6	9	7	4	5	3	2
9	2	8	6	4	7	3	1	5
4	3	7	1	5	2	8	6	9
1	6	5	8	3	9	2	4	7

Solution 43

1	7	9	8	3	6	5	2	4
2	4	8	1	5	9	3	6	7
6	3	5	4	2	7	1	8	9
7	1	6	5	4	2	9	3	8
3	5	2	9	7	8	4	1	6
8	9	4	3	6	1	7	5	2
5	8	3	6	9	4	2	7	1
4	6	7	2	1	3	8	9	5
9	2	1	7	8	5	6	4	3

Solution 44

7	9	2	8	5	3	6	1	4
6	4	1	7	2	9	3	8	5
3	5	8	1	4	6	2	7	9
5	8	7	9	6	2	1	4	3
9	1	3	4	7	8	5	6	2
2	6	4	3	1	5	7	9	8
8	7	9	2	3	1	4	5	6
4	2	5	6	8	7	9	3	1
1	3	6	5	9	4	8	2	7

Solution 45

7	9	6	1	4	8	3	2	5
5	8	3	6	2	7	9	1	4
1	2	4	9	5	3	6	8	7
3	6	8	2	7	5	1	4	9
4	7	9	3	1	6	8	5	2
2	5	1	8	9	4	7	6	3
6	4	5	7	3	1	2	9	8
8	3	2	4	6	9	5	7	1
9	1	7	5	8	2	4	3	6

Solution 46

6	7	2	1	8	4	9	5	3
5	3	9	2	7	6	1	4	8
1	8	4	9	5	3	6	2	7
9	1	6	3	4	5	8	7	2
3	2	8	6	1	7	5	9	4
7	4	5	8	9	2	3	6	1
2	5	1	7	3	9	4	8	6
8	9	7	4	6	1	2	3	5
4	6	3	5	2	8	7	1	9

Solution 47

1	9	7	4	2	3	6	8	5
5	2	4	6	1	8	3	7	9
8	3	6	9	5	7	2	4	1
6	1	9	7	8	4	5	2	3
2	4	3	1	6	5	7	9	8
7	5	8	3	9	2	1	6	4
4	8	1	5	7	6	9	3	2
9	7	2	8	3	1	4	5	6
3	6	5	2	4	9	8	1	7

Solution 48

7	6	3	4	9	8	5	2	1
5	4	8	2	6	1	7	9	3
1	9	2	3	7	5	6	4	8
9	3	4	1	5	6	8	7	2
8	7	6	9	4	2	1	3	5
2	5	1	7	8	3	9	6	4
3	8	7	5	2	9	4	1	6
6	2	9	8	1	4	3	5	7
4	1	5	6	3	7	2	8	9

Solution 49

1	6	5	8	3	2	9	4	7
8	7	2	1	4	9	6	3	5
9	4	3	6	5	7	1	8	2
7	9	4	2	1	3	5	6	8
6	5	1	4	9	8	7	2	3
3	2	8	7	6	5	4	1	9
5	1	9	3	8	4	2	7	6
2	3	6	5	7	1	8	9	4
4	8	7	9	2	6	3	5	1

Solution 50

8	6	4	1	5	2	3	7	9
5	9	1	6	7	3	4	2	8
2	3	7	8	9	4	5	1	6
3	4	5	9	6	1	2	8	7
7	1	6	2	4	8	9	5	3
9	8	2	5	3	7	1	6	4
6	5	8	3	2	9	7	4	1
4	2	9	7	1	6	8	3	5
1	7	3	4	8	5	6	9	2

SOLUTIONS

Solution 1

4	3	5	8	9	2	1	7	6
6	9	7	5	4	1	8	3	2
8	2	1	3	7	6	9	5	4
7	8	2	6	5	9	4	1	3
5	1	3	7	2	4	6	8	9
9	4	6	1	3	8	7	2	5
1	5	8	4	6	3	2	9	7
2	7	4	9	8	5	3	6	1
3	6	9	2	1	7	5	4	8

Solution 2

4	7	1	3	2	5	8	9	6
8	6	2	9	4	7	3	1	5
3	5	9	8	6	1	4	7	2
1	2	8	6	7	4	5	3	9
9	4	7	5	3	2	6	8	1
5	3	6	1	8	9	2	4	7
7	8	4	2	9	6	1	5	3
6	1	3	7	5	8	9	2	4
2	9	5	4	1	3	7	6	8

Solution 3

8	6	2	1	7	5	9	3	4
9	1	3	6	4	8	7	5	2
5	4	7	2	9	3	8	6	1
7	9	6	3	1	4	5	2	8
2	5	8	7	6	9	4	1	3
1	3	4	8	5	2	6	9	7
3	2	9	5	8	7	1	4	6
4	8	1	9	3	6	2	7	5
6	7	5	4	2	1	3	8	9

Solution 4

1	4	9	6	2	3	7	5	8
2	8	3	1	7	5	9	6	4
7	6	5	9	4	8	2	3	1
5	2	4	7	3	9	8	1	6
6	7	1	5	8	2	4	9	3
3	9	8	4	6	1	5	7	2
9	3	6	8	5	4	1	2	7
4	1	2	3	9	7	6	8	5
8	5	7	2	1	6	3	4	9

Solution 5

5	4	3	6	7	9	1	2	8
2	8	6	1	5	4	9	3	7
7	9	1	2	3	8	5	6	4
8	7	5	3	4	1	2	9	6
6	2	9	7	8	5	4	1	3
1	3	4	9	6	2	7	8	5
9	6	7	4	2	3	8	5	1
4	5	2	8	1	6	3	7	9
3	1	8	5	9	7	6	4	2

Solution 6

9	3	8	4	7	1	5	2	6
5	2	1	6	3	9	8	7	4
6	7	4	8	5	2	9	3	1
8	6	2	7	9	5	1	4	3
7	9	3	1	4	8	6	5	2
1	4	5	2	6	3	7	8	9
2	5	9	3	1	7	4	6	8
4	8	7	9	2	6	3	1	5
3	1	6	5	8	4	2	9	7

Solution 7

5	9	2	1	6	3	8	4	7
6	4	3	8	2	7	1	9	5
7	1	8	4	5	9	3	2	6
4	5	6	9	1	2	7	8	3
2	3	7	6	8	5	4	1	9
9	8	1	3	7	4	6	5	2
8	2	9	7	3	1	5	6	4
3	6	4	5	9	8	2	7	1
1	7	5	2	4	6	9	3	8

Solution 8

5	8	1	4	3	9	2	6	7
4	2	7	6	5	1	8	9	3
9	6	3	8	2	7	5	1	4
2	7	4	9	6	8	3	5	1
6	1	5	2	7	3	4	8	9
8	3	9	5	1	4	7	2	6
3	4	6	1	8	2	9	7	5
1	9	2	7	4	5	6	3	8
7	5	8	3	9	6	1	4	2

Solution 9

9	7	8	6	1	5	2	4	3
3	4	1	8	2	9	7	6	5
5	6	2	4	3	7	9	8	1
8	9	7	2	5	6	3	1	4
1	3	5	9	7	4	6	2	8
4	2	6	3	8	1	5	9	7
7	8	4	5	6	2	1	3	9
2	5	9	1	4	3	8	7	6
6	1	3	7	9	8	4	5	2

Solution 10

7	5	4	6	9	8	2	3	1
9	8	2	3	5	1	4	7	6
3	1	6	2	4	7	8	5	9
8	4	5	1	2	3	6	9	7
2	6	9	8	7	5	1	4	3
1	7	3	9	6	4	5	8	2
4	9	1	5	3	2	7	6	8
5	3	8	7	1	6	9	2	4
6	2	7	4	8	9	3	1	5

Solution 11

6	4	5	9	2	1	3	8	7
7	9	2	8	3	4	6	1	5
8	1	3	5	6	7	2	9	4
1	2	6	7	5	8	4	3	9
4	3	8	2	9	6	5	7	1
5	7	9	1	4	3	8	6	2
2	5	7	6	8	9	1	4	3
9	6	4	3	1	2	7	5	8
3	8	1	4	7	5	9	2	6

Solution 12

5	9	2	6	4	1	8	3	7
7	6	8	2	3	5	1	4	9
1	4	3	7	9	8	5	6	2
2	3	1	9	7	6	4	5	8
6	8	4	1	5	2	7	9	3
9	7	5	3	8	4	2	1	6
3	2	9	5	1	7	6	8	4
8	5	7	4	6	9	3	2	1
4	1	6	8	2	3	9	7	5

Solution 13

1	5	9	3	4	7	8	2	6
3	7	6	2	5	8	1	9	4
8	4	2	9	1	6	7	3	5
7	3	1	5	9	4	6	8	2
2	9	8	1	6	3	4	5	7
5	6	4	8	7	2	3	1	9
6	2	5	7	8	1	9	4	3
4	1	3	6	2	9	5	7	8
9	8	7	4	3	5	2	6	1

Solution 14

8	5	2	3	6	9	4	7	1
6	7	1	2	4	8	3	5	9
3	9	4	7	1	5	6	2	8
2	1	6	5	7	3	9	8	4
5	3	7	8	9	4	1	6	2
4	8	9	1	2	6	5	3	7
7	4	3	9	5	2	8	1	6
9	2	8	6	3	1	7	4	5
1	6	5	4	8	7	2	9	3

Solution 15

4	9	7	1	8	6	3	5	2
8	2	6	7	3	5	1	9	4
5	1	3	4	2	9	8	7	6
1	3	8	6	9	2	7	4	5
9	7	4	5	1	3	2	6	8
2	6	5	8	4	7	9	3	1
6	5	9	2	7	1	4	8	3
3	4	2	9	5	8	6	1	7
7	8	1	3	6	4	5	2	9

Solution 16

1	4	8	2	5	6	3	7	9
2	3	5	9	8	7	6	1	4
9	7	6	1	3	4	8	2	5
5	9	4	8	2	3	1	6	7
3	8	1	7	6	9	4	5	2
7	6	2	4	1	5	9	8	3
6	5	7	3	9	8	2	4	1
8	2	9	5	4	1	7	3	6
4	1	3	6	7	2	5	9	8

Solution 17

6	2	4	8	9	3	1	5	7
9	1	5	2	7	6	3	8	4
8	3	7	5	4	1	6	9	2
5	9	1	7	6	8	4	2	3
2	4	6	1	3	5	9	7	8
7	8	3	4	2	9	5	1	6
3	7	9	6	1	2	8	4	5
1	5	2	3	8	4	7	6	9
4	6	8	9	5	7	2	3	1

Solution 18

5	1	2	8	7	4	3	9	6
9	8	4	6	3	2	5	1	7
3	7	6	1	9	5	8	2	4
7	3	8	5	2	9	4	6	1
6	4	9	7	8	1	2	5	3
1	2	5	3	4	6	7	8	9
4	9	3	2	6	8	1	7	5
8	6	1	4	5	7	9	3	2
2	5	7	9	1	3	6	4	8

Solution 19

9	8	3	2	6	4	1	7	5
7	2	5	1	9	8	4	6	3
4	1	6	7	3	5	2	9	8
1	9	2	3	5	6	7	8	4
6	4	8	9	7	2	5	3	1
3	5	7	4	8	1	9	2	6
8	6	4	5	2	9	3	1	7
2	7	1	8	4	3	6	5	9
5	3	9	6	1	7	8	4	2

Solution 20

7	9	6	2	4	3	1	5	8
2	5	8	1	9	7	6	3	4
3	4	1	6	5	8	9	7	2
4	7	5	9	3	2	8	1	6
6	1	2	8	7	5	3	4	9
8	3	9	4	6	1	7	2	5
9	6	7	3	2	4	5	8	1
5	8	4	7	1	6	2	9	3
1	2	3	5	8	9	4	6	7

Solution 21

1	6	2	4	5	8	9	3	7
7	4	8	9	2	3	5	1	6
5	9	3	6	1	7	8	2	4
9	5	1	2	6	4	7	8	3
3	7	6	5	8	1	2	4	9
2	8	4	3	7	9	1	6	5
8	3	5	7	4	2	6	9	1
6	1	9	8	3	5	4	7	2
4	2	7	1	9	6	3	5	8

Solution 22

8	5	7	4	1	6	2	3	9
9	3	6	5	2	7	1	4	8
4	1	2	3	9	8	5	6	7
5	6	1	2	3	9	8	7	4
7	4	3	1	8	5	6	9	2
2	8	9	7	6	4	3	1	5
6	9	5	8	4	1	7	2	3
3	7	4	6	5	2	9	8	1
1	2	8	9	7	3	4	5	6

Solution 23

9	5	4	6	8	7	2	1	3
3	1	8	4	9	2	5	6	7
2	7	6	5	1	3	4	9	8
7	3	9	1	5	4	8	2	6
5	4	1	8	2	6	7	3	9
8	6	2	3	7	9	1	4	5
1	8	3	2	6	5	9	7	4
6	9	5	7	4	1	3	8	2
4	2	7	9	3	8	6	5	1

Solution 24

6	4	8	5	7	1	3	9	2
5	7	9	8	3	2	4	1	6
3	2	1	9	4	6	5	7	8
4	3	7	6	5	9	8	2	1
8	5	2	4	1	7	9	6	3
9	1	6	3	2	8	7	5	4
1	8	3	7	6	5	2	4	9
7	6	4	2	9	3	1	8	5
2	9	5	1	8	4	6	3	7

Solution 25

5	3	8	4	7	1	2	6	9
2	1	9	8	6	3	4	7	5
4	6	7	2	9	5	8	3	1
6	9	1	7	8	2	3	5	4
7	4	2	3	5	9	1	8	6
3	8	5	1	4	6	9	2	7
9	2	3	6	1	7	5	4	8
8	5	6	9	2	4	7	1	3
1	7	4	5	3	8	6	9	2

Solution 26

7	4	6	3	2	5	9	1	8
5	3	9	4	1	8	7	6	2
1	2	8	7	6	9	3	4	5
6	8	4	1	9	7	5	2	3
3	5	7	2	4	6	8	9	1
9	1	2	5	8	3	4	7	6
4	7	1	8	5	2	6	3	9
2	6	5	9	3	4	1	8	7
8	9	3	6	7	1	2	5	4

Solution 27

6	3	2	8	5	1	4	9	7
4	9	1	3	2	7	6	8	5
7	8	5	4	6	9	3	2	1
1	6	7	9	3	4	8	5	2
5	4	3	1	8	2	7	6	9
8	2	9	5	7	6	1	3	4
9	7	6	2	1	8	5	4	3
2	5	8	7	4	3	9	1	6
3	1	4	6	9	5	2	7	8

Solution 28

2	6	8	1	4	9	7	3	5
7	4	5	8	6	3	9	1	2
3	1	9	5	2	7	6	8	4
4	3	2	7	5	1	8	9	6
5	9	6	4	3	8	2	7	1
1	8	7	6	9	2	4	5	3
6	2	3	9	8	5	1	4	7
8	5	1	2	7	4	3	6	9
9	7	4	3	1	6	5	2	8

Solution 29

4	6	7	8	1	9	3	2	5
1	9	5	2	7	3	4	8	6
3	8	2	4	6	5	9	1	7
2	5	3	7	9	8	1	6	4
8	7	6	1	5	4	2	9	3
9	1	4	3	2	6	7	5	8
6	2	8	9	3	7	5	4	1
7	4	1	5	8	2	6	3	9
5	3	9	6	4	1	8	7	2

Solution 30

2	1	4	6	5	8	3	9	7
5	7	6	3	9	1	8	2	4
8	9	3	4	2	7	1	5	6
7	6	2	5	3	9	4	8	1
9	3	8	1	6	4	2	7	5
4	5	1	7	8	2	9	6	3
3	2	7	9	1	6	5	4	8
1	4	9	8	7	5	6	3	2
6	8	5	2	4	3	7	1	9

Solution 31

1	9	2	8	6	3	5	4	7
4	8	3	9	7	5	2	6	1
5	6	7	2	1	4	3	9	8
8	4	6	3	5	7	1	2	9
9	2	5	6	8	1	7	3	4
7	3	1	4	9	2	8	5	6
6	5	9	7	3	8	4	1	2
2	1	8	5	4	6	9	7	3
3	7	4	1	2	9	6	8	5

Solution 32

2	9	3	8	4	6	1	5	7
7	4	8	9	5	1	6	2	3
5	1	6	2	7	3	4	9	8
1	2	4	6	9	8	3	7	5
9	6	7	4	3	5	2	8	1
3	8	5	1	2	7	9	4	6
4	3	1	7	8	9	5	6	2
6	7	9	5	1	2	8	3	4
8	5	2	3	6	4	7	1	9

Solution 33

1	2	8	5	7	9	6	3	4
3	7	6	2	4	8	9	1	5
4	9	5	6	1	3	7	8	2
2	3	9	8	5	4	1	7	6
5	8	7	9	6	1	2	4	3
6	1	4	3	2	7	8	5	9
9	6	3	7	8	5	4	2	1
8	4	2	1	3	6	5	9	7
7	5	1	4	9	2	3	6	8

Solution 34

5	6	3	7	1	2	4	9	8
2	7	1	4	9	8	3	6	5
9	8	4	6	3	5	2	1	7
3	9	5	1	7	6	8	4	2
6	2	7	5	8	4	9	3	1
1	4	8	3	2	9	5	7	6
7	1	9	2	5	3	6	8	4
4	3	2	8	6	7	1	5	9
8	5	6	9	4	1	7	2	3

Solution 35

2	4	6	7	3	5	9	1	8
8	7	1	6	9	4	2	5	3
5	9	3	2	8	1	7	6	4
1	2	4	3	7	8	5	9	6
3	6	5	1	2	9	4	8	7
7	8	9	4	5	6	1	3	2
4	1	7	5	6	3	8	2	9
6	5	8	9	4	2	3	7	1
9	3	2	8	1	7	6	4	5

Solution 36

5	1	6	4	7	3	8	2	9
7	3	2	1	8	9	6	5	4
8	9	4	5	6	2	1	3	7
3	4	8	9	2	5	7	6	1
6	5	1	8	4	7	2	9	3
2	7	9	3	1	6	4	8	5
4	6	5	7	9	8	3	1	2
9	8	7	2	3	1	5	4	6
1	2	3	6	5	4	9	7	8

Solution 37

2	3	6	9	4	8	1	7	5
8	1	9	2	7	5	3	4	6
7	4	5	3	6	1	2	8	9
9	7	2	4	8	6	5	3	1
1	5	3	7	2	9	8	6	4
6	8	4	1	5	3	7	9	2
4	2	1	8	9	7	6	5	3
5	9	8	6	3	2	4	1	7
3	6	7	5	1	4	9	2	8

Solution 38

6	9	4	1	8	3	2	7	5
8	2	1	6	7	5	4	9	3
5	7	3	2	4	9	6	8	1
7	6	2	4	9	1	5	3	8
4	5	8	7	3	2	1	6	9
3	1	9	8	5	6	7	4	2
2	8	6	3	1	4	9	5	7
1	3	5	9	6	7	8	2	4
9	4	7	5	2	8	3	1	6

Solution 39

1	7	8	9	6	4	3	5	2
5	2	3	1	7	8	9	4	6
9	4	6	5	2	3	7	1	8
2	9	1	8	3	6	4	7	5
7	8	5	2	4	1	6	9	3
6	3	4	7	5	9	2	8	1
3	5	7	4	8	2	1	6	9
8	1	2	6	9	7	5	3	4
4	6	9	3	1	5	8	2	7

Solution 40

5	4	7	1	9	6	8	3	2
3	6	2	5	7	8	1	9	4
9	1	8	3	2	4	5	6	7
7	2	5	8	1	9	6	4	3
4	8	6	7	3	2	9	1	5
1	9	3	6	4	5	2	7	8
2	3	4	9	8	1	7	5	6
6	7	1	2	5	3	4	8	9
8	5	9	4	6	7	3	2	1

SOLUTIONS

Solution 1

6	2	5	4	9	8	3	7	1
4	8	1	2	7	3	6	9	5
9	3	7	5	6	1	2	4	8
3	4	6	1	5	2	7	8	9
7	5	9	3	8	6	4	1	2
2	1	8	9	4	7	5	6	3
1	9	4	6	2	5	8	3	7
8	6	2	7	3	9	1	5	4
5	7	3	8	1	4	9	2	6

Solution 2

1	8	9	4	5	2	6	7	3
4	2	3	7	8	6	5	1	9
6	5	7	9	3	1	4	2	8
8	1	5	6	2	7	9	3	4
7	4	6	8	9	3	2	5	1
3	9	2	5	1	4	8	6	7
2	7	8	1	6	9	3	4	5
9	3	4	2	7	5	1	8	6
5	6	1	3	4	8	7	9	2

Solution 3

8	1	7	9	6	2	4	5	3
3	5	4	7	1	8	6	9	2
9	2	6	3	5	4	1	8	7
2	6	3	1	7	5	9	4	8
7	9	1	4	8	3	5	2	6
4	8	5	6	2	9	3	7	1
5	7	9	8	3	6	2	1	4
6	4	8	2	9	1	7	3	5
1	3	2	5	4	7	8	6	9

Solution 4

3	9	5	6	1	7	8	4	2
8	4	6	9	3	2	5	1	7
2	1	7	5	4	8	6	9	3
4	5	3	7	8	6	9	2	1
9	7	2	1	5	4	3	8	6
6	8	1	3	2	9	4	7	5
7	3	8	4	6	1	2	5	9
1	6	4	2	9	5	7	3	8
5	2	9	8	7	3	1	6	4

Solution 5

7	2	8	4	3	6	9	1	5
9	1	6	8	2	5	3	4	7
4	3	5	1	9	7	6	8	2
2	6	1	7	4	8	5	9	3
8	4	9	6	5	3	2	7	1
5	7	3	9	1	2	4	6	8
1	8	2	3	6	9	7	5	4
3	9	4	5	7	1	8	2	6
6	5	7	2	8	4	1	3	9

Solution 6

4	7	5	8	2	3	1	6	9
1	8	3	5	9	6	4	7	2
2	6	9	1	4	7	5	3	8
3	4	7	6	8	9	2	5	1
9	1	6	4	5	2	7	8	3
8	5	2	7	3	1	9	4	6
6	3	1	9	7	4	8	2	5
7	2	8	3	1	5	6	9	4
5	9	4	2	6	8	3	1	7

Solution 7

9	3	7	8	4	5	1	6	2
1	8	4	2	7	6	3	5	9
2	6	5	1	3	9	4	8	7
4	2	6	3	8	1	7	9	5
5	7	9	6	2	4	8	3	1
8	1	3	9	5	7	2	4	6
3	9	8	7	6	2	5	1	4
7	5	1	4	9	3	6	2	8
6	4	2	5	1	8	9	7	3

Solution 8

8	3	2	6	9	1	4	7	5
5	7	1	2	3	4	8	6	9
9	4	6	5	7	8	3	1	2
4	9	7	8	1	5	2	3	6
1	2	8	3	4	6	9	5	7
3	6	5	9	2	7	1	8	4
2	8	4	7	6	3	5	9	1
6	1	3	4	5	9	7	2	8
7	5	9	1	8	2	6	4	3

Solution 9

8	7	3	1	5	2	6	4	9
5	2	6	4	9	8	3	1	7
9	1	4	6	7	3	8	5	2
6	5	8	2	1	9	4	7	3
4	9	7	3	8	6	1	2	5
1	3	2	5	4	7	9	8	6
2	4	9	8	3	5	7	6	1
7	8	5	9	6	1	2	3	4
3	6	1	7	2	4	5	9	8

Solution 10

1	2	9	5	4	7	3	6	8
8	7	5	6	2	3	1	9	4
6	4	3	8	1	9	7	2	5
4	3	8	2	9	6	5	1	7
5	6	7	4	3	1	9	8	2
2	9	1	7	5	8	4	3	6
7	1	2	9	8	4	6	5	3
9	5	6	3	7	2	8	4	1
3	8	4	1	6	5	2	7	9

Solution 11

6	3	8	5	4	1	7	9	2
7	1	2	6	3	9	8	5	4
9	4	5	2	7	8	1	3	6
4	7	1	3	6	2	9	8	5
5	6	3	8	9	7	4	2	1
2	8	9	4	1	5	3	6	7
3	2	7	9	5	4	6	1	8
1	5	6	7	8	3	2	4	9
8	9	4	1	2	6	5	7	3

Solution 12

1	4	7	5	3	2	6	9	8
5	8	6	4	1	9	2	7	3
9	3	2	8	7	6	4	5	1
4	1	8	2	9	3	5	6	7
6	5	3	1	4	7	8	2	9
7	2	9	6	5	8	1	3	4
8	7	1	3	2	5	9	4	6
3	6	5	9	8	4	7	1	2
2	9	4	7	6	1	3	8	5

Solution 13

5	3	7	2	8	6	1	4	9
1	2	6	5	9	4	3	8	7
9	4	8	1	7	3	6	5	2
4	8	1	7	3	2	5	9	6
3	9	2	8	6	5	4	7	1
7	6	5	9	4	1	8	2	3
8	5	9	6	1	7	2	3	4
6	7	3	4	2	8	9	1	5
2	1	4	3	5	9	7	6	8

Solution 14

9	4	1	6	3	5	8	2	7
5	3	8	9	2	7	6	4	1
2	6	7	4	1	8	9	3	5
1	9	3	7	4	2	5	8	6
6	7	2	5	8	9	4	1	3
8	5	4	3	6	1	7	9	2
4	2	5	1	9	6	3	7	8
3	8	6	2	7	4	1	5	9
7	1	9	8	5	3	2	6	4

Solution 15

2	6	1	9	5	4	7	3	8
8	7	9	3	2	1	5	6	4
3	5	4	6	7	8	1	9	2
4	9	2	8	1	5	3	7	6
5	3	7	2	4	6	9	8	1
1	8	6	7	9	3	4	2	5
7	1	3	5	6	2	8	4	9
9	2	5	4	8	7	6	1	3
6	4	8	1	3	9	2	5	7

Solution 16

9	4	8	7	6	1	3	2	5
7	6	3	2	4	5	8	9	1
5	1	2	3	8	9	4	7	6
1	8	4	9	7	3	5	6	2
3	2	7	8	5	6	9	1	4
6	9	5	4	1	2	7	3	8
4	7	6	1	3	8	2	5	9
2	3	1	5	9	4	6	8	7
8	5	9	6	2	7	1	4	3

Solution 17

4	7	1	3	2	9	5	8	6
9	2	8	7	5	6	3	1	4
3	5	6	1	4	8	7	2	9
1	9	5	8	3	2	4	6	7
6	8	4	9	1	7	2	3	5
2	3	7	5	6	4	1	9	8
5	4	3	6	8	1	9	7	2
7	6	2	4	9	3	8	5	1
8	1	9	2	7	5	6	4	3

Solution 18

7	8	4	3	5	2	1	6	9
5	9	6	1	7	8	2	3	4
3	2	1	6	4	9	7	5	8
8	7	2	4	6	3	5	9	1
1	6	5	9	8	7	4	2	3
9	4	3	5	2	1	8	7	6
4	3	7	8	9	5	6	1	2
6	5	9	2	1	4	3	8	7
2	1	8	7	3	6	9	4	5

Solution 19

5	4	9	1	8	2	6	7	3
3	8	6	7	4	9	5	2	1
7	1	2	5	6	3	9	4	8
1	7	5	3	9	6	2	8	4
6	2	3	8	5	4	7	1	9
8	9	4	2	7	1	3	6	5
4	5	1	9	2	7	8	3	6
2	6	8	4	3	5	1	9	7
9	3	7	6	1	8	4	5	2

Solution 20

7	4	9	1	5	3	2	6	8
8	2	5	9	6	4	1	3	7
6	1	3	7	8	2	9	5	4
3	7	6	5	1	8	4	9	2
5	8	4	3	2	9	7	1	6
1	9	2	6	4	7	3	8	5
2	3	1	8	7	6	5	4	9
9	6	7	4	3	5	8	2	1
4	5	8	2	9	1	6	7	3

Solution 21

7	3	5	9	4	1	8	2	6
6	2	1	5	7	8	3	4	9
9	4	8	3	6	2	7	1	5
4	6	2	7	3	5	9	8	1
8	9	7	4	1	6	2	5	3
5	1	3	8	2	9	4	6	7
2	7	6	1	8	3	5	9	4
1	5	4	2	9	7	6	3	8
3	8	9	6	5	4	1	7	2

Solution 22

5	7	3	4	1	9	2	8	6
4	6	1	8	2	5	9	7	3
2	8	9	6	3	7	4	1	5
1	3	7	2	4	8	5	6	9
9	5	8	7	6	3	1	2	4
6	4	2	5	9	1	8	3	7
3	9	6	1	5	2	7	4	8
7	1	4	9	8	6	3	5	2
8	2	5	3	7	4	6	9	1

Solution 23

9	4	2	5	7	8	6	1	3
6	7	1	3	4	9	2	5	8
3	5	8	2	1	6	7	4	9
2	9	5	1	3	4	8	7	6
4	6	3	8	5	7	1	9	2
1	8	7	9	6	2	4	3	5
8	2	4	7	9	5	3	6	1
7	3	9	6	8	1	5	2	4
5	1	6	4	2	3	9	8	7

Solution 24

5	2	1	3	7	8	6	9	4
3	8	6	1	4	9	7	5	2
9	7	4	6	5	2	1	8	3
6	1	3	2	9	5	8	4	7
2	5	7	8	3	4	9	6	1
8	4	9	7	6	1	2	3	5
4	9	8	5	1	7	3	2	6
1	3	2	4	8	6	5	7	9
7	6	5	9	2	3	4	1	8

Solution 25

9	5	3	4	8	7	2	6	1
8	6	4	1	3	2	5	7	9
2	7	1	6	5	9	4	3	8
6	1	8	2	9	3	7	5	4
4	9	7	8	6	5	3	1	2
3	2	5	7	4	1	9	8	6
1	4	2	3	7	6	8	9	5
7	8	9	5	1	4	6	2	3
5	3	6	9	2	8	1	4	7

Solution 26

4	5	6	9	7	1	2	3	8
2	1	8	4	3	6	7	9	5
9	3	7	5	8	2	1	6	4
7	2	3	8	1	9	5	4	6
8	9	4	7	6	5	3	2	1
5	6	1	3	2	4	8	7	9
3	8	9	1	4	7	6	5	2
6	7	5	2	9	8	4	1	3
1	4	2	6	5	3	9	8	7

Solution 27

4	3	1	2	6	9	8	5	7
6	8	7	5	3	1	4	9	2
5	9	2	4	8	7	6	1	3
7	6	9	8	5	3	1	2	4
1	5	3	7	4	2	9	6	8
8	2	4	1	9	6	7	3	5
9	7	6	3	2	4	5	8	1
3	4	5	6	1	8	2	7	9
2	1	8	9	7	5	3	4	6

Solution 28

9	8	6	7	2	3	1	5	4
2	7	5	9	4	1	6	3	8
4	1	3	6	5	8	7	9	2
5	9	8	2	6	4	3	7	1
7	2	1	8	3	9	5	4	6
3	6	4	1	7	5	8	2	9
6	3	7	4	1	2	9	8	5
8	5	2	3	9	6	4	1	7
1	4	9	5	8	7	2	6	3

Solution 29

2	8	5	6	1	9	7	4	3
4	9	6	5	3	7	8	2	1
7	1	3	8	2	4	9	6	5
8	4	7	9	6	5	1	3	2
5	3	9	2	4	1	6	8	7
6	2	1	7	8	3	5	9	4
1	5	2	4	9	8	3	7	6
3	6	8	1	7	2	4	5	9
9	7	4	3	5	6	2	1	8

Solution 30

9	1	6	3	7	8	4	2	5
3	5	7	2	4	6	8	1	9
8	4	2	1	9	5	6	3	7
6	8	9	5	2	1	7	4	3
5	2	4	7	6	3	9	8	1
1	7	3	4	8	9	2	5	6
7	6	5	8	1	4	3	9	2
4	9	1	6	3	2	5	7	8
2	3	8	9	5	7	1	6	4

Solution 31

3	8	6	7	4	1	2	5	9
9	1	7	2	8	5	6	4	3
2	5	4	3	6	9	7	8	1
8	7	2	9	5	3	1	6	4
6	9	3	8	1	4	5	7	2
1	4	5	6	7	2	9	3	8
4	2	1	5	3	7	8	9	6
5	6	9	4	2	8	3	1	7
7	3	8	1	9	6	4	2	5

Solution 32

1	9	5	8	6	4	3	7	2
3	4	7	9	2	5	6	8	1
8	2	6	1	7	3	5	9	4
7	1	4	6	3	2	9	5	8
9	8	3	7	5	1	4	2	6
5	6	2	4	9	8	1	3	7
4	3	9	2	8	6	7	1	5
6	5	8	3	1	7	2	4	9
2	7	1	5	4	9	8	6	3

Solution 33

8	5	9	7	1	2	6	3	4
2	3	4	6	8	9	7	5	1
7	1	6	5	4	3	8	9	2
6	9	2	3	7	8	1	4	5
1	7	5	9	2	4	3	8	6
4	8	3	1	6	5	9	2	7
9	2	1	4	3	7	5	6	8
3	4	7	8	5	6	2	1	9
5	6	8	2	9	1	4	7	3

Solution 34

4	5	1	7	9	6	2	3	8
2	3	7	5	8	4	9	6	1
6	9	8	3	1	2	5	4	7
7	2	9	4	6	1	3	8	5
5	8	4	9	3	7	6	1	2
1	6	3	2	5	8	4	7	9
9	7	2	8	4	3	1	5	6
8	4	6	1	2	5	7	9	3
3	1	5	6	7	9	8	2	4

Solution 35

7	9	6	5	4	2	3	8	1
8	5	1	7	3	9	2	4	6
4	3	2	8	6	1	9	5	7
6	1	3	2	8	4	7	9	5
5	8	7	6	9	3	4	1	2
9	2	4	1	7	5	6	3	8
3	7	8	4	5	6	1	2	9
2	6	9	3	1	8	5	7	4
1	4	5	9	2	7	8	6	3

Solution 36

8	7	4	6	5	9	1	2	3
9	5	6	2	3	1	4	8	7
1	3	2	4	8	7	9	6	5
7	1	5	3	6	2	8	9	4
3	2	9	1	4	8	7	5	6
6	4	8	7	9	5	2	3	1
4	6	1	8	2	3	5	7	9
2	9	7	5	1	6	3	4	8
5	8	3	9	7	4	6	1	2

Second Edition

Dental Instruments

A Pocket Guide

To access your Student Resources, visit the Web address below:

http://evolve.elsevier.com/Boyd/dentalinstruments/

Evolve Student Learning Resources for *Boyd: Dental Instruments: A Pocket Guide*, second edition offers the following features:

- **Assessments**

  The Assessments allow students to test their knowledge by answering true or false, multiple choice, or matching questions about images from each chapter in the book. Students can see how many questions they answer correctly; the correct answers are provided for questions they miss.

- **Drag-and-Drop Exercises**

  The Drag-and-Drop Exercises test the student's skill at selecting the correct instrument and arranging them in the proper sequence for a tray setup. A selection of instruments is shown, and a type of dental procedure is specified. The student must select the correct instruments and put them in proper order of use on the tray.

- **Weblinks**

  A variety of weblinks are provided so the student can pursue further study.

Second Edition

Dental Instruments

A Pocket Guide

Linda R. Bartolomucci Boyd, CDA, RDA, BA
Dental Assisting Program
Diablo Valley College
Pleasant Hill, California

ELSEVIER
SAUNDERS
11830 Westline Industrial Drive
St. Louis, Missouri 63146

DENTAL INSTRUMENTS: A POCKET GUIDE, ED 2
ISBN 1-4160-2329-1

International Standard Book Number 1-4160-2329-1

Publishing Director: Linda Duncan
Executive Editor: Penny Rudolph
Developmental Editor: Courtney Sprehe
Publishing Services Manager: Linda McKinley
Project Manager: Rich Barber
Designer: Amy Buxton

Printed in the United States of America

Last digit is the print number: 9 8 7 6 5 4 3 2 1

Dedication

I dedicate this edition to all my family, who recognize the value of love, prayer, and education. I especially dedicate this textbook to my sons, Michael and Matthew, and to my daughter-in-law, Rebecca. They have always given me encouragement in my endeavors and have loved me unconditionally, especially during the writing of this textbook. And special thanks to my grandson, Christian Michael Boyd, who gives me such joy and has taught me the simplicity of learning.

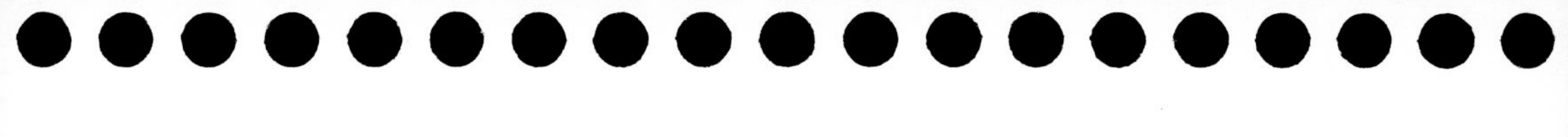

Consultants

Andrew Hartzell
President
G. Hartzell & Son
Concord, California

Joyce M. Litch, RDH, DDS, MSD
Private Practice of Periodontics
San Jose, California

Preface

Dental instruments are an intricate part of the dental practice. Basic dental instruments have remained relatively unchanged throughout the years, but design modifications have been made to accommodate developments in the dental field. For example, special coatings are available, such as the titanium coating found on composite instruments, that allow instruments to be adapted to the different types of materials used in today's dental office.

As the world's technology has evolved, so has the technology for the equipment used in dentistry. This second edition of *Dental Instruments: A Pocket Guide* includes both traditional and new instruments, as well as some of the newer equipment used in dental practices. Also, a chapter on sterilization equipment has been added.

It is imperative that the clinician have a thorough knowledge and understanding of all instruments, because dental practices rely on tray setups for procedures. To help the reader master the identification and use of dental instruments, this text includes both common and specialty instruments. Certain chapters focus on the instruments used in all dental practices, such as the components of the basic tray setup, the anesthetic syringe and its parts, evacuation devices, dental dams, handpieces, burs, and sterilization equipment. Other chapters are designed around various dental procedures, such as instruments used in hygiene, amalgam, and composite procedures. The dental specialty chapters include instruments used in fixed prosthodontics, orthodontics, endodontics, and periodontics. Two chapters discuss oral surgery. Many chapters include an example of a tray setup, which shows the instruments presented in the chapter.

Simplification is the key to studying and understanding each instrument and its functions. The flip-book, flashcard design of this text can help the reader memorize instruments and then identify them at a glance, because a photograph or illustration is provided on the top page, and a full description of the instrument is given on the bottom page, including the name, function, and key characteristics. Many instruments have both a full photograph and a close-up of the working end or ends of the instrument. As readers learn the instruments, they can use the text for self-testing. An Evolve web site, a terrific learning tool, is available on the Internet for both students and instructors.

I am confident that this text can help students to more easily learn the dental instruments, dental equipment, and tray setups that clinicians use in dental practices. It is imperative that students begin their career in the dental profession with a thorough knowledge of dental instruments and equipment. This text can certainly help them achieve that goal.

Linda R. Bartolomucci Boyd

Acknowledgments

I am extremely grateful to the several people who have assisted me in developing the second edition of this textbook. First and foremost, I want to thank all students. Their zest for learning has encouraged me in my efforts to make this text a great process for learning dental instruments. I truly appreciate all the dentists and their staff members who were willing to answer my questions, especially Timothy Farley, DDS. I would also like to thank all the dentists who gave me such great support and who allowed me to borrow instruments for photographs. A special thanks to Kyle Van Brocklin, DDS, and his registered dental assistant, Nicole Campbell, who allowed me to take photographs of equipment in their offices.

I would like to thank Andy Hartzell and his excellent staff at G. Hartzell & Son for their graciousness in lending me most of the instruments used in the photographs; also Phyllis Martina for helping me obtain the photographs I needed from Hu-Friedy Instrument Co. I would like to thank Ken Cook for his dedication and artistry in taking the photographs for this textbook.

I owe boundless thanks to my colleagues, including periodontist Joyce M. Litch, RDH, DDS, MSD, whom I consulted for the chapters on hygiene instruments and periodontal instruments; she was so giving of her time. Cathy Clarke freely gave both time and endless encouragement in helping me research the sterilization aspects of this text. I am grateful to all my colleagues who were so encouraging and supportive during the phases of this second edition and to Jill Wilson for her constant assistance in whatever I needed to complete this text.

My thanks to my editor, Penny Rudolph, whose enthusiasm and vision of this book remain the same as mine, and to my developmental editor, Courtney Sprehe, for all her encouragement and hard work in getting the text to production.

I could not have written this second edition without the love, support, and prayers of all my family and friends: my son Michael, my daughter-in-law, Rebecca, and my grandson, Christian, who gave me such joy when I needed some encouragement; my son Matthew, who was always there for me anytime of the day or night; my brother Ray, my sister Meri, and my cousin Elaine, who gave their constant support and love; and my very dear and best friend, John LaFountain, whose love and encouragement saw me through all the phases of this book.

Linda R. Bartolomucci Boyd

Note to the Students

This text is designed to help you master the identification and function of instruments and equipment used in dental practices. The 17 chapters cover instruments required for clinical procedures in both general and specialty practices.

As you can see, the text is formatted in the flash card style. For the instrument pages, each instrument (or group of instruments) is pictured on the top page; the function and special characteristics of the instrument are listed on the bottom page. Some instruments on the top page have numbered parts. In these cases, the bottom page identifies the parts matching the numbers on the instrument. As you master the name and function of an instrument, you can test yourself. Fold the book in half, showing only the picture of the instrument. Then, from memory, try to name the instrument and describe its function and special characteristics.

Verify your answer by checking the bottom page. Keep in mind that it is important to be able to name the instrument, as well as describe its function. You can also test yourself on the Evolve web site (the URL is given on p. ii) by using the Assessment Questions from each chapter and the drag-and-drop exercises.

After mastering the individual instruments, you must be able to select and place instruments in order of use for specific dental procedures. At the end of most chapters there is an example of a tray setup that shows the instruments covered in that chapter. The array may include instruments from other chapters to portray a complete tray setup. For example, some of the instruments from Chapter 1, such as the basic setup (i.e., mouth mirror, explorer, and cotton forceps), are included on all tray setups. Also, the tray setups in this text include only instruments and not the auxiliary items that would be used for dental procedures.

The design elements of flash card–style learning, comprehensive chapters for specific dental procedures, and examples of tray setups can help you master an important and intricate part of dental practice. I wish you all success in the field of dentistry. I know you will be a great asset to the dental profession.

Linda R. Bartolomucci Boyd

About the Evolve Site

The Evolve web site for *Dental Instruments: A Pocket Guide* is a great addition to the text, and both faculty and students can benefit from it. To get started on the Evolve site, the student or instructor just logs on to and follows the instructions provided.

For Students

The Evolve site for students has two main parts: assessment quizzes for each chapter and interactive drag-and-drop exercises (a new feature for the second edition). The assessments allow students to test their knowledge by answering questions about each chapter. Students are able to see how many questions they answer correctly, and the correct answers are provided for any questions they miss. The drag-and-drop exercises can test the student's skill at selecting the correct instruments and arranging them in the proper sequence for a tray setup. For these exercises a selection of instruments is shown, and the type of dental procedure is specified.

The student must select the correct instruments and put them in the proper order of use on the tray. The student is given feedback on whether or not their answer is correct. The Evolve site also features a downloadable test form and web links for further study.

For Faculty

The Evolve site for faculty is a vital adjunct for instructors using this text. The web site can be used in a number of ways for teaching and as a source of different tools for measuring students' learning proficiency.

For example, pictures from all 17 chapters can be downloaded and used in a Power Point presentation. This is a great way to present each instrument and to discuss its use with students. These pictures in Power Point can also be used to test students' recognition of the instrument, along with their knowledge of its function and special characteristics. To help with this process, I have developed a test sheet composed of a table with three columns, one for the name, one for the function, and one for the special characteristics. This test sheet can be downloaded and adapted to the instructor's specific needs.

The instructor site also provides a test bank of questions. The questions, which are all multiple choice, appear in Examview, a program that allows the instructor to customize quizzes and tests. In some cases I have provided different questions about the same instrument.

This gives the instructor a choice in the style of question, as well as a variety of ways to measure a student's proficiency.

In addition to these features, the faculty site also includes all the material that appears on the student site.

The Evolve site is a wonderful asset to *Dental Instruments: A Pocket Guide*. I have found it extremely useful both in my presentations and for testing students. I hope that instructors find the web site an invaluable complement to their teaching efforts, and that students find it a helpful tool for measuring their progress in mastering dental instruments.

Linda R. Bartolomucci Boyd

Contents

Photograph/Illustration Credits

Photographer: Kenneth A. Cook, III, Pleasanton, California

Photographs/illustrations of the following instruments were provided courtesy of the following:

Alfa Medical, Hempstead, New York
Sterilizers—Dry Heat (Static Air and Rapid Heat Transfer)

Barnstead International/Harvey, Dubuque, Iowa
Sterilizer—Chemiclave (Unsaturated Chemical Vapor)

DL Bird, DS Robinson
Bird/Robinson: *Torres and Ehrlich modern dental assisting*, ed 8, Philadelphia, 2005, WB Saunders.
Implant Scaler (Disposable Tips)
Three-Number Instrument
Tofflemire/Matrix Band Retainer

Coltène/Whaledent, Cuyahoga Falls, Ohio
Gutta-Percha

Danville Engineering, San Ramon, California
Air Abrasion Unit and Handpiece

DENTSPLY Caulk, Milford, Delaware
Automatrix System

DENTSPLY Professional, York, Pennsylvania
Bur
Diamond Bur—Flame
Diamond Bur—Flat-End Cylinder
Diamond Bur—Flat-End Taper
Diamond Bur—Wheel
Electric Handpiece Unit and Handpiece Attachments
Finishing Bur
High-Speed Handpiece

Inverted Cone Bur
Pear-Shaped Bur
Prophy Slow-Speed Handpiece
Prophy Slow-Speed Handpiece with Prophy Angle Attachment
Round Bur
Straight Fissure Bur—Crosscut
Straight Fissure Bur—Plain Cut
Taper Fissure Bur—Crosscut
Taper Fissure Bur—Plain Cut
Ultrasonic Scaling Unit (Power Scaler)

DENTSPLY Tulsa Dental, Tulsa, Oklahoma
Anterior Clamp
Premolar Clamp
Universal Clamp—Mandibular
Universal Clamp—Maxillary

Garrison Dental Solutions, Spring Lake, Michigan
Sectional Matrix System

G. Hartzell & Son, Concord, California
Provided many of the instruments used in the professional photography

Hu-Friedy, Chicago, Illinois
Cassettes
Color Coding for Instruments
Nitrile Utility Gloves
Parts Box for Sterilization
Process Indicator Tape and Dispensing Unit
Sterilization Management System
Ultrasonic Scaler Instrument Tip—Supragingival
Ultrasonic Scaler Instrument Tip—Subgingival
Ultrasonic Scaler Instrument Tip—Furcation
Ultrasonic Scaler Instrument Tip—Universal

Ivoclar Vivadent, ICDE, Amherst, New York
Amalgamator

Johnson: *Color atlas of endodontics*, Philadelphia, 2002, WB Saunders.
Gutta-Percha Warming Unit

KaVo America Corp., Lake Zurich, Illinois
Fiberoptic High-Speed Handpiece
Slow-Speed Motor with Straight Handpiece Attachment

Midmark Corp., Versailles, Ohio
Ultrasonic Cleaning Unit
Sterilizer—Autoclave (Saturated Steam)

Practicon Dental, Greenville, North Carolina
Laboratory Coat
Protective Glasses (Eye Wear) and Protective Mask

Premier Dental, Plymouth Meeting, Pennsylvania
Reamer
Root Canal File—K Type
Root Canal File—Hedstrom

SciCan, Toronto, Ontario
Sterilizer—Autoclave ("Flash")

Stryker Corp., Kalamazoo, Michigan
Surgical Electric Handpiece Unit and Implant Handpiece

SybronEndo, Orange, California
Electronic Apex Locator
Vitalometer/Pulp Tester

CHAPTER 1

Basic Dental Instruments

2

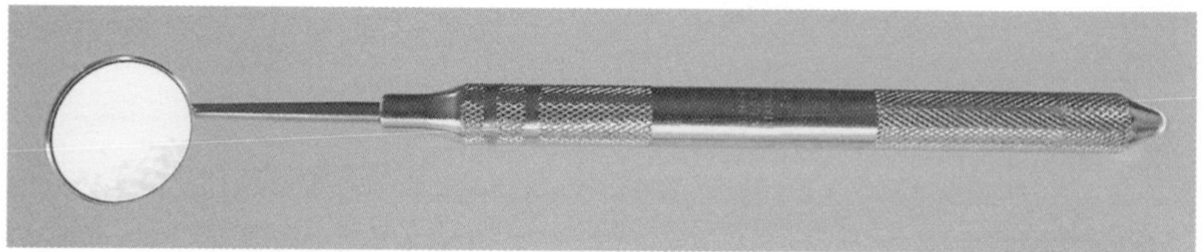

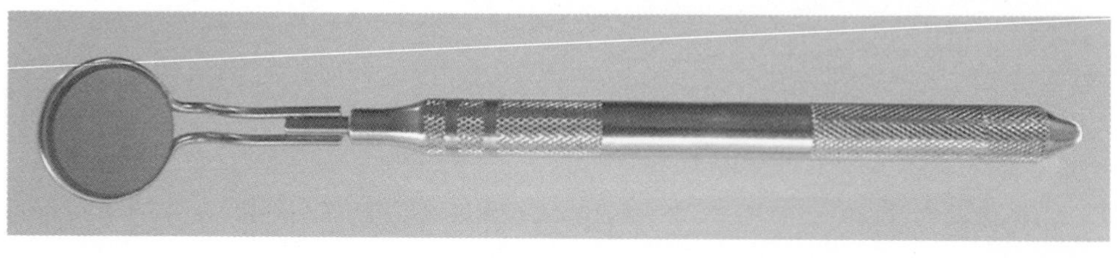

INSTRUMENT

Mouth Mirror

FUNCTION

To provide indirect vision
To retract lips, cheeks, and tongue
To reflect light into the mouth

CHARACTERISTICS

Front surface mirrors—Accurate, distortion-free image
Flat surface mirrors—Used in disposable models
Concave mirrors—Magnify image
Double-sided mirrors—Used to retract tongue or cheek and view intraoral cavity simultaneously
Range of sizes
Commonly used sizes: No. 4 and no. 5
Single ended
Different mirror handles available
Used with most tray setups

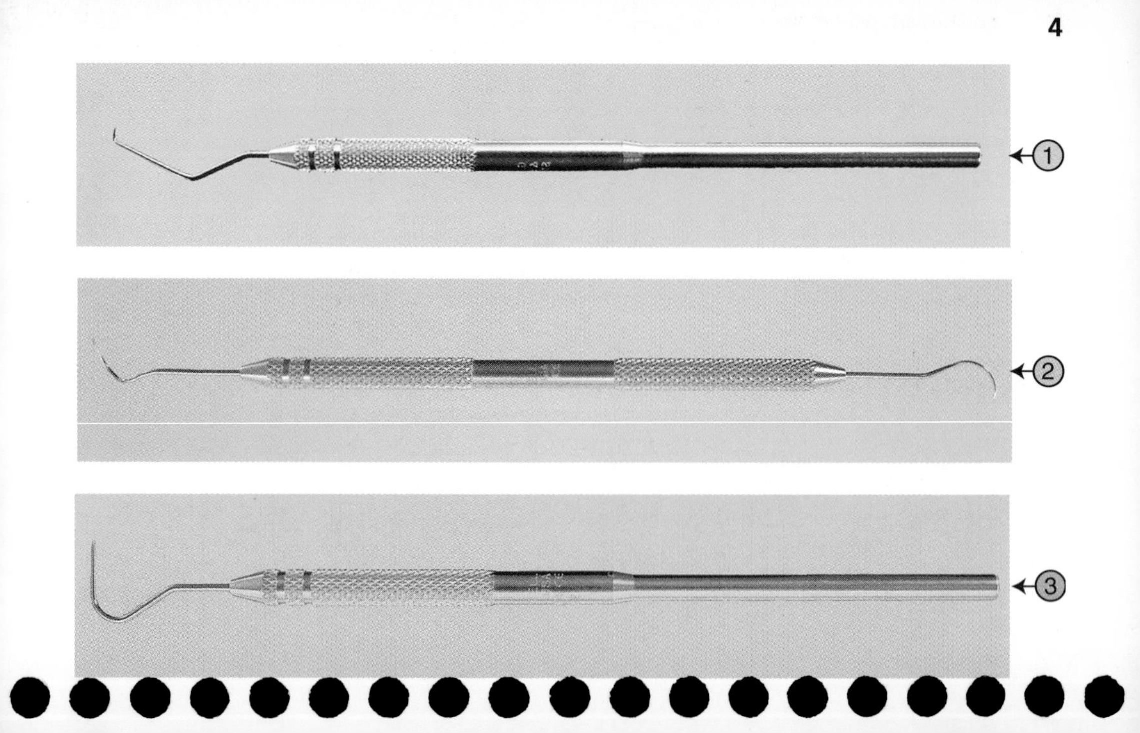
1
2
3

Explorers

FUNCTION To examine teeth for decay (caries), calculus, furcations, or other abnormalities

CHARACTERISTICS Pointed tips; sharp, thin, flexible
Single or double ended

- Double-ended models—May have different styles of working ends; also may have explorer on one end and periodontal probe on the other

Used with most tray setups
Variety of sizes and types:

1. Orban
2. Pigtail
3. Shepherd's hook

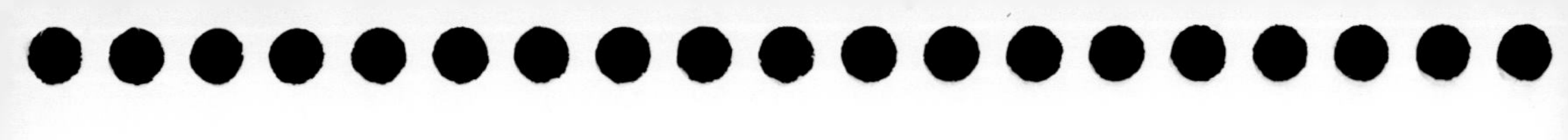

INSTRUMENT

Cotton Forceps (Pliers)

FUNCTION To grasp material and/or transfer it into and out of the oral cavity

CHARACTERISTICS Plain or serrated tips
Pointed or rounded tips
Locking forceps (see Chapter 11)
Range of sizes available
Used with most tray setups

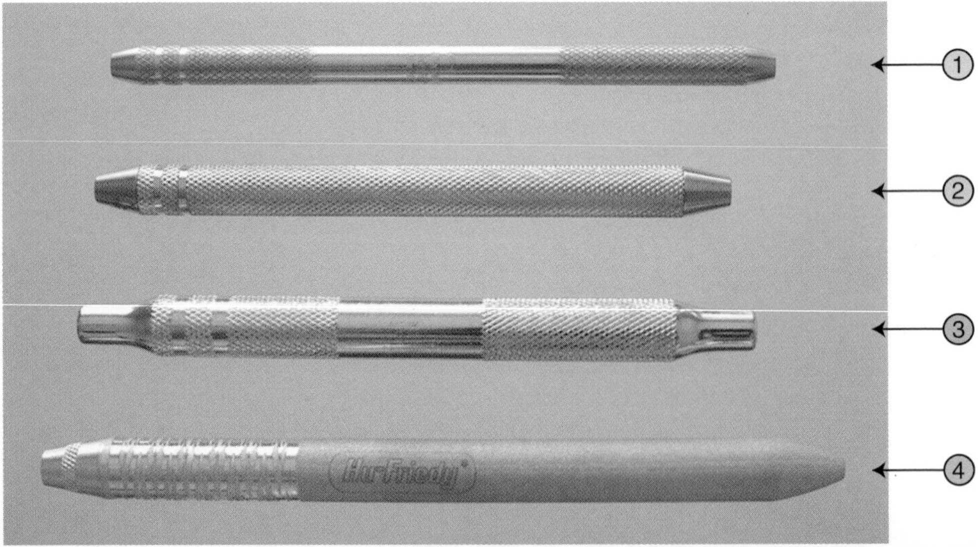

①

②

③

④

INSTRUMENT

Instrument Handles

FUNCTION To hold (grasp) instrument

CHARACTERISTICS Single or double ended

Removable working ends (replaceable and interchangeable)

Examples: Mouth mirror, scaler

Nonremovable working ends also available

Larger diameter models—Help lighten grasp and maximize control

Alternating diameter models—Lessen stress associated with carpal tunnel syndrome

Lighter weight models—Minimize fatigue

Variety of sizes, styles, and textures:

① Small, round $\frac{1}{4}$-inch stainless steel

② Standard, $\frac{5}{16}$-inch hollow stainless steel

③ Lightweight, $\frac{3}{8}$-inch slip-resistant pattern

④ Satin Steel model—Lightweight, ergonomically designed

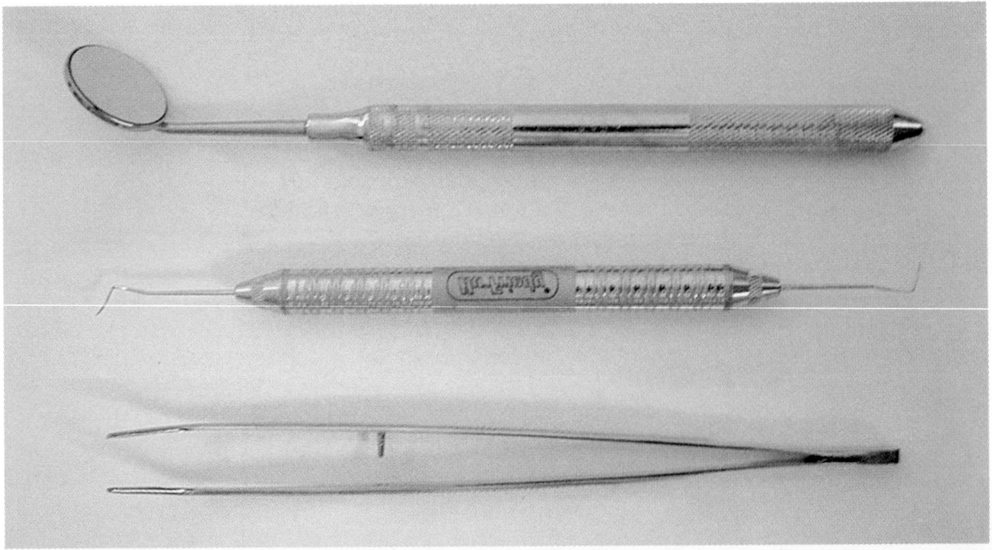

10

TRAY SETUP

Basic

FROM TOP TO BOTTOM

Mouth mirror, explorer, cotton forceps

CHAPTER 2

Enamel Cutting Instruments

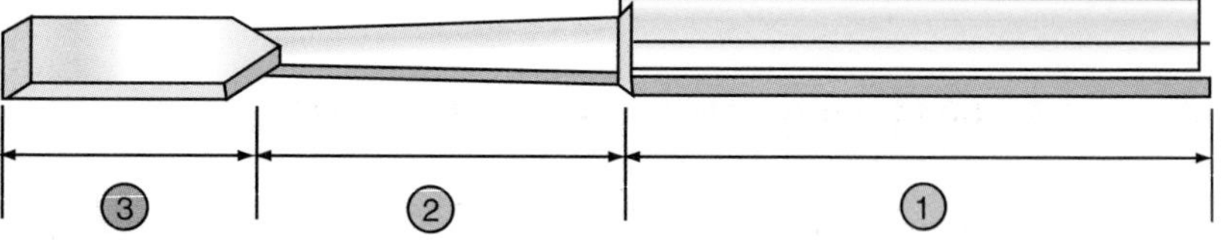
3
2
1

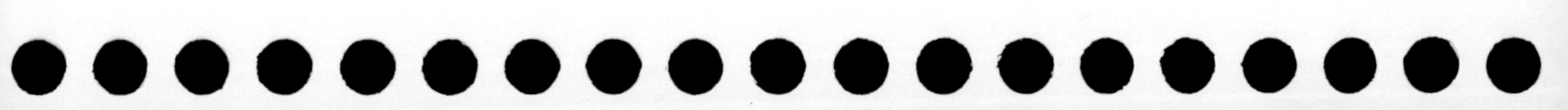

Parts of an Instrument

① **HANDLE** Grasping end of instrument
Variety of sizes and styles

② **SHANK** Connects handle to working end of instrument
May be straight or may have one or more angles to accommodate specific areas of the mouth

③ **WORKING END** May have cutting edge, bevel, point, nib, or beaks

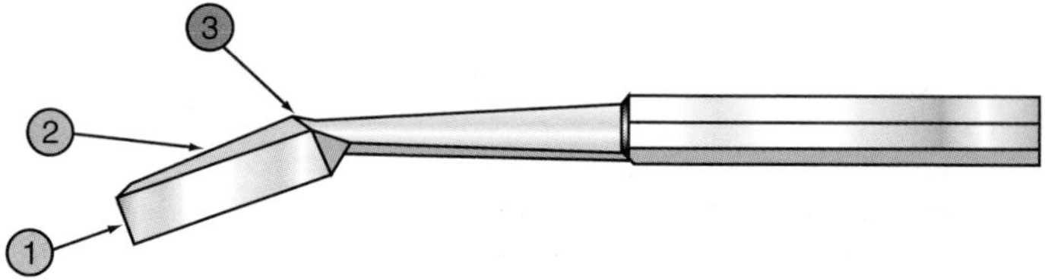

16

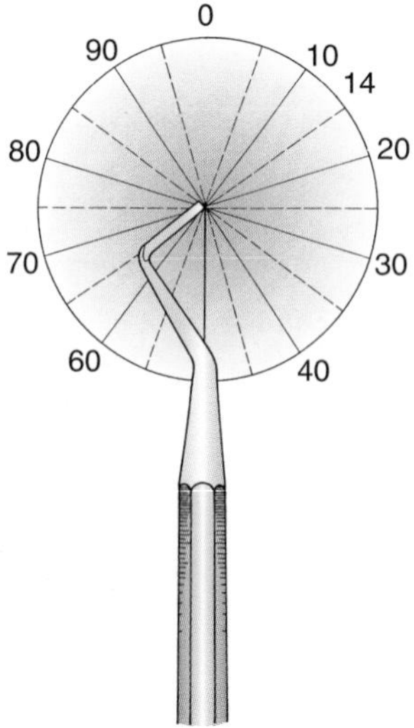

0
10
14
20
30
40
60
70
80
90

3
2
1

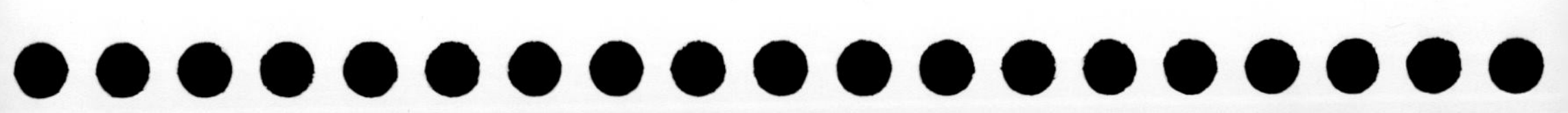

INSTRUMENT

Three-Number Instrument*

FUNCTION Numbers on handle indicate width, length, and angle of blade.

① Indicates width of blade in tenths of millimeters
Example: 20 indicates a width of 2 mm

② Indicates length of blade in millimeters
Example: 8 indicates a length of 8 mm

③ Indicates angle of blade from long axis of shaft
Example: 12 indicates an angle of 12 degrees

The designation for the instrument described above would be 20–8–12.

Examples: Enamel hatchet, enamel hoe

*The instrument number formula was designed by Dr. G.V. Black, Northwestern University.

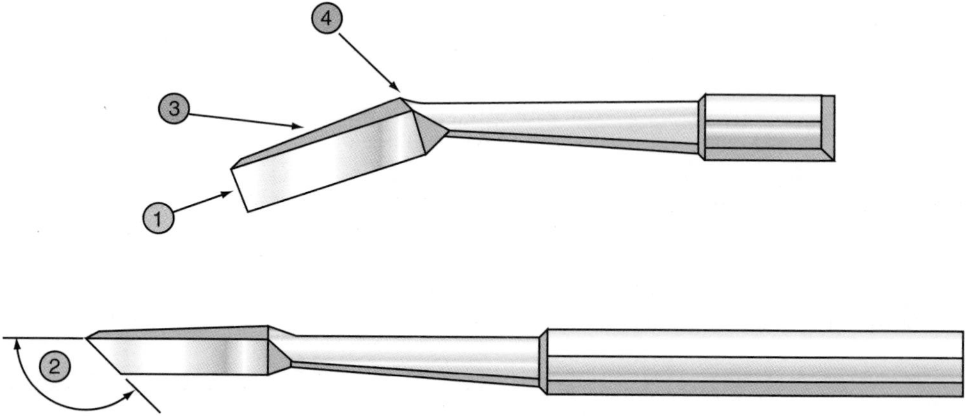

Four-Number Instrument*

FUNCTION Numbers on handle indicate width of blade, angle of cutting edge, length of blade, and angle of blade.

① Indicates width of blade in tenths of millimeters
Example: 20 indicates a width of 2 mm

② Indicates angle of cutting edge of blade in relation to handle
Example: 95 indicates a cutting edge angle of 95 degrees

③ Indicates length of blade in millimeters
Example: 8 indicates a length of 8 mm

④ Indicates angle of blade from long axis of shaft
Example: 12 indicates a blade angle of 12 degrees

The designation for the instrument described above would be 20–95–8–12.

Examples: Angle former, gingival margin trimmers

*The instrument number formula was designed by Dr. G.V. Black, Northwestern University.

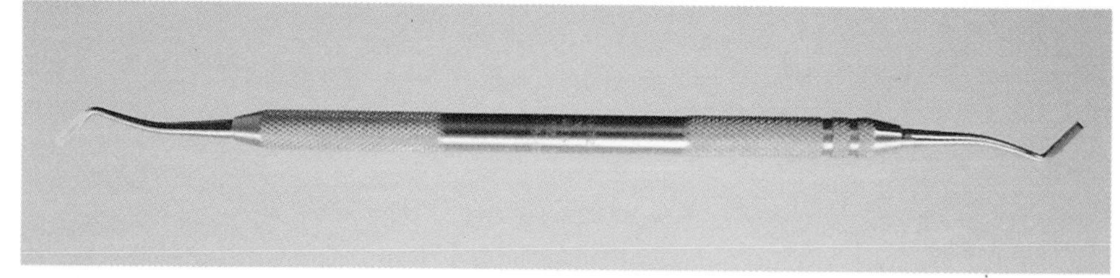

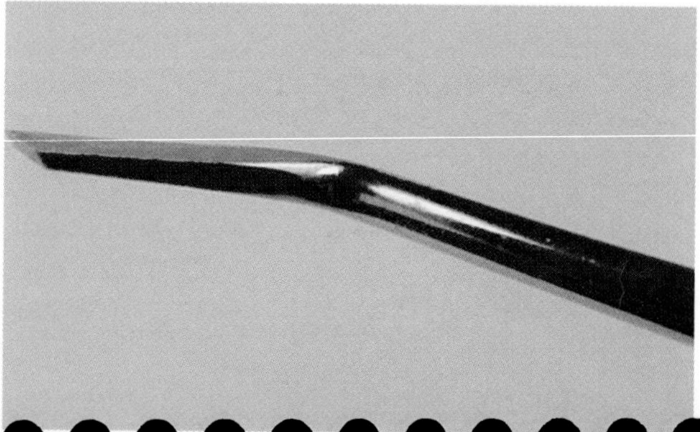

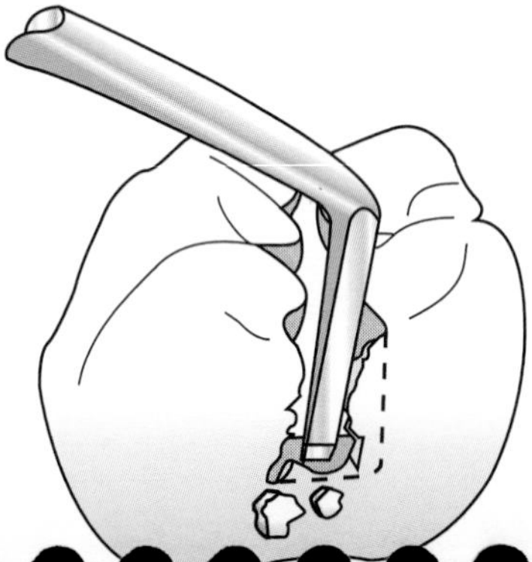

INSTRUMENT

Enamel Hatchet

FUNCTION

To clean and smooth walls in cavity preparation
To remove enamel not supported by dentin

CHARACTERISTICS

Used with push motion
Cutting edge on same plane as handle
Single or double ended

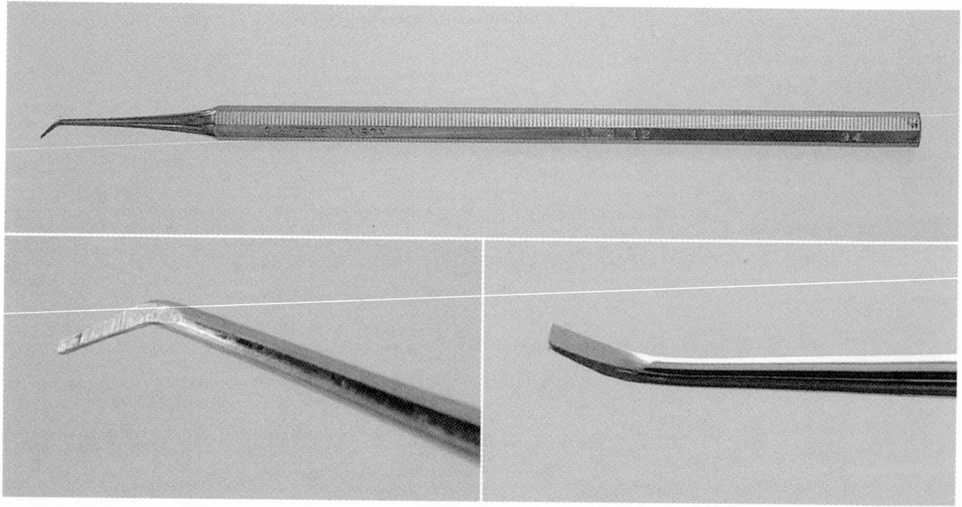

INSTRUMENT

Enamel Hoe

FUNCTION

To clean and smooth floor and walls in cavity preparation
To form or accentuate line angles in cavity preparation

CHARACTERISTICS

Used with pulling motion
Cutting edge or blade almost perpendicular to handle

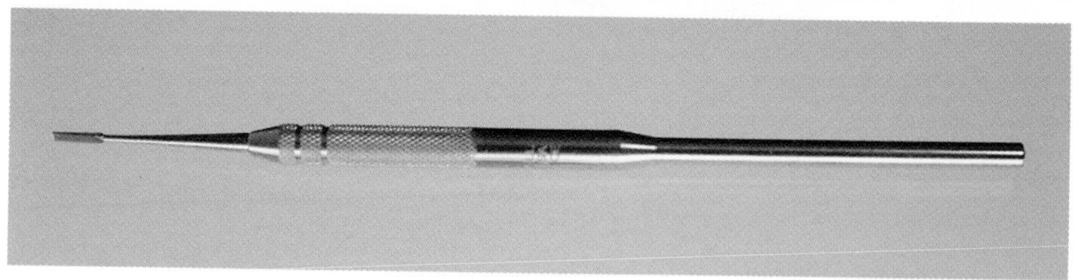

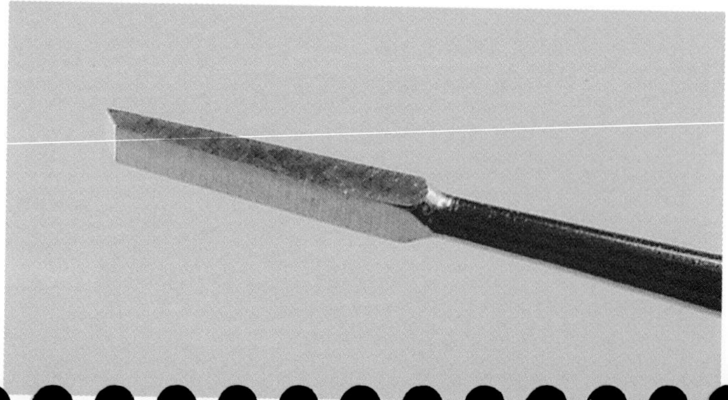

INSTRUMENT

Straight Chisel

FUNCTION To plane and cleave enamel in cavity preparation

CHARACTERISTICS Used with push motion
Single-bevel cutting edge
Single or double ended

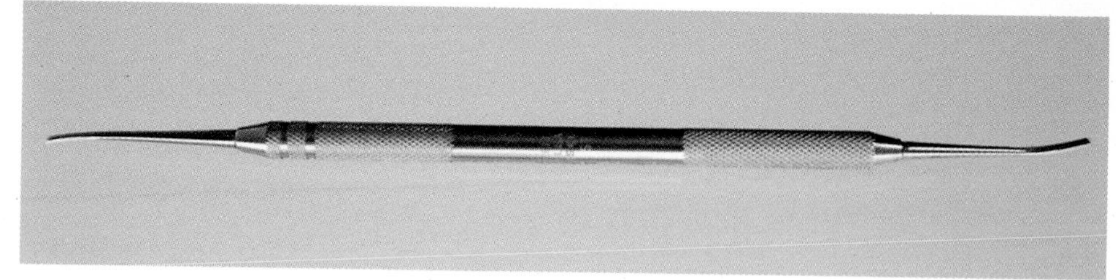

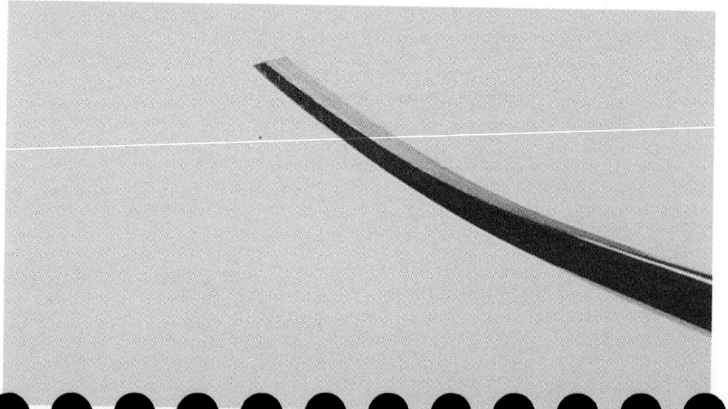

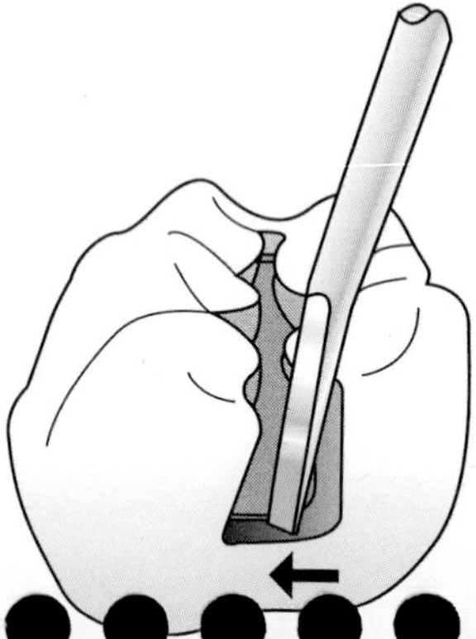

INSTRUMENT

Wedelstaedt Chisel

FUNCTION To plane and cleave enamel in cavity preparation

CHARACTERISTICS Used with push motion
Curved blade
Single-bevel cutting edge
Single or double ended

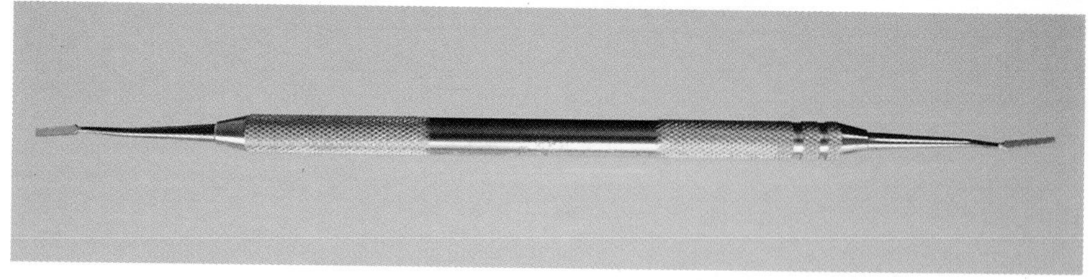

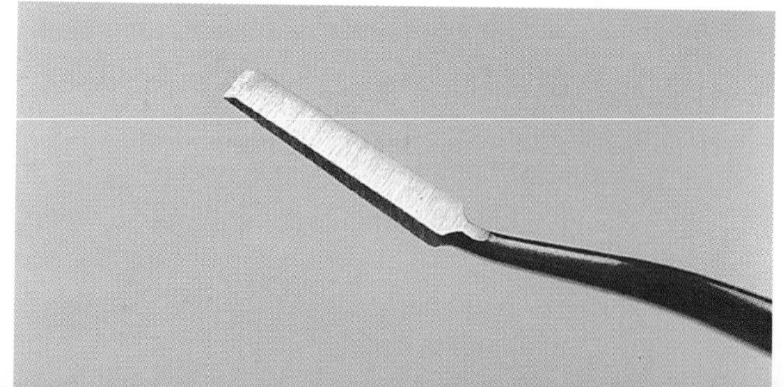

INSTRUMENT

Binangle Chisel

FUNCTION To plane and cleave enamel in cavity preparation

CHARACTERISTICS Used with push motion
Two angles for cutting edges
Single or double ended

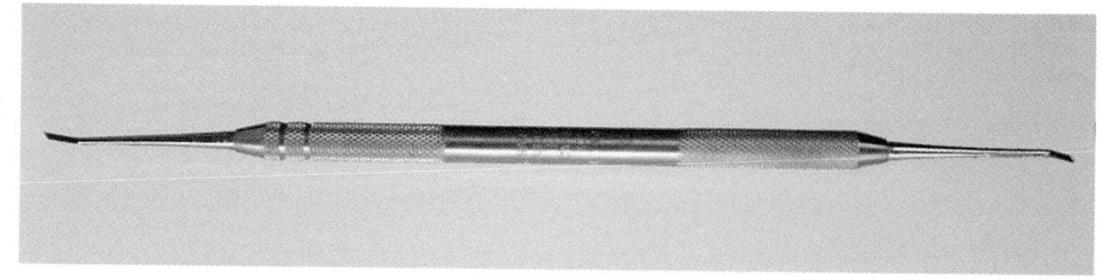

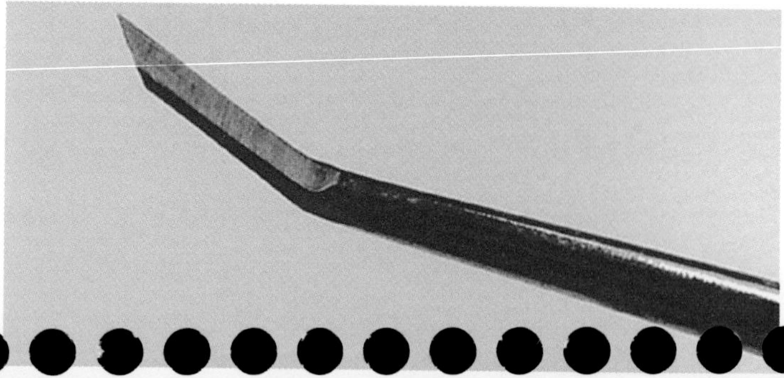

INSTRUMENT

Angle Former

FUNCTION To accentuate line and point angles in internal outline and retention in cavity preparation

CHARACTERISTICS Cutting edge at an angle
Single or double ended

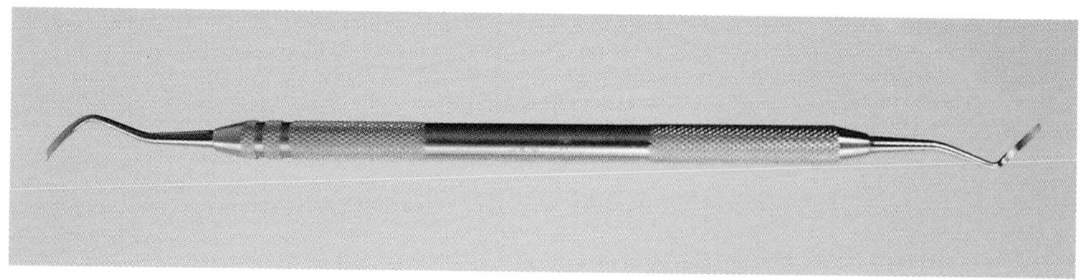

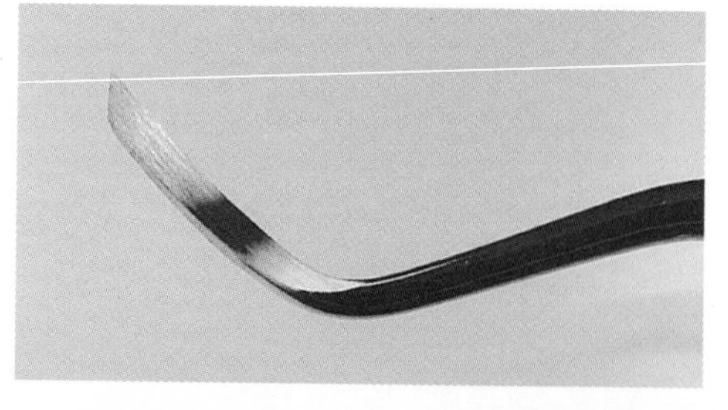

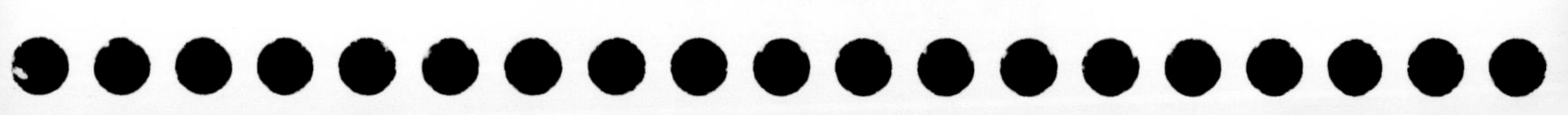

INSTRUMENT

Gingival Margin Trimmer—Mesial

FUNCTION To bevel cervical walls of mesial retention areas

CHARACTERISTICS Curved blade
Cutting edge at angle to blade
Double ended (one end curves to the right, the other to the left)

34

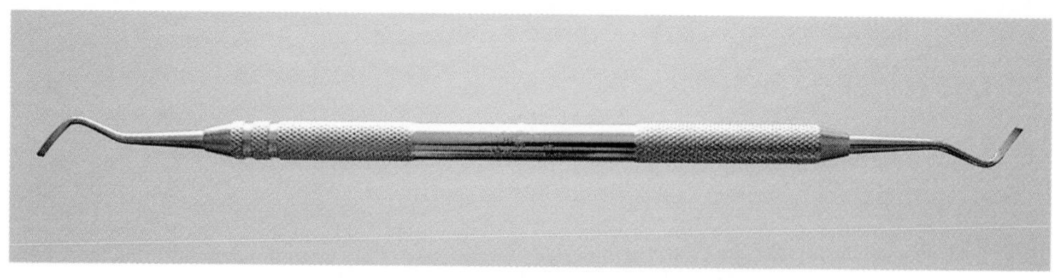

INSTRUMENT

Gingival Margin Trimmer—Distal

FUNCTION To bevel cervical walls of distal retention areas

CHARACTERISTICS Curved blade
Cutting edge at angle to blade
Double ended (one end curves to the right, the other to the left)

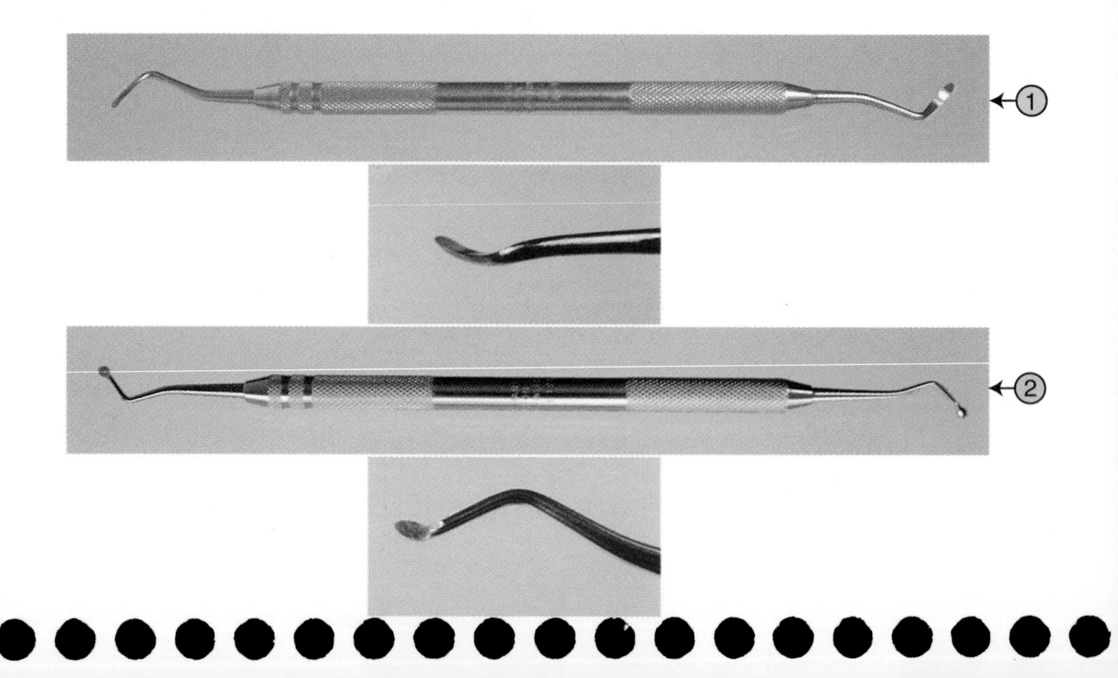
1
2

INSTRUMENT

Spoon Excavators

FUNCTION

To remove carious dentin

Secondary functions:

- To remove temporary crowns
- To remove temporary cement in temporary restoration
- To remove permanent crown during try-in

CHARACTERISTICS

Spoon-shaped with cutting edge

Range of sizes:

1. Large
2. Small

Single or double ended

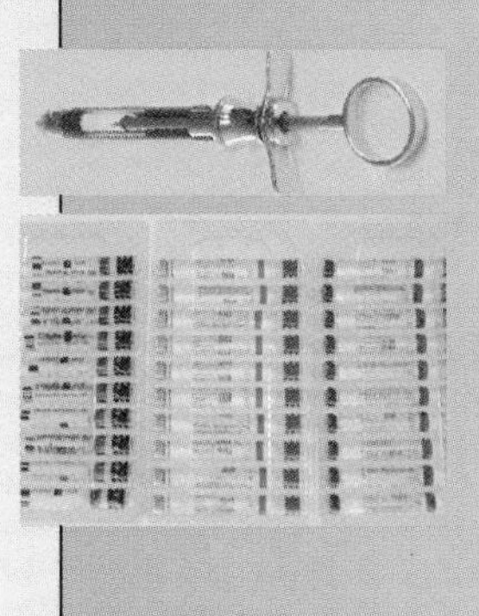

CHAPTER 3

Local Anesthetic Syringe and Components

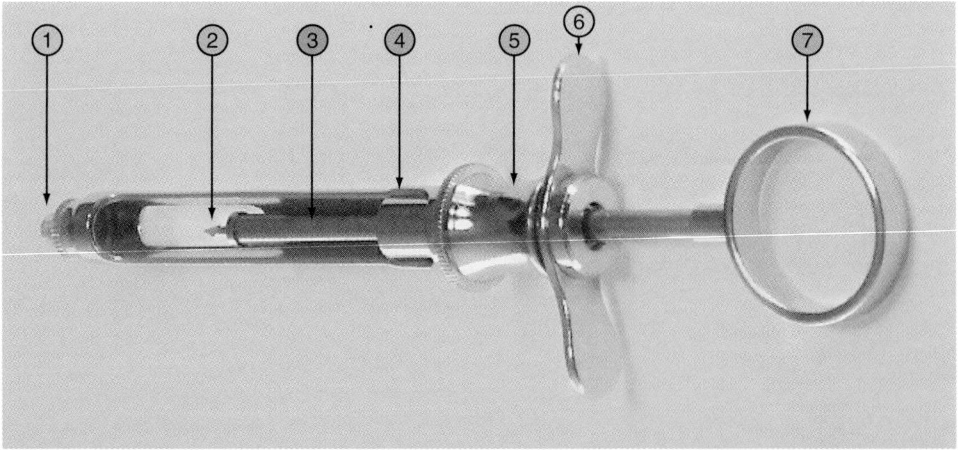

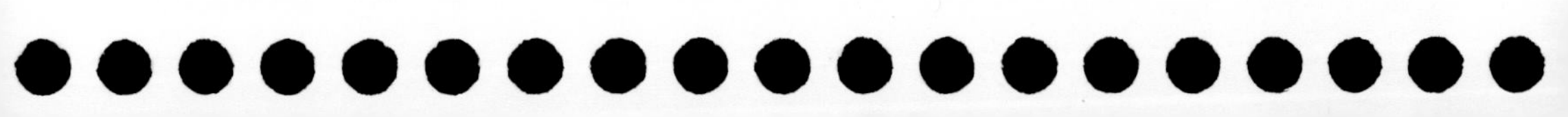

Anesthetic Aspirating Syringe

FUNCTION To administer a local anesthetic

CHARACTERISTICS Parts:

① Threaded tip
② Harpoon
③ Piston rod
④ Barrel of syringe
⑤ Finger grip
⑥ Finger bar
⑦ Thumb ring

PRACTICE NOTES

1. Disposable syringes equipped with needles and preloaded with anesthetic are available.
2. Syringes with harpoons are considered aspirating syringes.

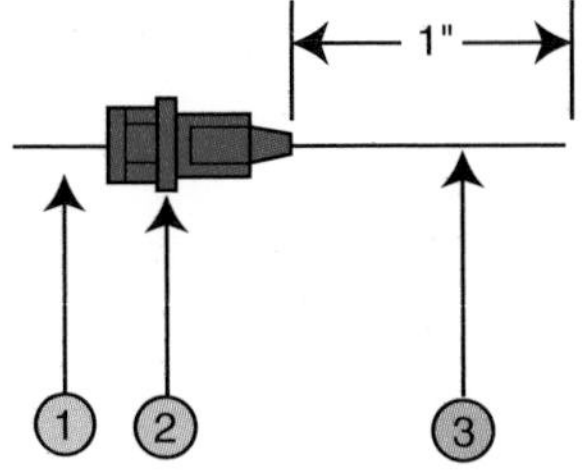
1"
1
2
3

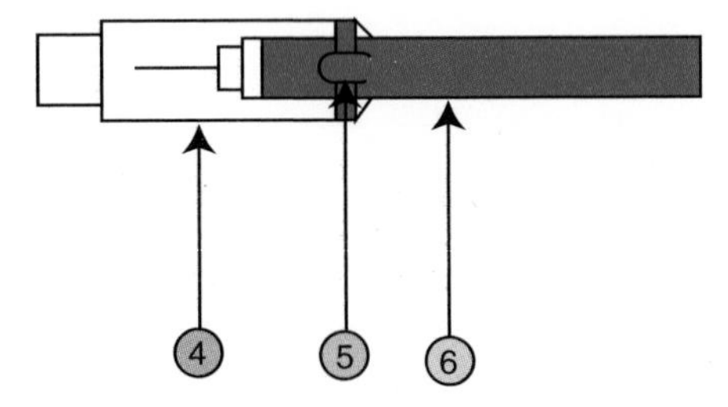
4
5
6

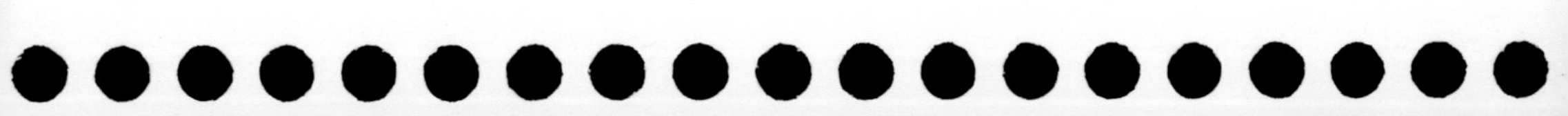

Short Needle

FUNCTION To administer anesthetic by infiltration injection on maxillary arch

CHARACTERISTICS Parts:

① Cartridge end of needle
② Needle hub
③ Injection end of needle
④ Protective cap
⑤ Seal on cap
⑥ Needle guard

1 inch long

Variety of gauges

- Gauge number—Identifies diameter (thickness) of needle
- Larger gauge number—Indicates thinner needle (e.g., 30 gauge is thinner than 25 gauge)

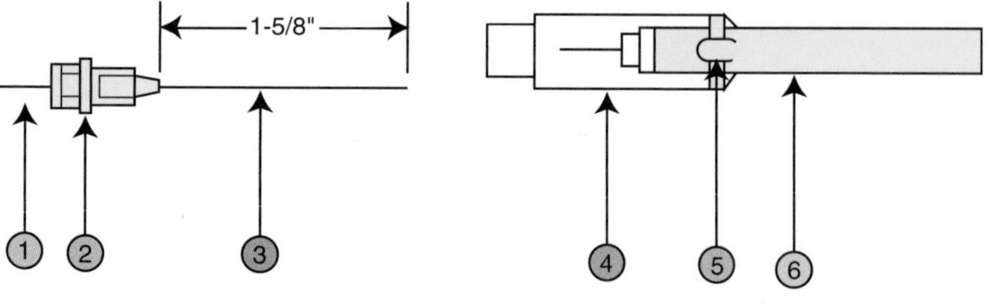
1-5/8"
1
2
3
4
5
6

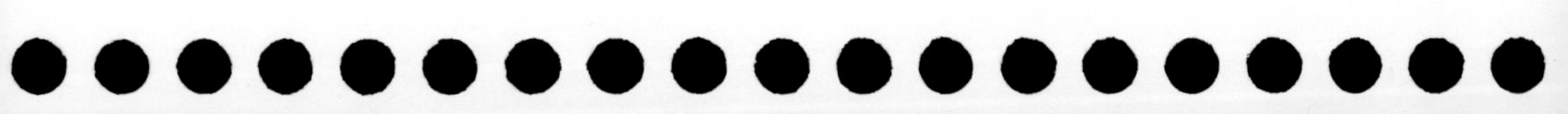

Long Needle

FUNCTION To administer anesthetic by block injection on mandibular arch

CHARACTERISTICS Parts:

① Cartridge end of needle
② Needle hub
③ Injection end of needle
④ Protective cap
⑤ Seal on cap
⑥ Needle guard

1⅝ inches long

Variety of gauges

- Gauge number—Identifies diameter (thickness) of needle
- Larger gauge number—Indicates thinner needle (e.g., 30 gauge is thinner than 25 gauge)

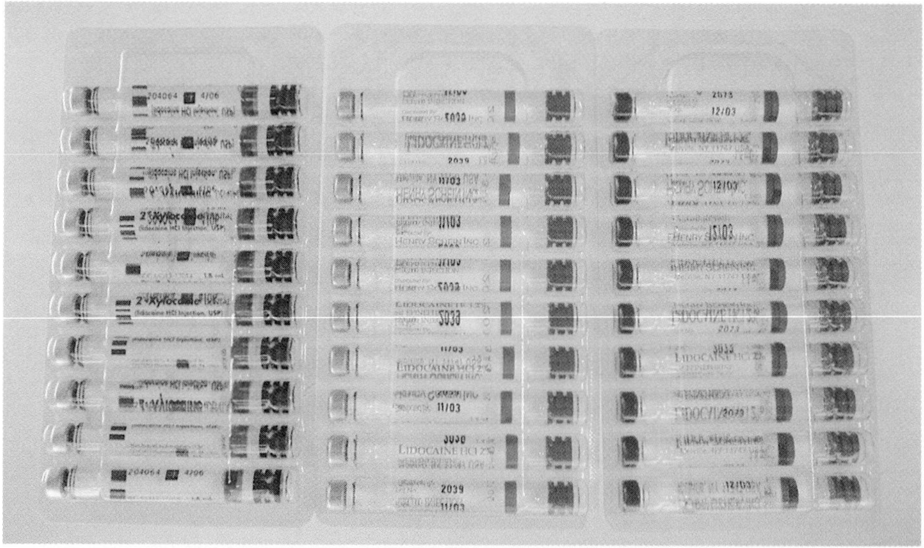
204064 4/06
2% Xylocaine
(lidocaine HCl Injection, USP)
LIDOCAINE HCl 2%
2039
11/03
12/03

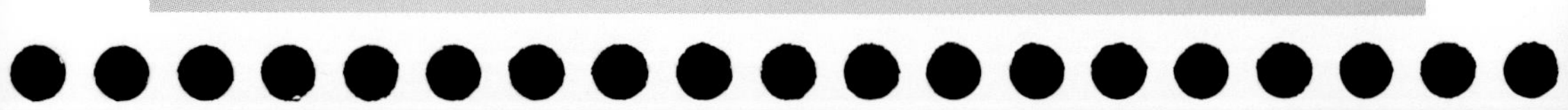

Anesthetic Cartridge

FUNCTION To hold liquid anesthetic for injection

CHARACTERISTICS Contains 1.8 ml of anesthetic solution

Rubber stopper—Inserts into harpoon of syringe

Aluminum cap with rubber diaphragm—Inserts into needle attached to syringe

Several types of anesthetic solution available

Color code of cartridge—Identifies type of anesthetic (type used depends on patient's health history and dental procedures performed)

1. When looking at the ratio of epinephrine, the lower the second number, the higher the percentage of vasoconstrictor.
2. Longer lasting anesthetic has a higher percentage of vasoconstrictor.
3. Anesthetic is available without a vasoconstrictor.

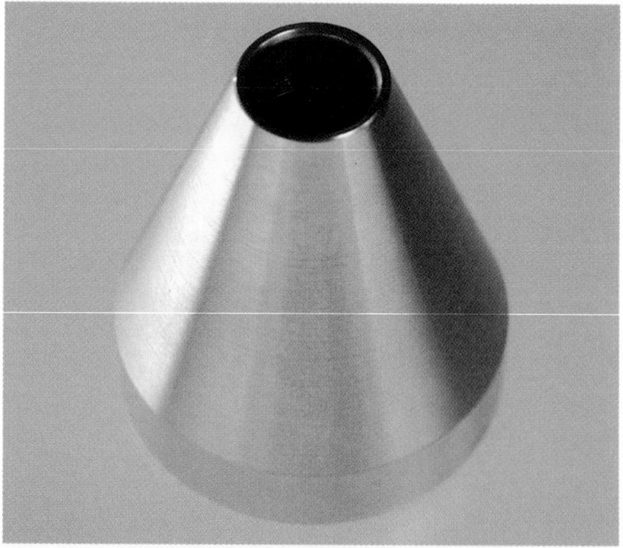

INSTRUMENT

Needle Stick Protector—Jenker™

FUNCTION To hold needle sheath for one-hand recapping after injection

CHARACTERISTICS Low center of gravity for stability in recapping
Helps prevent needle stick accidents

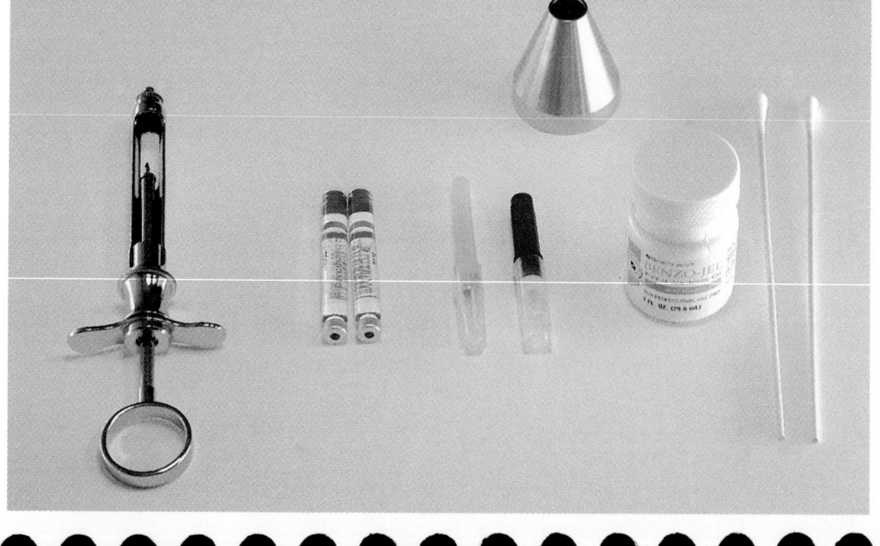
BENZO-JEL
1 FL. OZ. (29.6 ml)

TRAY SETUP

Local Anesthetic Syringe

FROM LEFT TO RIGHT

Anesthetic aspirating syringe, anesthetic cartridges, long needle, short needle, needle stick protector, topical anesthetic, cotton swabs

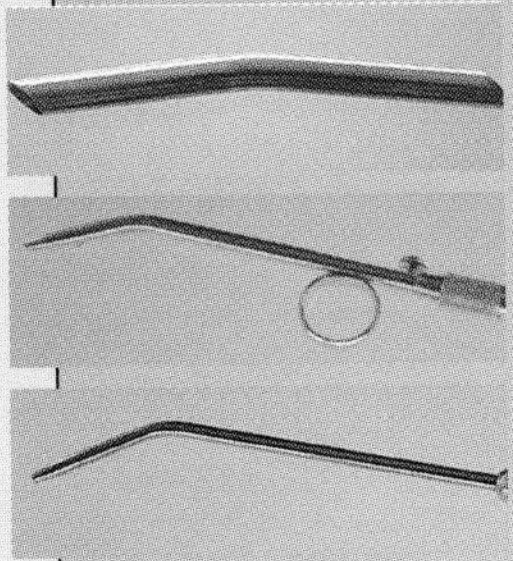

CHAPTER 4

Evacuation Devices and Air/Water Syringe

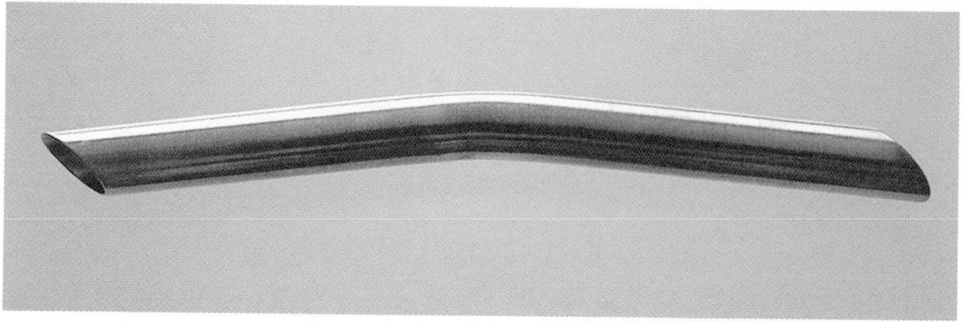

INSTRUMENT

High-Velocity (Volume) Evacuation (HVE) Tip

FUNCTION To evacuate large volumes of fluid and debris from the oral cavity

CHARACTERISTICS Straight or slightly angled at one or both ends
Stainless steel, autoclavable plastic, or disposable plastic
Attaches to high-velocity tubing on dental unit

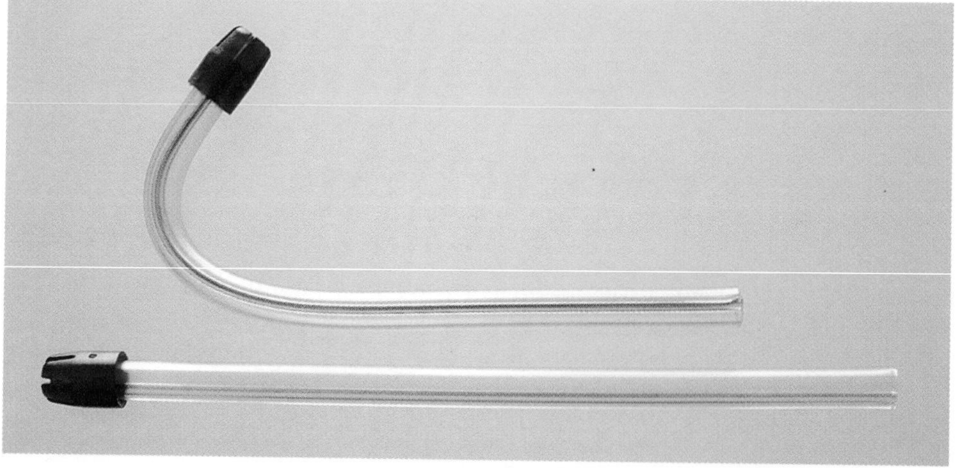

56

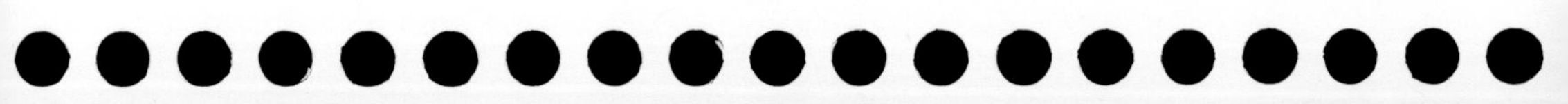

Low-Velocity (Volume) Evacuation Tip/Saliva Ejector

FUNCTION To evacuate smaller volumes of fluid from the oral cavity

CHARACTERISTICS Disposable plastic for single use
Can be bent for placement under tongue and in other areas of mouth or can be used straight
Attaches to low-velocity tubing on dental unit
Variety of styles

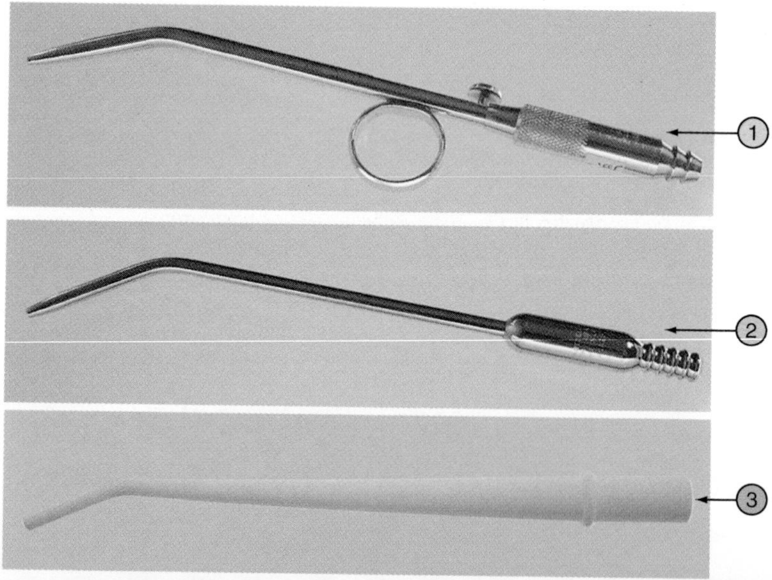

1

2

3

High-Velocity (Volume) Surgical Evacuation Tip

FUNCTION To evacuate fluid from oral cavity and surgical site

CHARACTERISTICS Stainless steel, autoclavable plastic, disposable plastic
Narrowed tip (accommodates surgical site)
Attaches to high-velocity tubing on dental unit
May require connecting tube for adaptation to surgical evacuation tip
Stainless steel surgical tips narrow at insertion of tubing; additional tubing is necessary to connect to high velocity on dental unit.
① and ② Autoclavable tips
③ Disposable tip

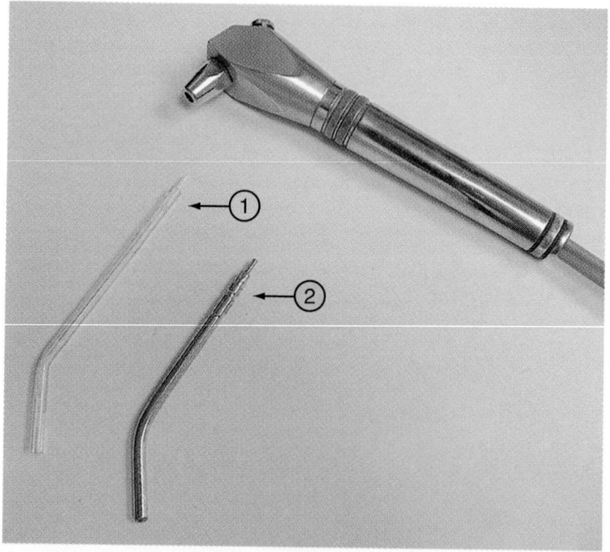

60

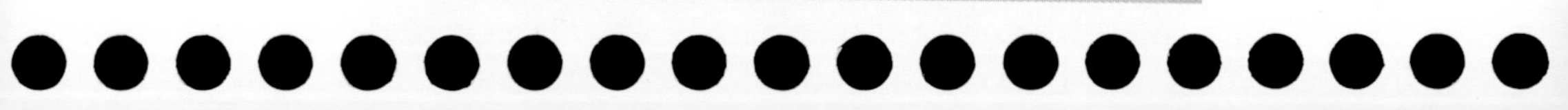

INSTRUMENT

Air/Water Syringe with Removable Tip

FUNCTION To rinse and dry specific teeth or entire oral cavity

CHARACTERISTICS Three-way syringe—Air, water, or spray with water and air

Syringe tip—Attaches to air/water syringe on dental unit

① Disposable plastic syringe tip for single use

② Autoclavable metal syringe tip

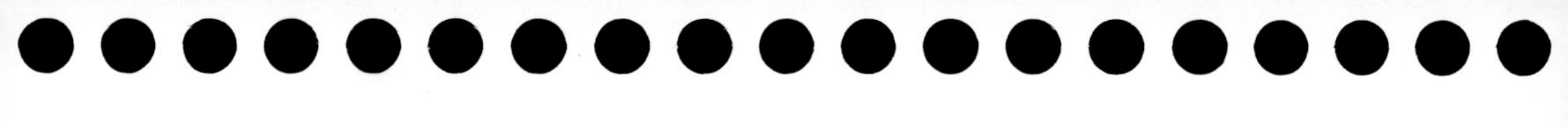

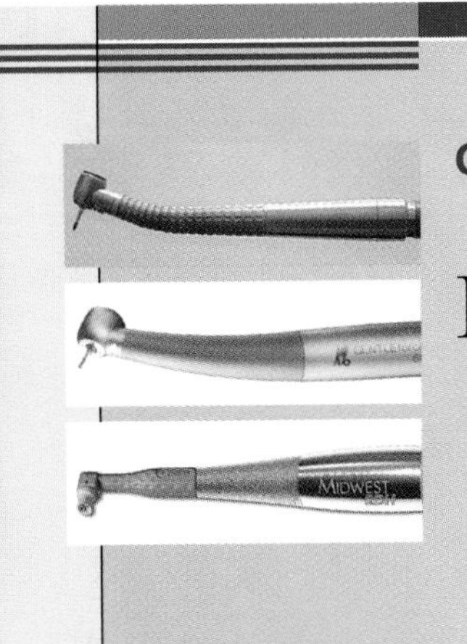

CHAPTER 5

Dental Handpieces

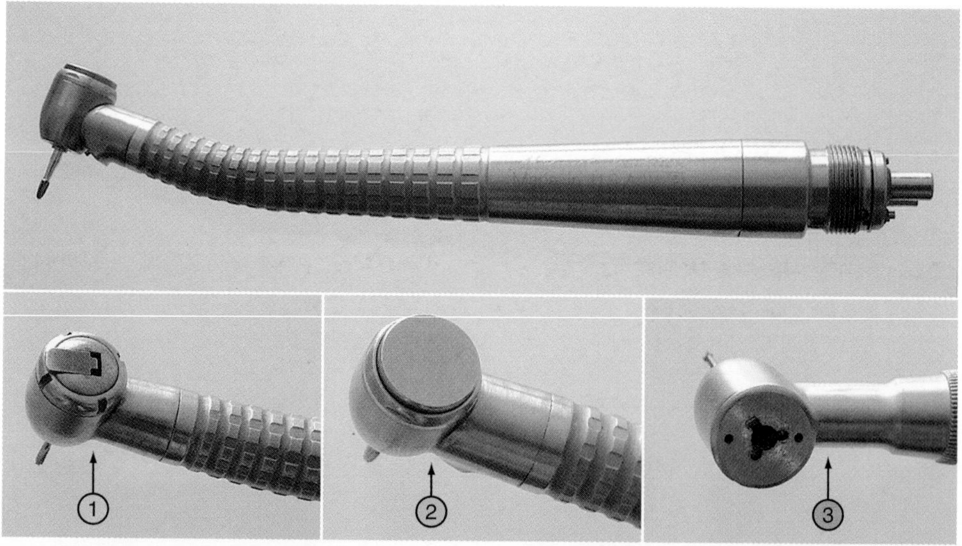

1
2
3

High-Speed Handpiece

FUNCTION

To use with bur to cut tooth with decay or other dental anomalies

Example: Cavity preparation for restoration or crown

To use with bur for adjusting crowns and bridges for final fit

CHARACTERISTICS

Handpiece is run by air pressure at a maximum speed of 450,000 rotations per minute.

On high-speed handpiece, bur generates extreme amount of heat.

Instrument sprays water/air or air on bur for cooling purposes to prevent damage to pulp.

Handpiece attaches to tubing on dental unit.

Different styles of securing bur are available:

① Power level chuck
② Push-button chuck
③ Conventional chuck

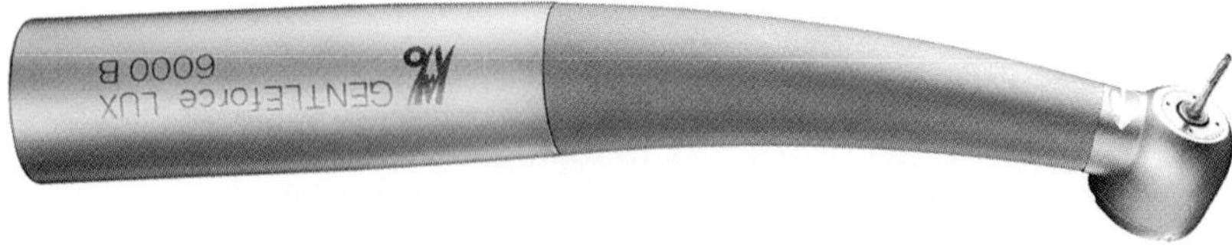
GENTLEforce LUX
6000 B

INSTRUMENT

Fiberoptic High-Speed Handpiece

FUNCTION
To illuminate tooth during preparation for restoration
To provide light intraorally during use of handpiece

CHARACTERISTICS
Light(s) at head of handpiece
Lights working area while handpiece rotates
Same characteristics as high-speed handpiece
Attaches to tubing on dental unit

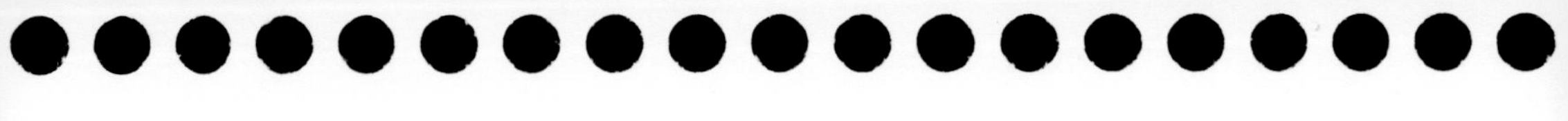

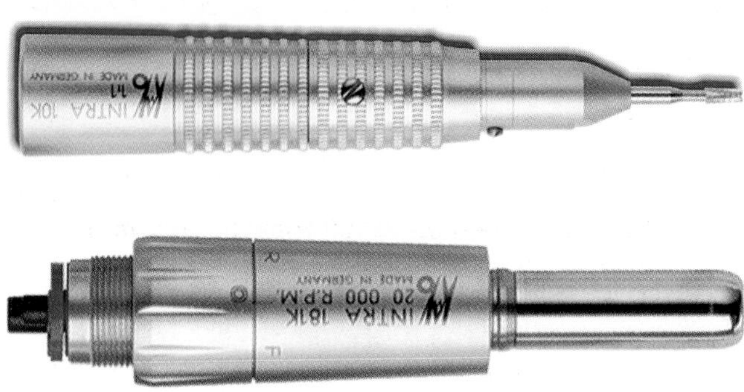
INTRA 10K
1:1
MADE IN GERMANY
INTRA 181K
20 000 R.P.M.
MADE IN GERMANY

INSTRUMENT

Slow-Speed Motor with Straight Handpiece Attachment

FUNCTION

To use with slow-speed attachments
To use straight attachment with long-shank straight bur

CHARACTERISTICS

Maximum speed of 30,000 rotations per minute; used as adjunct to high-speed handpiece
Contra-angle or prophy angle attachments—Designed for intraoral use
Straight attachment—Usually used outside oral cavity
Slow-speed handpiece, motor—Attaches to tubing on dental unit

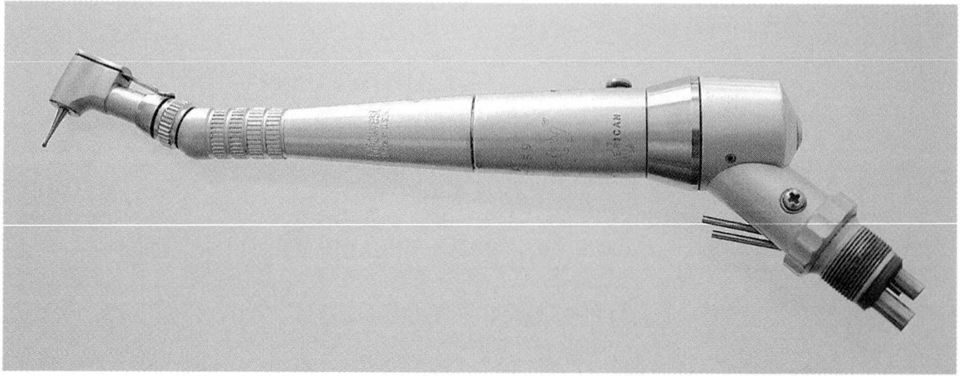

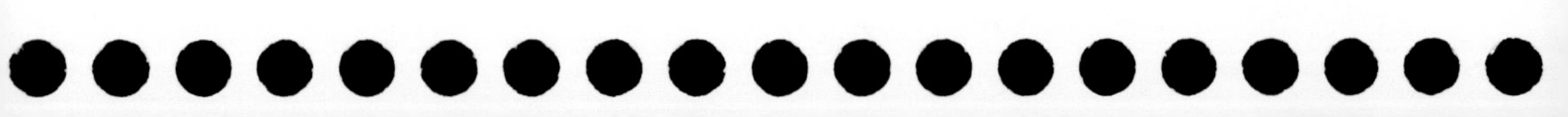

INSTRUMENT

Slow-Speed Motor with Contra-Angle Handpiece Attachment

FUNCTION

To use with burs for intraoral and extraoral procedures:

- To remove decay
- To refine cavity preparation
- To adjust occlusal restorations
- To polish amalgam restorations
- To adjust provisional and permanent crowns and bridges
- To adjust partials and dentures

CHARACTERISTICS

Attaches to straight handpiece

Slow-speed handpiece and motor—Attaches to tubing on unit

Types:

- Latch type—Latch-type bur or latch-type prophylaxis polishing cup or brush
- Friction grip—Friction-grip bur

DENSPLY
MIDWEST
RDH

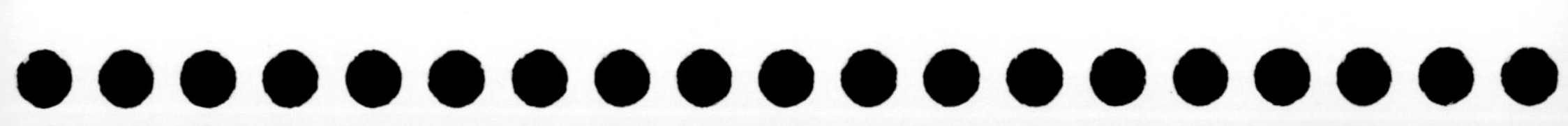

INSTRUMENT

Prophy Slow-Speed Handpiece* with Disposable Prophy Angle Attachment

FUNCTION To polish teeth with prophy cup or brush attachment

CHARACTERISTICS Prophy angle attaches to motor
Prophy handpiece and motor attaches to tubing on dental unit.
Lightweight design to reduce hand and wrist fatigue.
Ergonomic shape for natural hand positioning.

---

*Referred to as *RDH* (registered dental hygienist) *prophy handpiece*.
Pictured: MIDWEST® RDH® Hygiene Handpiece for Disposable Prophy Angles.

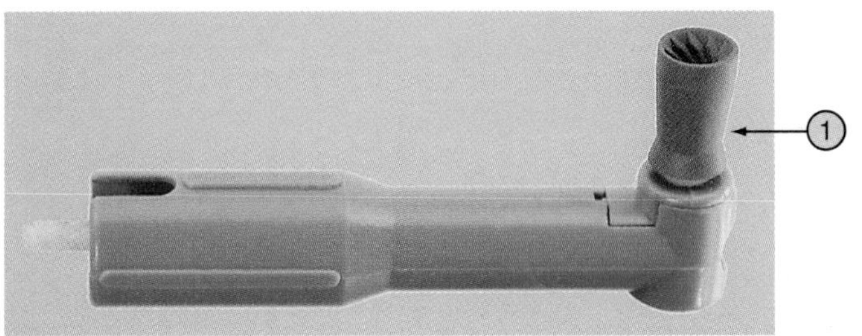
①

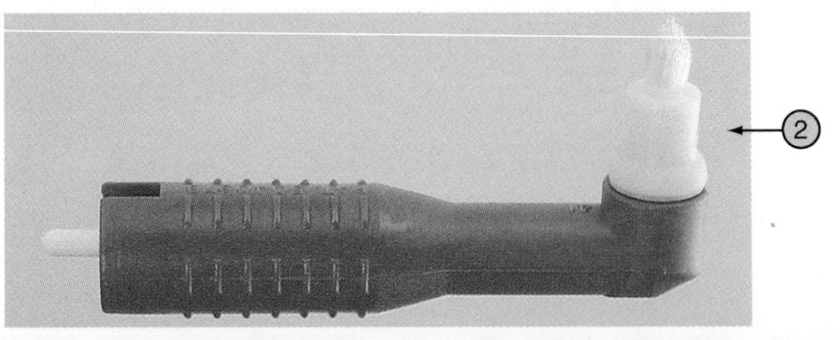
②

INSTRUMENT

Disposable Prophy Angle Attachments for Slow-Speed Handpiece

FUNCTION To polish teeth with prophylaxis cup and brush

CHARACTERISTICS Attaches to straight or prophy handpiece

Types:

① Disposable prophy cup—For polishing all surfaces of teeth

② Disposable prophy brush—For polishing occlusal surfaces and deep grooves on lingual surfaces of anterior teeth

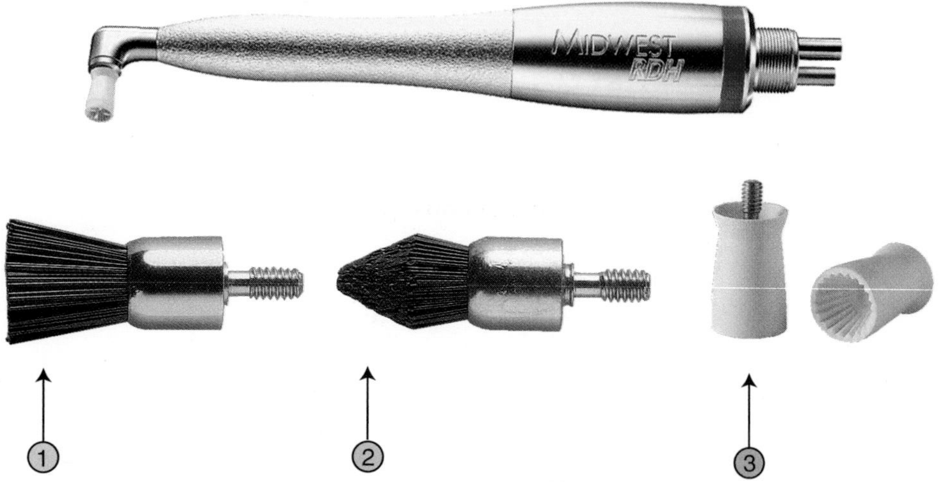

MIDWEST
RDH
1
2
3

INSTRUMENT

Prophy Slow-Speed Handpiece*

FUNCTION To polish teeth with prophy cup or brush

CHARACTERISTICS Prophy angle is one piece.
Disposable screw-type prophy cup or brush attaches to prophy angle slow-speed handpiece.
Lightweight design to reduce hand and wrist fatigue.
Ergonomic shape for natural hand positioning.
Attachments:

① Flat-end brush
② Tapered-end brush
③ Prophy cup

*Referred to as *RDH* (registered dental hygienist) *prophy handpiece*.
Pictured: MIDWEST® RDH® Hygiene Handpiece with Prophy Right Angle.

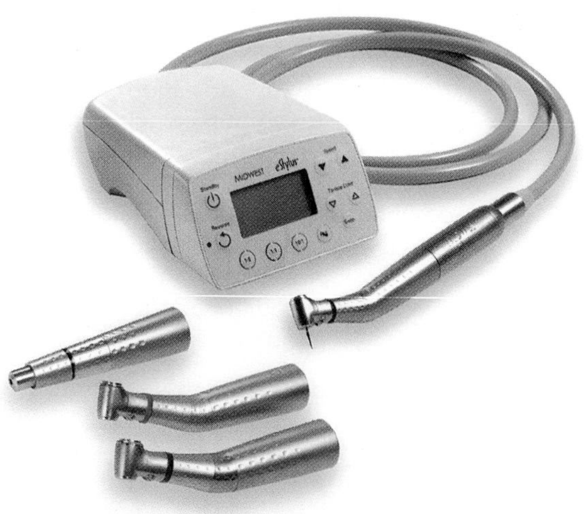
MIDWEST
eStylus

INSTRUMENT

Electric Handpiece Unit and Handpiece Attachments

FUNCTION

To use with bur for intraoral cavity preparation
To use with endodontic nickel-titanium rotary instruments
To use with bur for trimming of provisional crowns
To use with bur for adjusting permanent restorations, crowns, and bridges

CHARACTERISTICS

Speed (i.e., rotations per minute [rpm]) can be set before procedure.

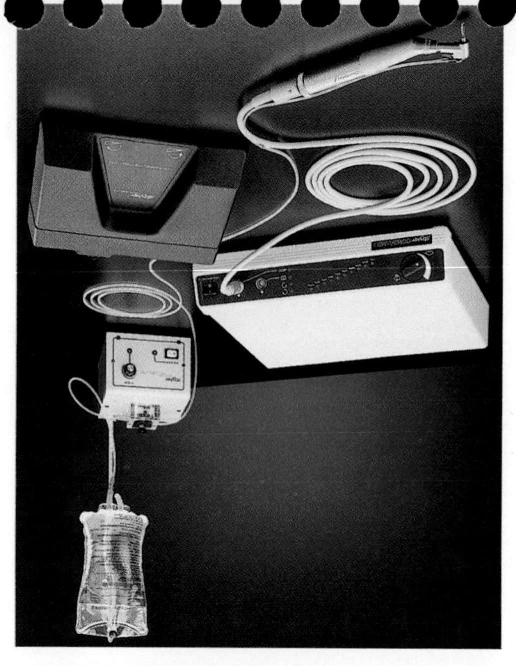

INSTRUMENT

Surgical Electrical Handpiece Unit and Implant Handpiece

FUNCTION
To use with depth drills for implants
To use with sterile water for cooling drilling system

CHARACTERISTICS
Air driven
Latch-type attachment on handpiece
Maximum speed of 85,000 rotations per minute (rpm)
Lower speed (e.g., 810 rpm) used for implant
Attachment available for splitting impacted teeth

Prep Start ™
40
60
80
100
120
140
psi
DANVILLE ENGINEERING

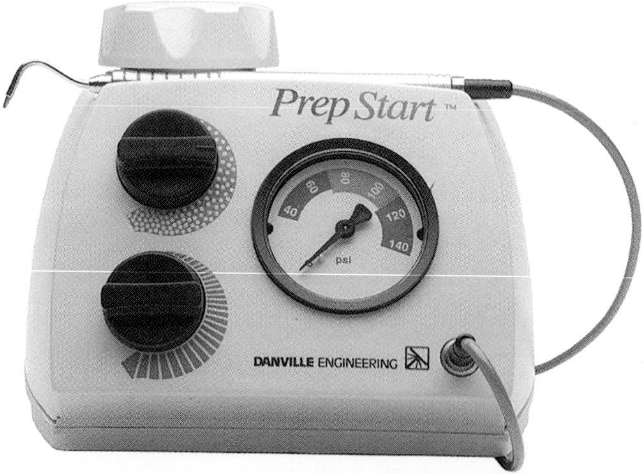

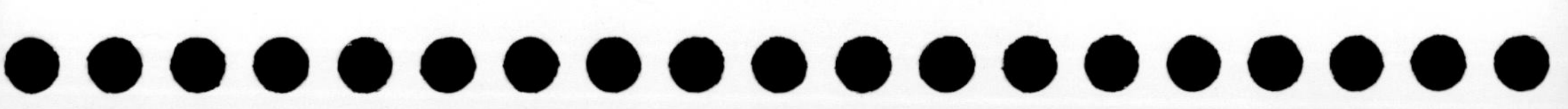

INSTRUMENT

Air Abrasion Unit and Handpiece

FUNCTION

To use for class I or class VI cavities instead of handpiece
To use for preparation of occlusal surface for sealants

CHARACTERISTICS

Handpiece uses high pressure of alpha-alumina particles through small device that removes decay and/or prepares pit and fissures for sealants or restoration.
Minimal use of anesthesia is required.

84

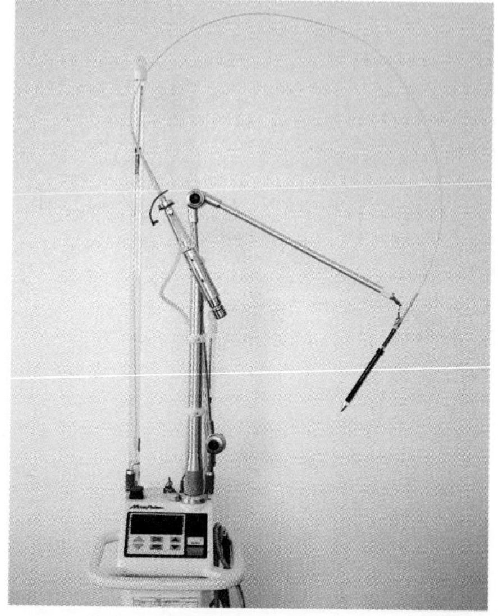

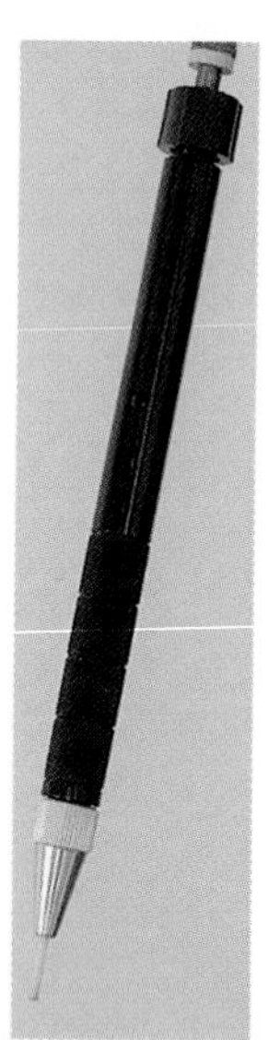

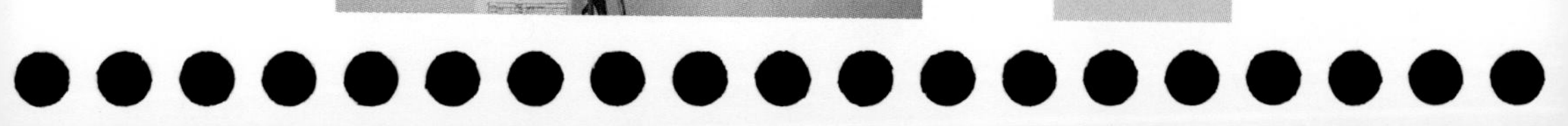

INSTRUMENT

Laser Handpiece Unit and Laser Handpiece

FUNCTION To cut, vaporize, or cauterize soft tissue

Examples:

To remove lesions or tumors

To reduce excess tissue

To control bleeding

CHARACTERISTICS New technological device

Works by means of a highly concentrated light source

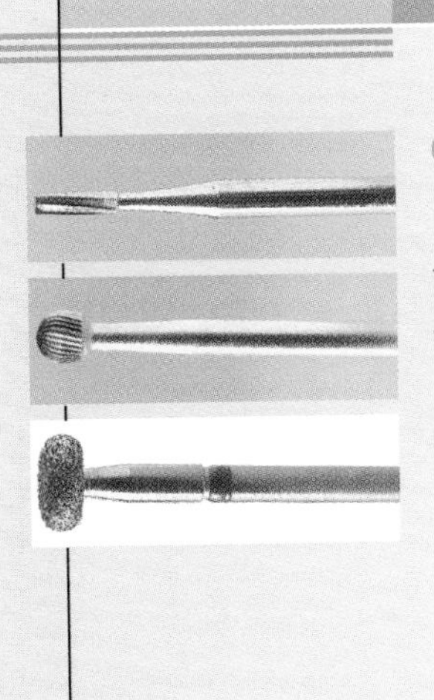

CHAPTER 6

Burs for High-Speed and Low-Speed Handpieces

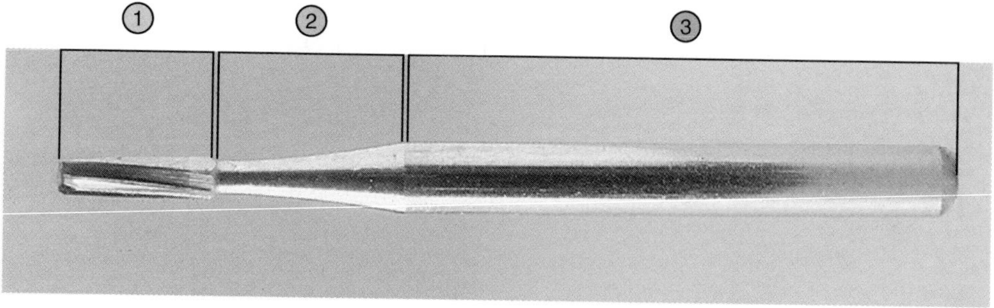

3

2

1

INSTRUMENT

Bur

FUNCTION To be used in high-speed or low-speed handpiece

CHARACTERISTICS Parts

① **Head:** Part of bur that cuts, polishes, or finishes
Available in a variety of shapes and sizes
Examples:
Fit a variety of shanks
Examples:
- No. 2 round bur in friction grip shank
- No. 2 round bur in latch-type shank
- No. 2 round bur in straight shank

Pictured: MIDWEST Bur

Bur (continued)

CHARACTERISTICS

Parts (continued)

② **Neck:** Part of bur that tapers to connect shank to head

③ **Shank:** Part of bur that is inserted into handpiece

- Length and style vary depending on handpiece used.
- Bur with straight, long shank fits into straight slow-speed handpiece.
- Bur with latch-type shank fits into contra-angle slow-speed handpiece.
- Friction grip bur fits into high-speed handpiece; chuck tightens bur into the handpiece.

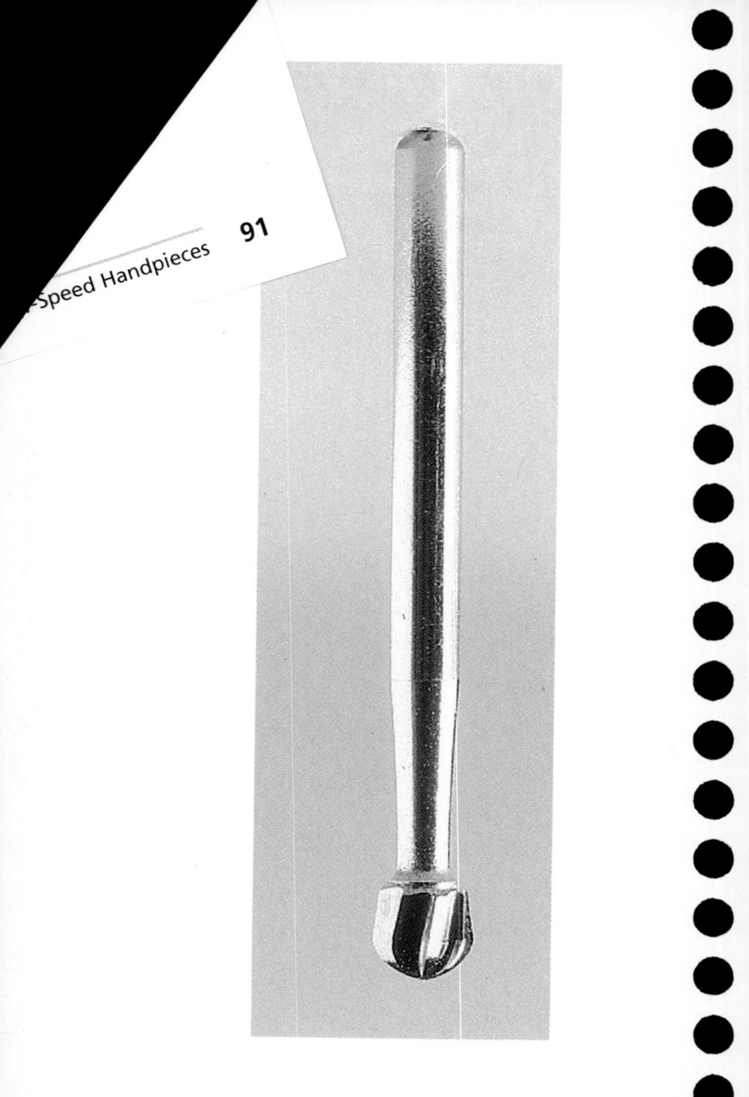

INSTRUMENT

Round Bur

FUNCTION To remove caries from tooth structure
To open tooth for endodontic treatment

CHARACTERISTICS Range of sizes
Commonly used sizes: No. ¼ to no. 8

Pictured: MIDWEST Round Bur

94

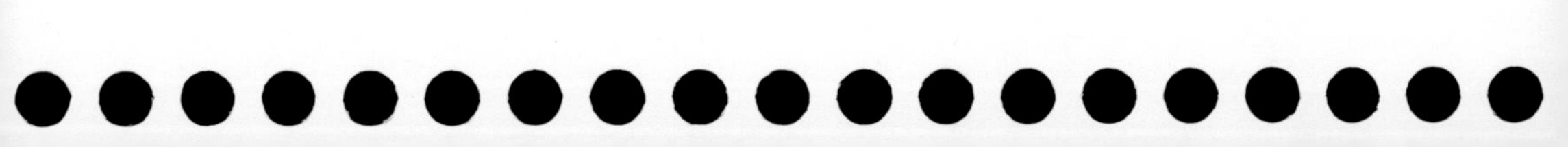

Pear-Shaped Bur

FUNCTION

To open tooth for a restoration
To remove caries

CHARACTERISTICS

Frequently used in preparation of composite restorations
Range of sizes
  Commonly used sizes: No. 330 to no. 333
Bur head available in long
  Example: No. 333L

Pictured: MIDWEST Pear-Shaped Bur

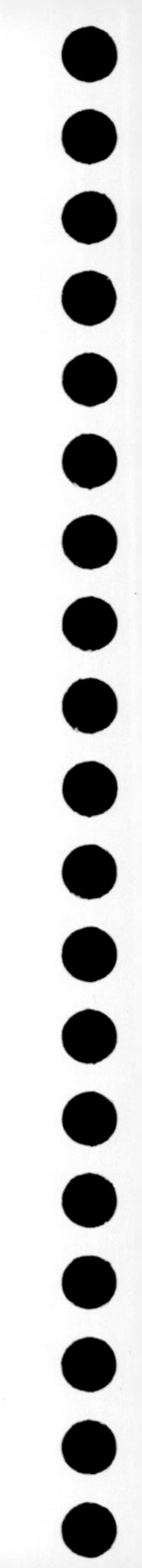

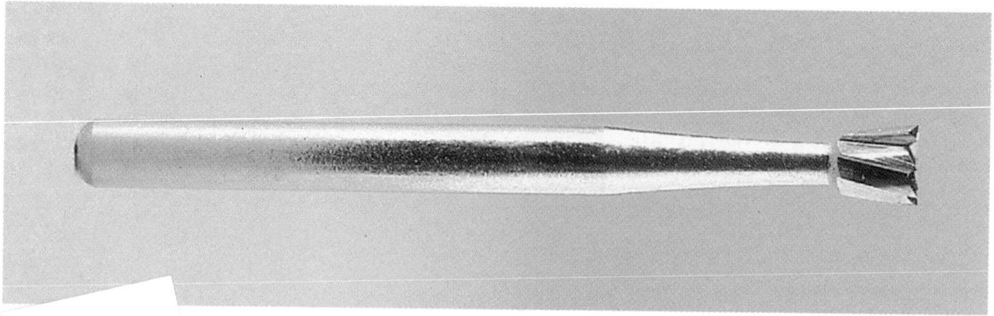

INSTRUMENT

Inverted Cone Bur

FUNCTION To remove caries
To establish retention in tooth for cavity preparation

CHARACTERISTICS Range of sizes
Commonly used sizes: No. 33½ to no. 39

Pictured: MIDWEST Inverted Cone Bur

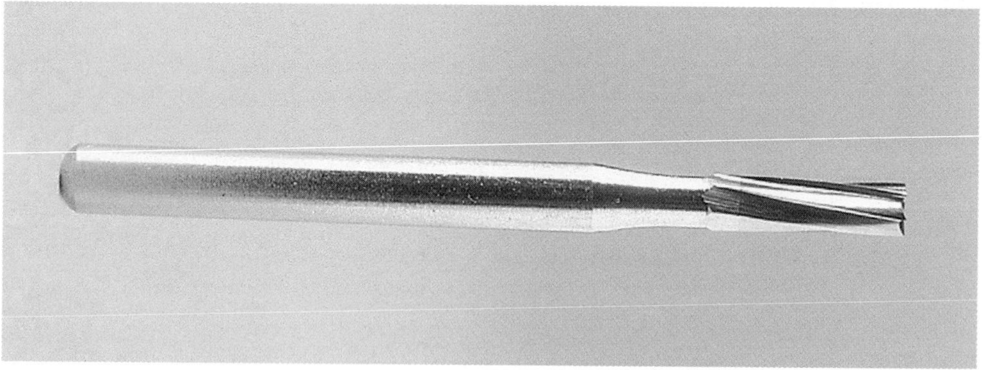

Straight Fissure Bur—Plain Cut

FUNCTION

To cut cavity preparation
To form inner walls of cavity preparation
To place retention grooves in walls of cavity preparation

CHARACTERISTICS

Cutting part of bur—Has parallel sides
Range of sizes
Commonly used sizes: No. 56 to no. 58
May have short or long shank for adaptation to a variety of cavity preparations; *S* at end of number indicates short shank, *L* indicates long shank
Examples: No. 56S, no. 56L

Pictured: MIDWEST Straight Fissure Bur—Plain Cut

100

Tapered Fissure Bur—Plain Cut

FUNCTION

To cut cavity preparation
To form angles in walls of cavity preparation
To place retention grooves in walls of cavity preparation

CHARACTERISTICS

Cutting part of bur—Has tapered sides
Range of sizes
  Commonly used sizes: No. 168 to no. 171
May have short or long shank for adaptation to a variety of cavity preparations; *S* at end of number indicates short shank, *L* indicates long shank
  Example: No. 168S, no. 171L

Pictured: MIDWEST Tapered Fissure Bur—Plain Cut

102

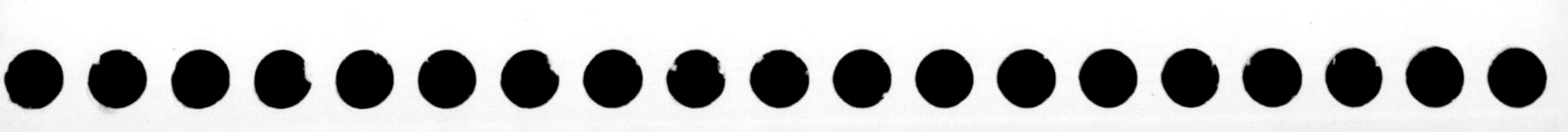

Straight Fissure Bur—Crosscut

FUNCTION

To cut cavity preparation
To form walls of cavity preparation
To place retention grooves in walls of cavity preparation

CHARACTERISTICS

Cutting part of bur—Has parallel sides with horizontal cutting edges
Range of sizes
Commonly used sizes: No. 556 to no. 558
May have long shank for adaptation to a variety of cavity preparations; *L* at end of number indicates long shank
Example: No. 556L

Pictured: MIDWEST Straight Fissure Bur—Crosscut

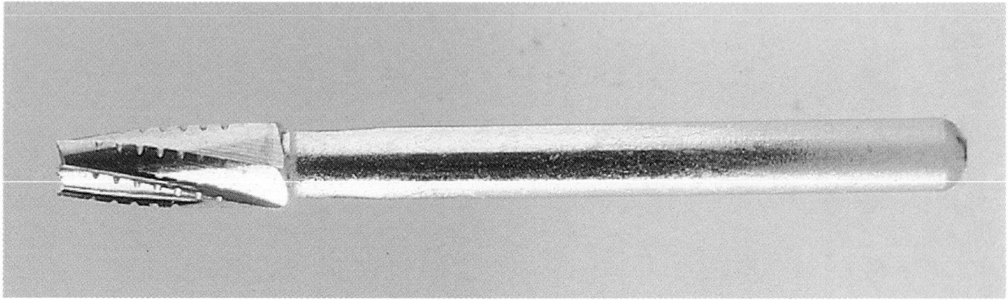

Tapered Fissure Bur—Crosscut

FUNCTION

To cut cavity preparation
To form angles in walls of cavity preparation
To place retention grooves in walls of cavity preparation

CHARACTERISTICS

Cutting part of bur—Has tapered sides with horizontal cutting edges
Range of sizes
  Commonly used sizes: No. 699 to no. 703
May have long shank for adaptation to a variety of cavity preparations; *L* at end of number indicates long shank
  Example: No. 701L

Pictured: MIDWEST Tapered Fissure Bur—Crosscut

106

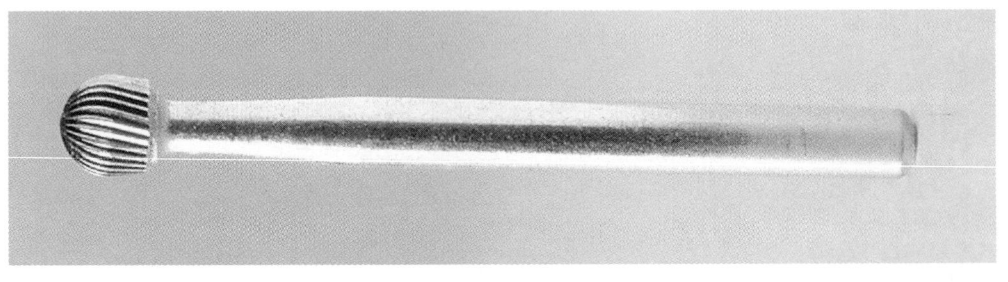

INSTRUMENT

Finishing Bur

FUNCTION To finish composite restoration
To finish restoration by restoring anatomy in tooth
To equilibrate or adjust occlusion

CHARACTERISTICS Variety of shapes and sizes

Pictured: MIDWEST Finishing Bur

108

INSTRUMENT

Diamond Bur—Flat-End Taper

FUNCTION To reduce a tooth for crown preparation when a square shoulder is needed

CHARACTERISTICS Range of grits (coarse to superfine); grit designated by color band on shank of diamond bur or by letter after name of diamond bur
Superfine diamond burs—Used for finishing restorations
Variety of shapes and sizes

Pictured: MIDWEST Diamond Bur—Flat-End Taper

110

INSTRUMENT

Diamond Bur—Flat-End Cylinder

FUNCTION To reduce a tooth for crown preparation when parallel walls and flat floors are needed

CHARACTERISTICS Range of grits (coarse to superfine); grit designated by color band on shank of diamond bur or by letter after name of diamond bur

Superfine diamond burs—Used for finishing restorations

Variety of shapes and sizes

Pictured: MIDWEST Diamond Bur—Flat-End Cylinder

112

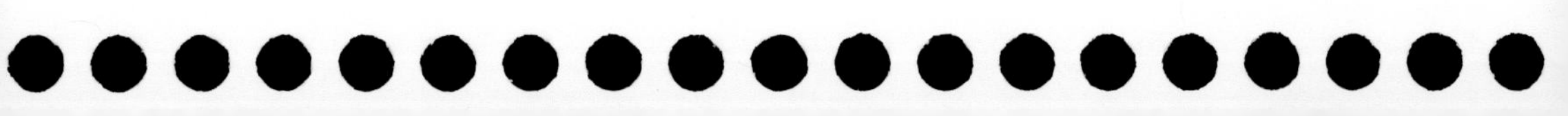

INSTRUMENT

Diamond Bur—Flame

FUNCTION To reduce a tooth for crown preparation for subgingival margins

CHARACTERISTICS Range of grits (coarse to superfine); grit designated by color band on shank of diamond bur or by letter after name of diamond bur
Superfine diamond burs—Used for finishing restorations
Variety of shapes and sizes

Pictured: MIDWEST Diamond Bur—Flame

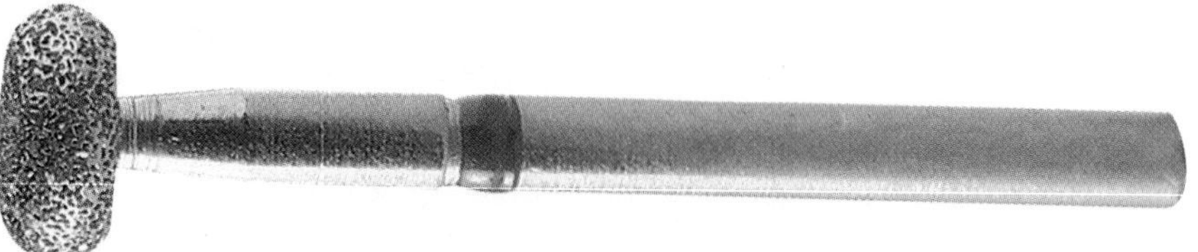

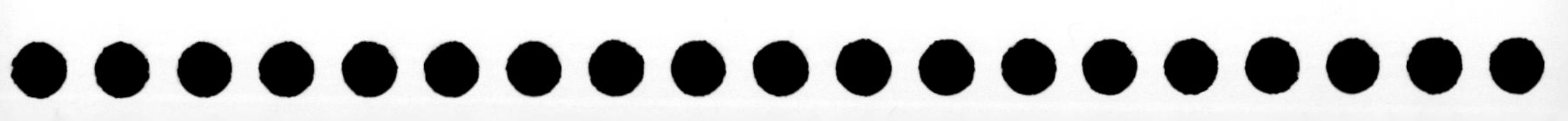

INSTRUMENT

Diamond Bur—Wheel

FUNCTION To reduce a tooth for crown preparation on lingual aspect of anterior teeth and to reduce bulk of incisal edges

CHARACTERISTICS Range of grits (coarse to superfine); grit designated by color band on shank of diamond bur or by letter after name of diamond bur
Superfine diamond burs—Used for finishing restorations
Variety of shapes and sizes

Pictured: MIDWEST Diamond Bur—Wheel

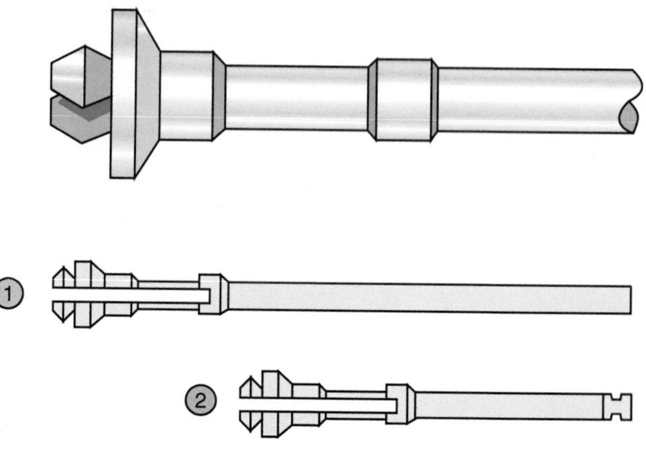
1
2

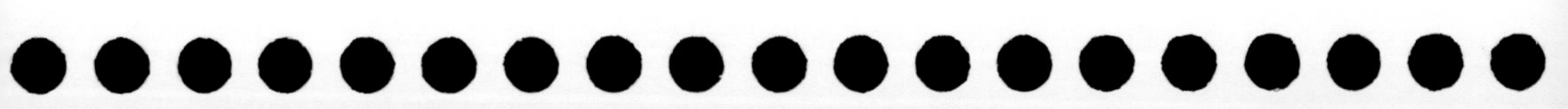

INSTRUMENT

Mandrel—Snap On

FUNCTION To attach discs to mandrel for finishing and polishing inside or outside oral cavity (device is inserted into handpiece)

CHARACTERISTICS Shank types:

1. Long shank—For straight slow-speed handpiece
2. Short latch-type shank—For contra-angle slow-speed handpiece

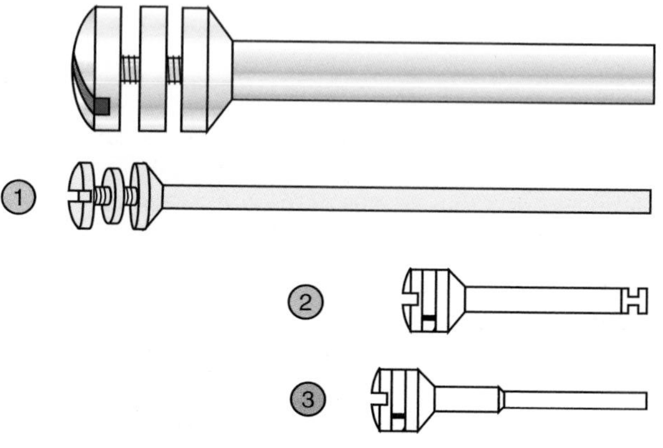
1
2
3

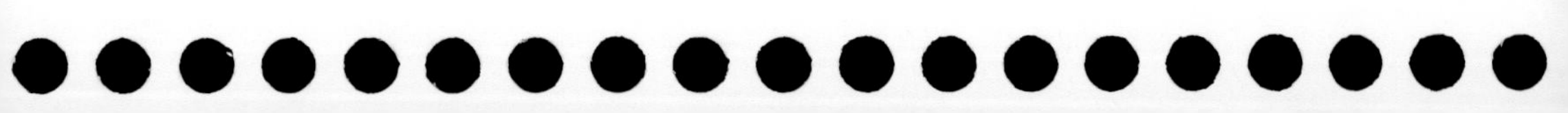

Mandrel—Screw On

FUNCTION To attach discs to mandrel for finishing and polishing inside or outside oral cavity (device is inserted into handpiece)

CHARACTERISTICS Shank types:

① Long shank—For straight slow-speed handpiece
② Short latch-type shank—For contra-angle or right-angle slow-speed handpiece
③ Friction grip shank—For high-speed handpiece

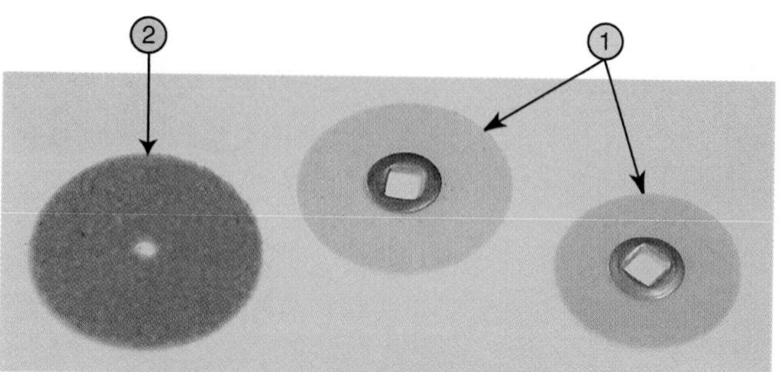
2
1

MEDIUM ½
COARSE ½

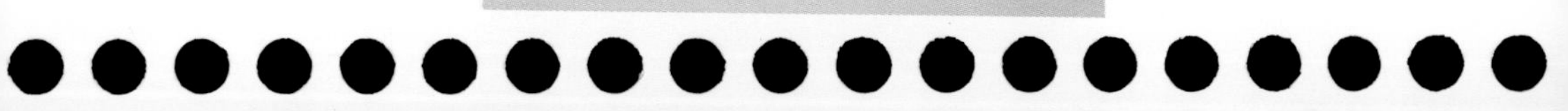

Sandpaper Disc

FUNCTION

To contour restorative material
To polish restorative material (extra fine grit)

CHARACTERISTICS

Range of grits (coarse to extra fine)
Two types
① Snap on (metal center)
② Screw on
Sandpaper disc organizer has a range of sizes.

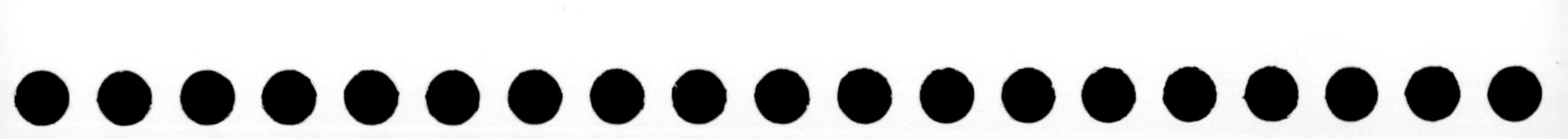

Composite Disc

FUNCTION To contour restorative material (coarse grit)
To polish or smooth restorative material (extrafine grit)

CHARACTERISTICS Made from synthetic material to accommodate composite restorations
Range of grits (coarse to extrafine)
Variety of sizes
Two types available
- Snap on (pictured)
- Screw on

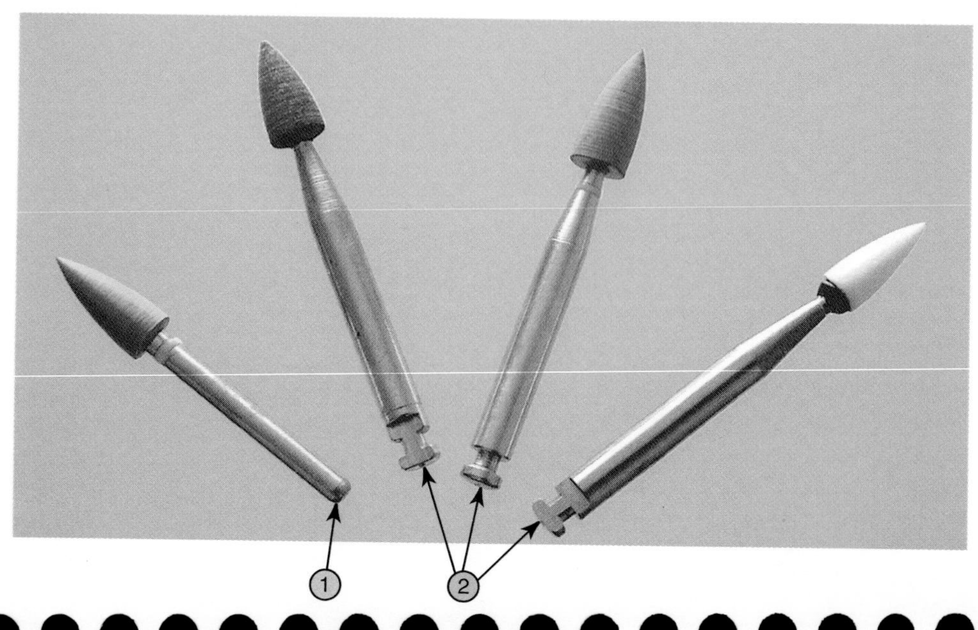
1
2

Rubber Points

FUNCTION To polish restorations, amalgam, composite, gold

CHARACTERISTICS Types of polishing grits:

- Brown points (brownies)—Abrasive
- Green points (greenies)—Less abrasive than brownies
- White points—Polishing point

Variety of shanks available for all types of rubber points

① Friction grip
② Latch type

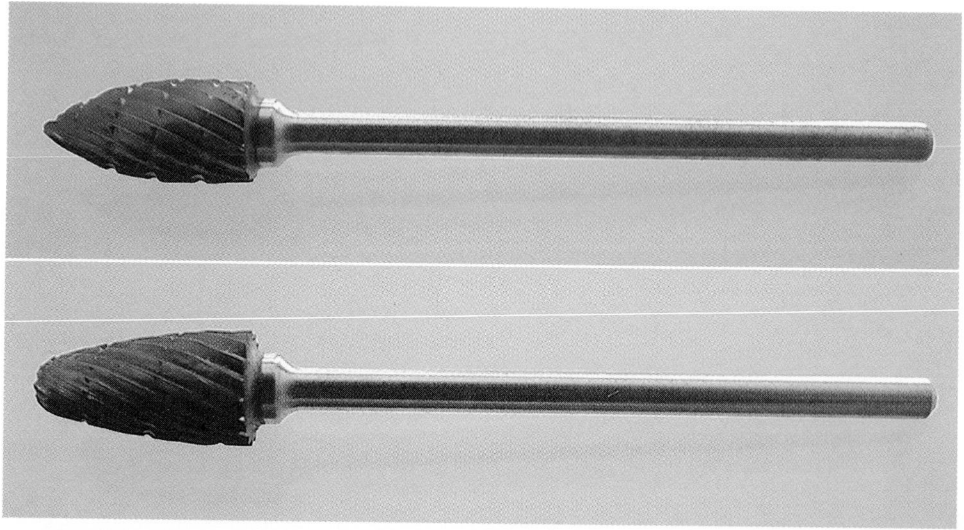

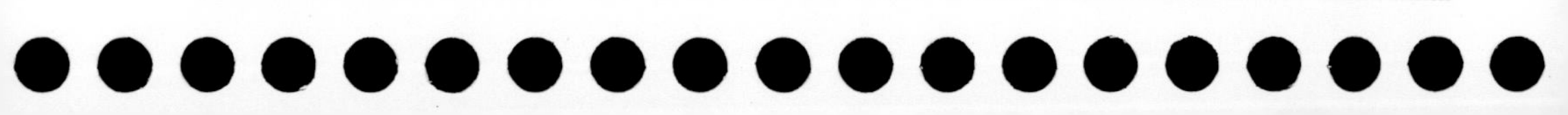

INSTRUMENT

Laboratory Bur—Acrylic Bur

FUNCTION To cut models or trim acrylic in laboratory

CHARACTERISTICS Long shank—For attachment to straight handpiece
Variety of sizes and shapes

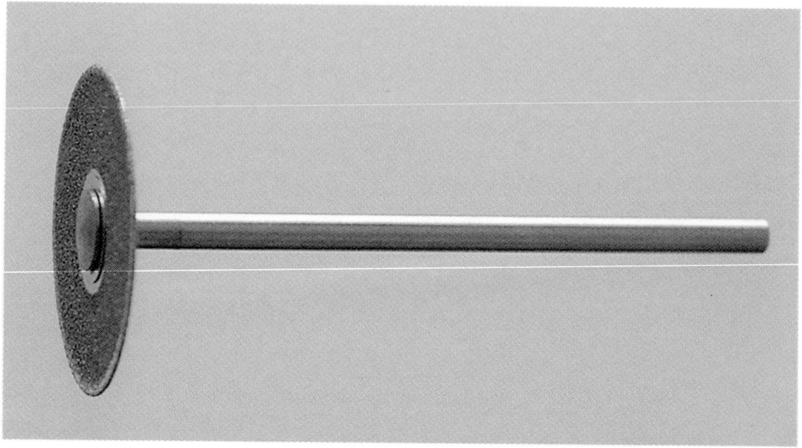

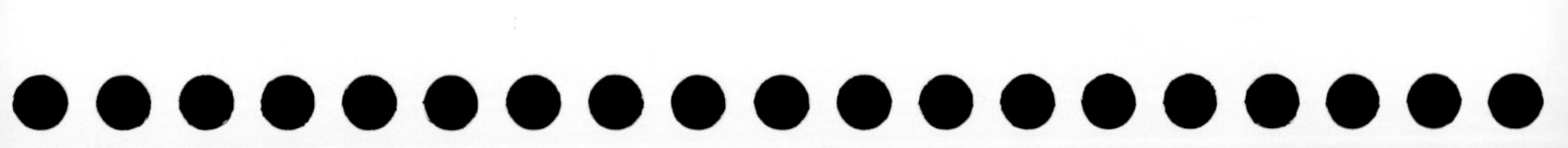

INSTRUMENT

Laboratory Bur—Diamond Disc

FUNCTION To contour or cut models in the laboratory

CHARACTERISTICS Single-sided or double-sided cutting edge

FG
FG
FG
FG
RA
RA

Magnetic Bur Block with Burs

FUNCTION To be used on dental tray setups

CHARACTERISTICS Magnetic to hold burs in place
Holds friction grip and latch-type burs
Can be sterilized in autoclave
Variety of shapes and sizes

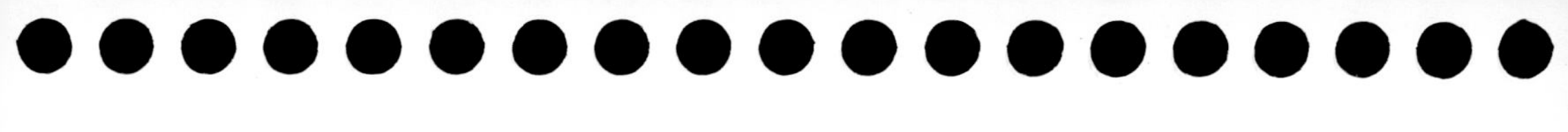

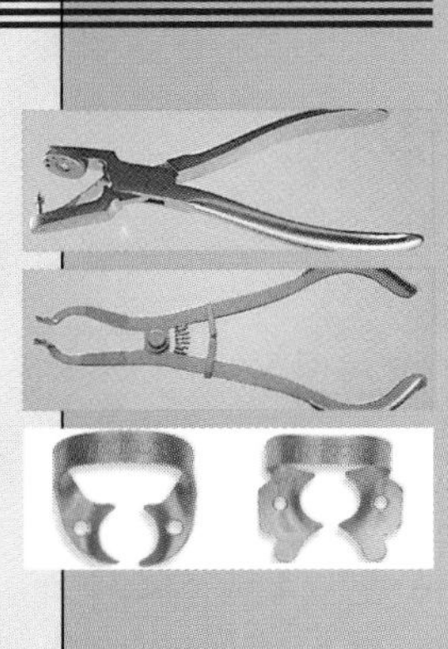

CHAPTER 7

Dental Dam Instruments

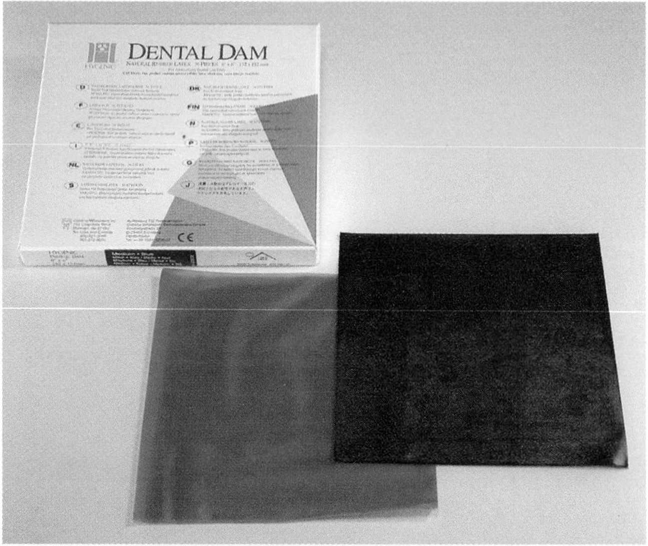

Dental Dam

FUNCTION To isolate teeth for dental procedures

CHARACTERISTICS Sizes—4 × 4, 5 × 5, 6 × 6, or continuous roll
Gauge or thickness—Thin, medium, heavy
Colors—Gray, green, blue, pastels
Latex free available

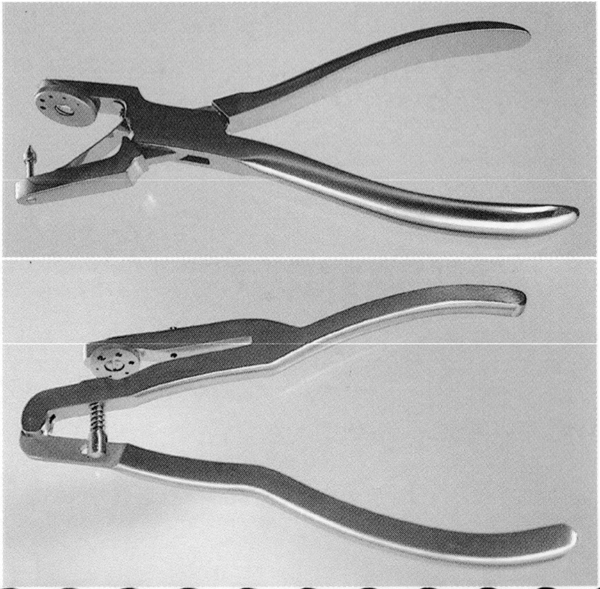

Dental Dam Punch

FUNCTION To punch holes in dental dam for each individual tooth

CHARACTERISTICS Designated hole size for each tooth:

No. 5—Anchor tooth (largest)

No. 4—Molars

No. 3—Premolars

No. 2—Maxillary and mandibular cuspids and maxillary central and laterals

No. 1—Mandibular central and laterals (smallest)

PRACTICE NOTES

1. The oral cavity is examined before holes are punched to accommodate the patient's specific dentition.
2. A space of 3 to 3.5 mm is maintained between holes.

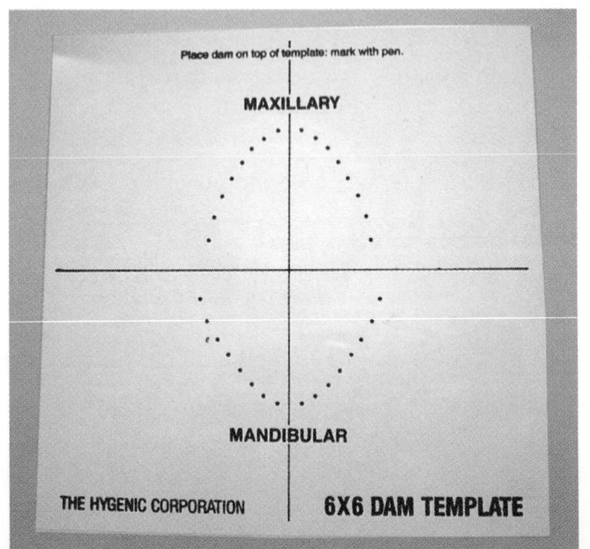
Place dam on top of template: mark with pen.
MAXILLARY
MANDIBULAR
THE HYGENIC CORPORATION
6X6 DAM TEMPLATE

INSTRUMENT

Dental Dam Template

FUNCTION To use as a guide for marking and punching holes in correct position on dental dam

CHARACTERISTICS Made of durable plastic

PRACTICE NOTES

1. The oral cavity is examined before holes are marked and punched to adjust positioning to the patient's specific dentition.
2. The dental·dam is placed on the template, and the points where holes should be punched are marked with a pen.

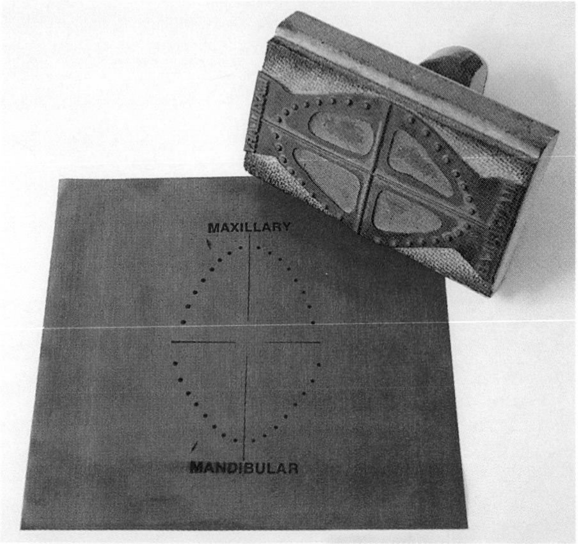

MAXILLARY
MANDIBULAR

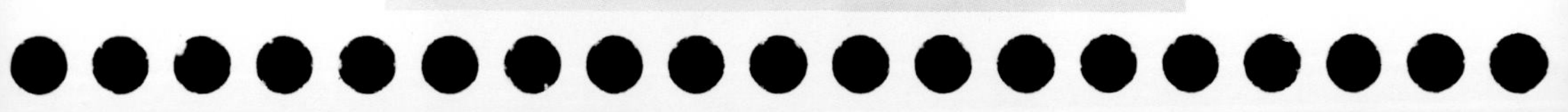

Dental Dam Stamp

FUNCTION To mark holes on dental dam

CHARACTERISTICS Has 32 dots that represent the adult dentition
Used as guide for punching holes in correct position

PRACTICE NOTES

1. The oral cavity is examined before holes are marked and punched to adjust positioning to the patient's specific dentition.

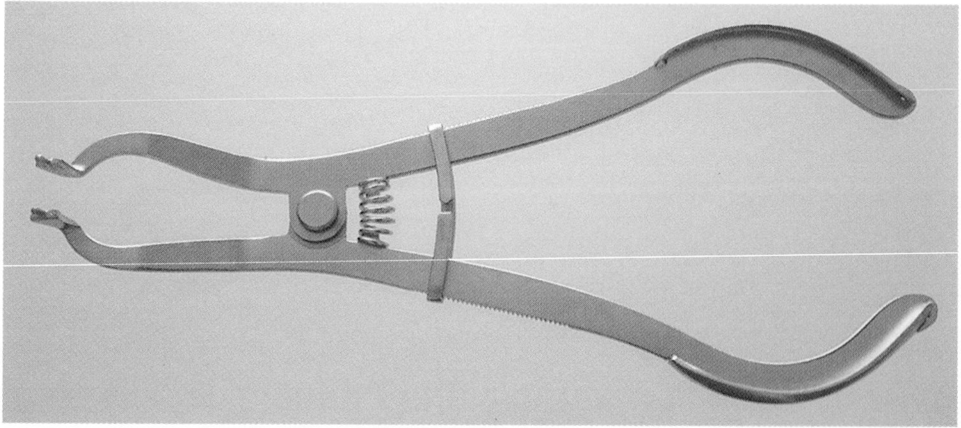

142

INSTRUMENT

Dental Dam Forceps

FUNCTION To place dental dam clamp on tooth and to remove clamp after procedure

CHARACTERISTICS Beaks on forceps fit into dental dam clamp
Forceps open with spring motion
Bar between handle holds forceps in place while clamp is seated

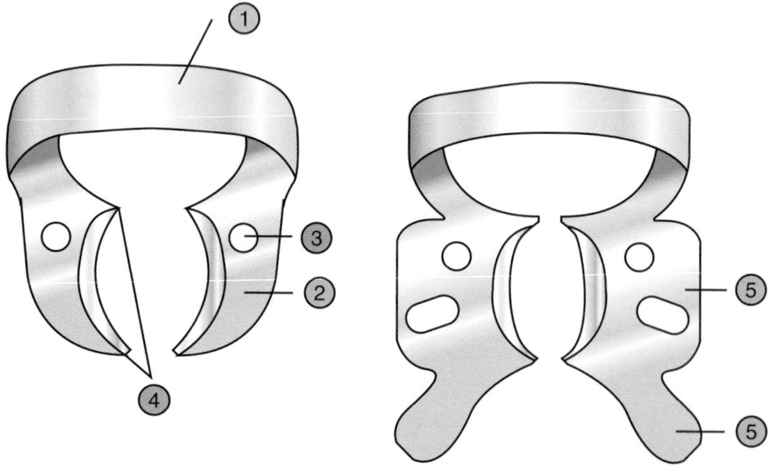

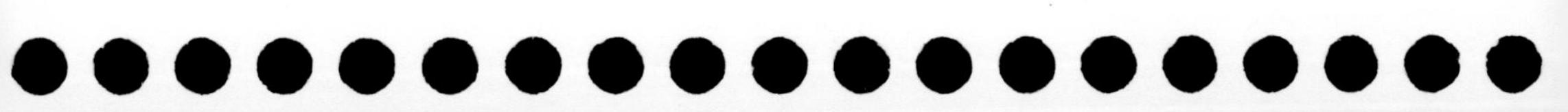

Dental Dam Clamp

FUNCTION To anchor and stabilize dental dam

CHARACTERISTICS Parts

① **Bow:** Placed toward distal part of tooth
② **Jaws:** Have four prongs that secure clamp on tooth
③ **Holes:** On jaws; designated for beaks on forceps to place clamp on tooth
④ **Prongs:** Designed to secure clamp on cervical part of tooth, beyond the height of contour
⑤ **Winged clamps:** Have extension of metal on jaws to hold dental dam away for better visibility (wingless clamps do not have extra extension of metal)

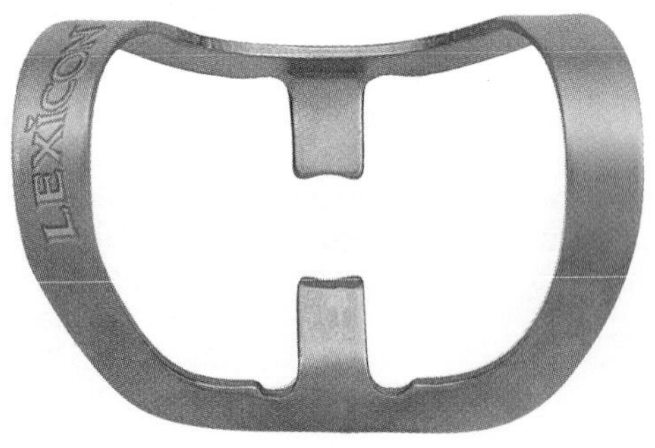
LEXICON

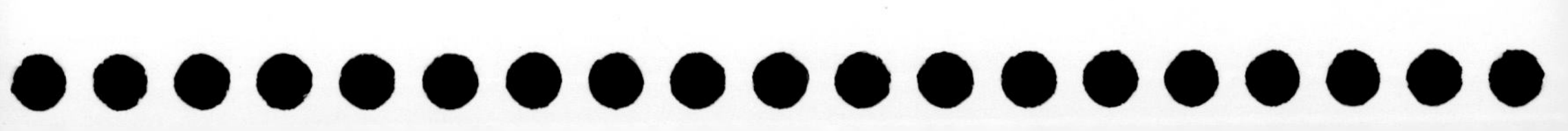

Anterior Clamp

FUNCTION To anchor and stabilize dental dam

CHARACTERISTICS Used only on anterior teeth
Example: Wingless clamp
Range of sizes

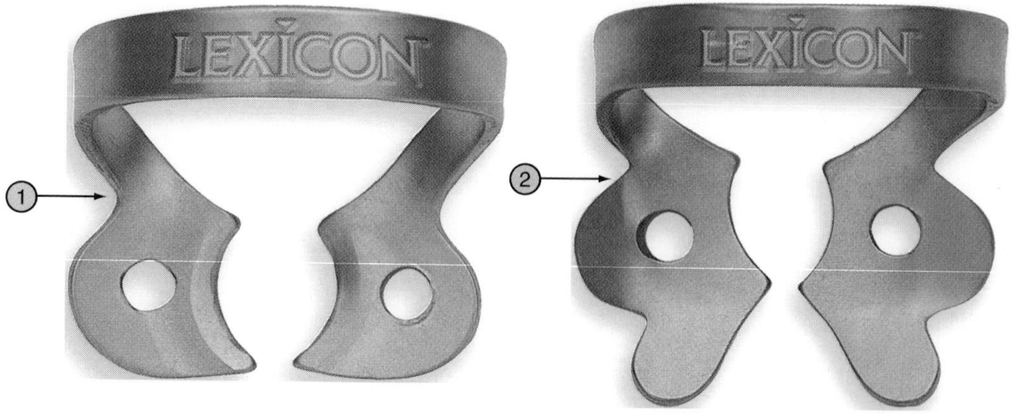

LEXICON

LEXICON

1

2

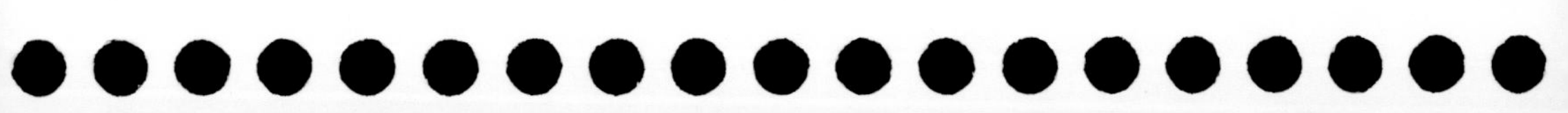

Premolar Clamp

FUNCTION To anchor and stabilize dental dam

CHARACTERISTICS Clamp used determined by tooth size
Range of sizes
Variety of styles

Examples:

① Wingless clamp
② Winged clamp

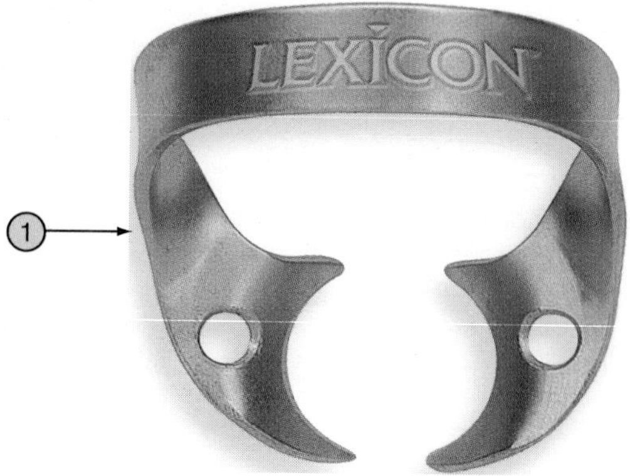

LEXICON

1

LEXICON

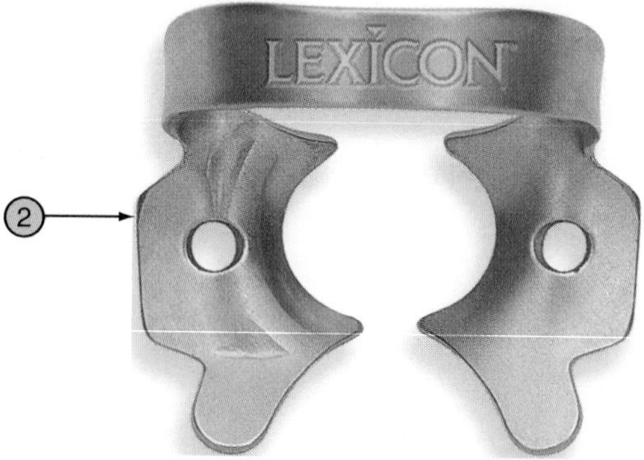

2

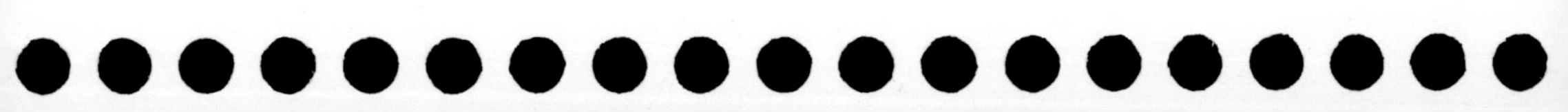

Universal Clamp—Maxillary

FUNCTION To anchor and stabilize dental dam

CHARACTERISTICS Used on right or left posterior molars
Range of sizes
Variety of styles

Examples:

① Wingless clamp*
② Winged clamp

*Manufacturer suggests that wingless universal clamp may be used for both maxillary and mandibular.

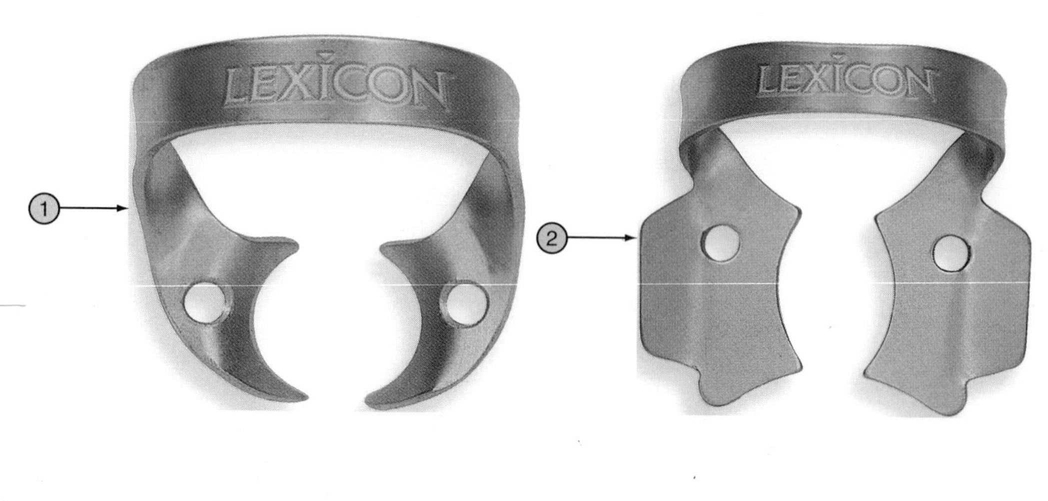
1
LEXICON
2
LEXICON

Universal Clamp—Mandibular

FUNCTION To anchor and stabilize dental dam

CHARACTERISTICS Used on right or left posterior molars
Range of sizes
Variety of styles

Examples:
① Wingless clamp*
② Winged clamp

*Manufacturer suggests that wingless universal clamp may be used for both maxillary and mandibular.

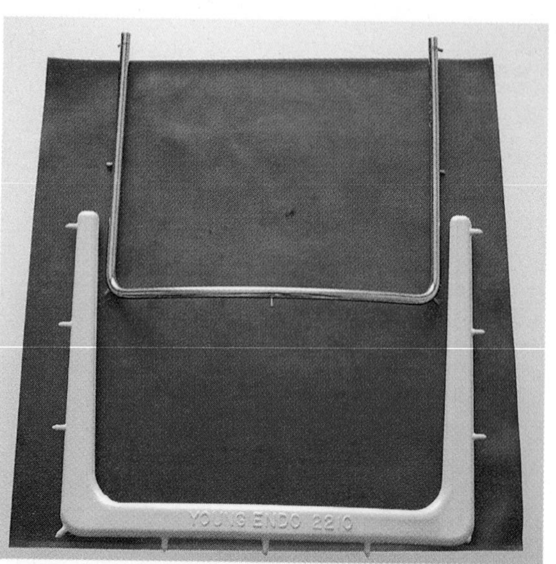
YOUNG ENDO 2210

INSTRUMENT

Dental Dam Frame

FUNCTION To hold dental dam away from teeth

CHARACTERISTICS Metal or plastic
Plastic frame—May be left on during radiographic exposures

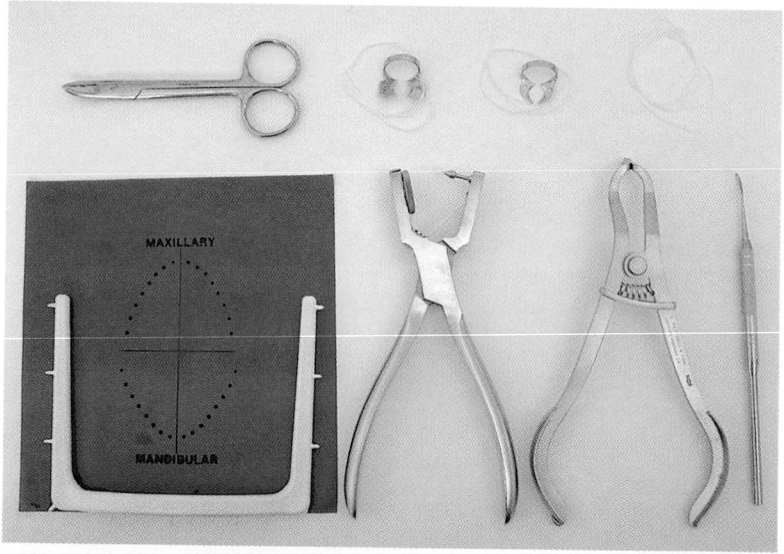

156

Dental Dam

TOP (LEFT TO RIGHT)

Crown and bridge scissors, dental dam clamps with ligature ties, stabilizing ligatures

BOTTOM (LEFT TO RIGHT)

Stamped dental dam, plastic dental dam frame, dental dam punch, dental dam forceps, beavertail burnisher

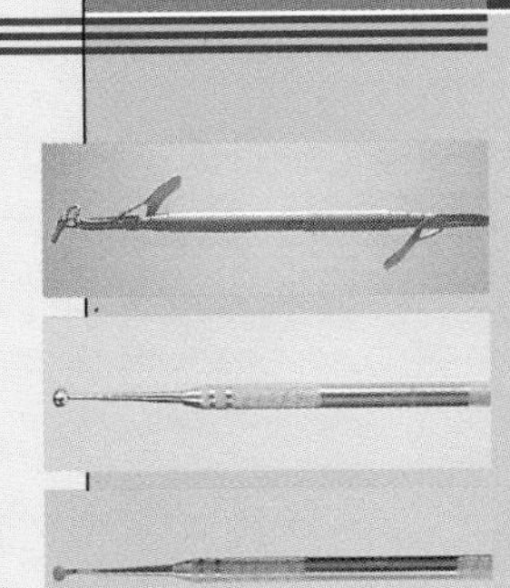

CHAPTER 8

Amalgam Instruments

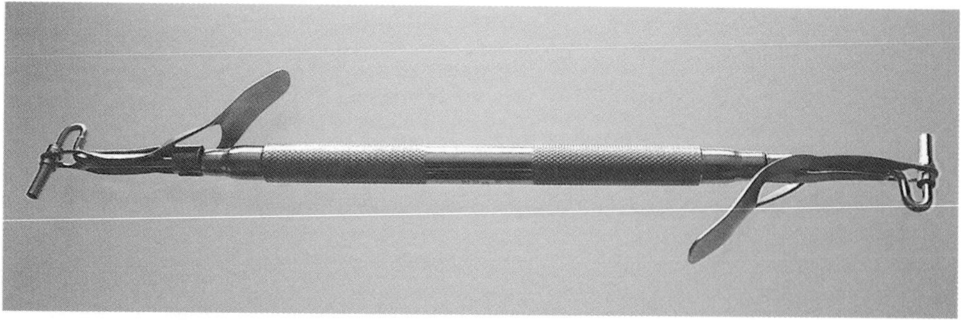

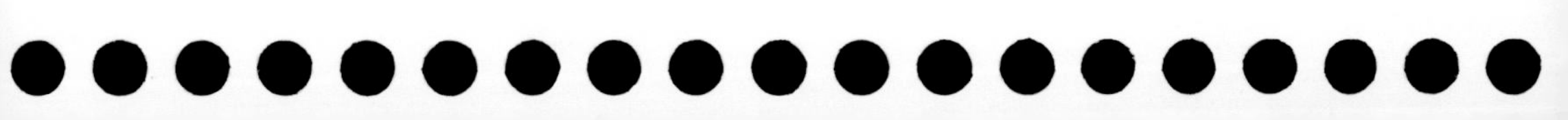

Amalgam Carrier

FUNCTION To carry and dispense amalgam for cavity preparation

CHARACTERISTICS Single or double ended

- Double ended—One small end, one large end

PRACTICE NOTES

1. Amalgam is placed in hollow tubes and then transferred to the cavity preparation (the inside of the hollow tubes is coated with metal or Teflon).
2. Amalgam sticks in the carrier if it is not released immediately after the tubes are filled.

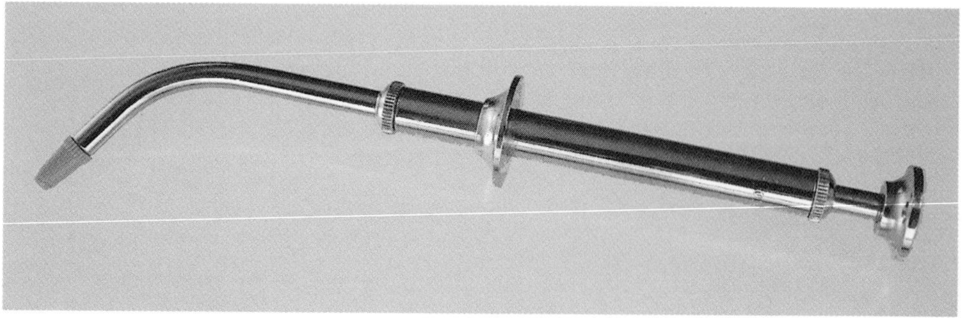

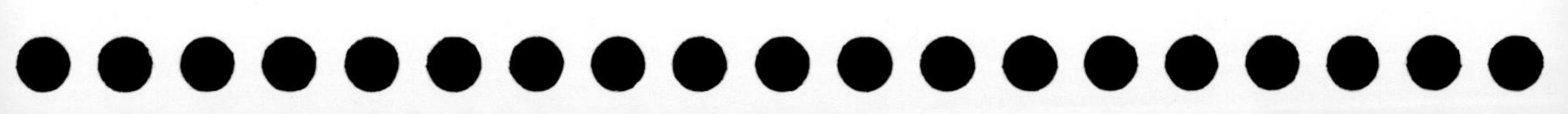

Amalgam Carrier—Plunger Style

FUNCTION To carry and dispense amalgam for cavity preparation

CHARACTERISTICS Single ended

PRACTICE NOTES

1. Amalgam is placed in hollow tubes and then transferred to the cavity preparation (the inside of the hollow tubes is coated with metal or Teflon).
2. Amalgam sticks in the carrier if it is not released immediately after the tubes are filled.

164

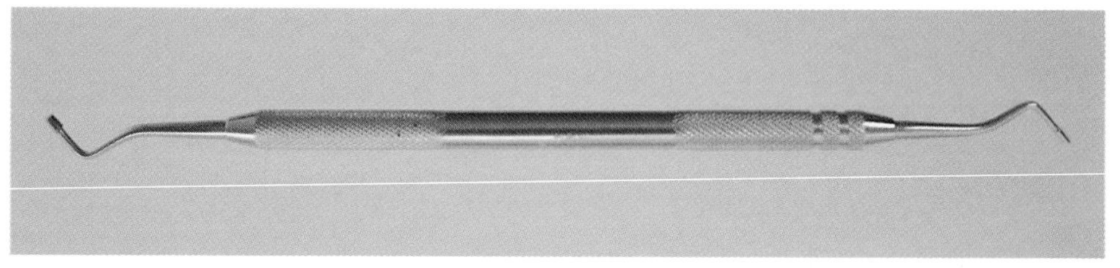

Smooth Condenser (Plugger)

FUNCTION To pack and condense amalgam into cavity preparation (also condenses other restorative materials)

CHARACTERISTICS Smooth ends
Round, flat, or diamond shaped
Single or double ended
- Double ended—One small end, one large end

Back action condenser with right-angle working ends—Accommodates difficult areas
Range of sizes

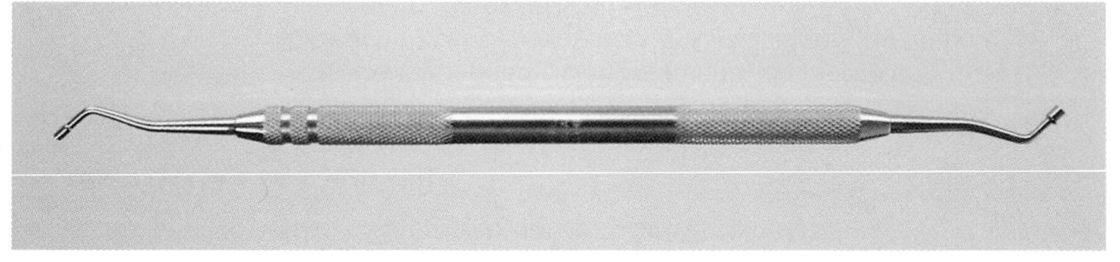

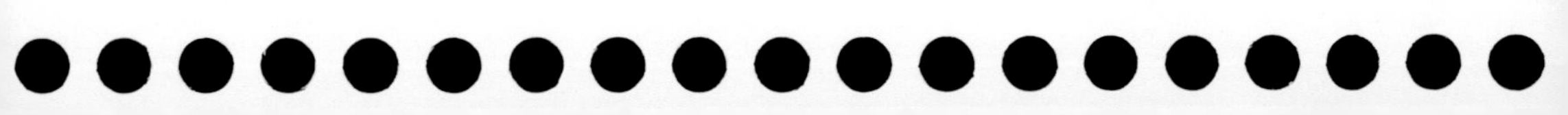

Serrated Condenser (Plugger)

FUNCTION To pack and condense amalgam into cavity preparation (also condenses other restorative materials)

CHARACTERISTICS Serrated ends

Round, flat, or diamond shaped

Single or double ended

- Double ended—One small end, one large end

Back action condenser with right-angle working ends—Accommodates difficult areas

Range of sizes

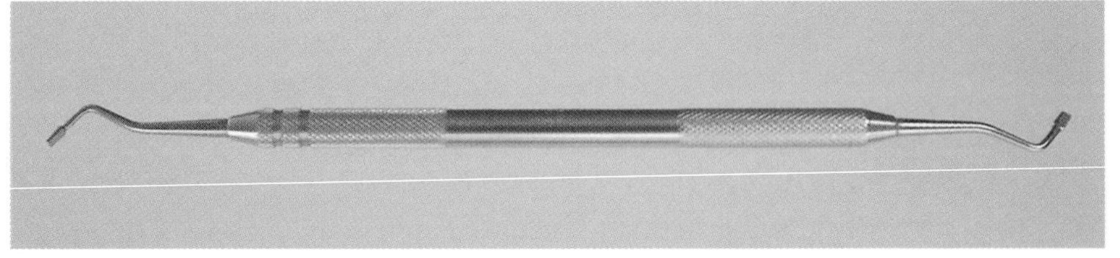

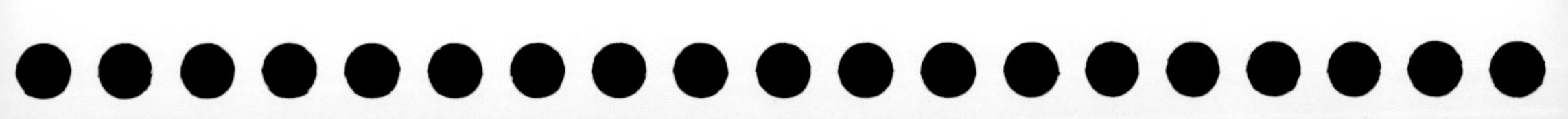

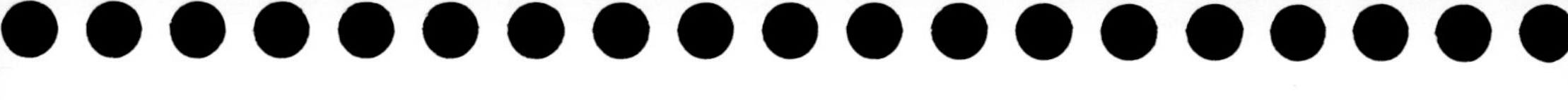

INSTRUMENT

Interproximal Condenser

FUNCTION To pack and condense amalgam into interproximal areas of cavity preparation (also condenses other restorative materials)

CHARACTERISTICS Ends shaped to fit mesial or distal areas of cavity preparation
Smooth or serrated ends
Range of sizes

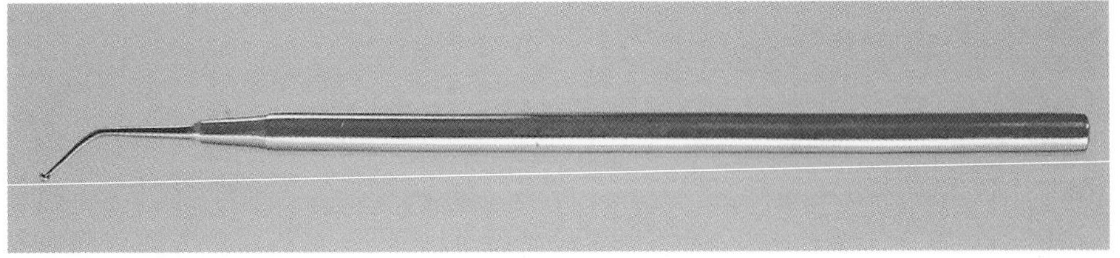

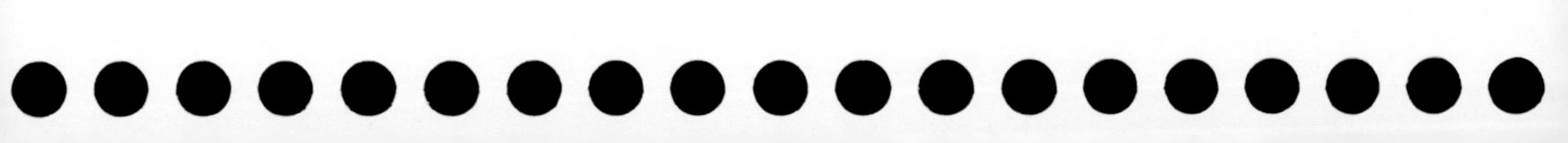

INSTRUMENT

Liner Applicator

FUNCTION To place calcium hydroxide or glass ionomer in cavity preparation

CHARACTERISTICS Short or long handle
Single or double ended

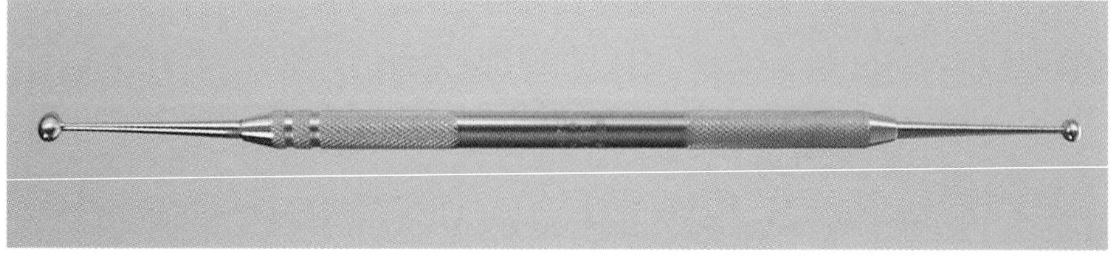

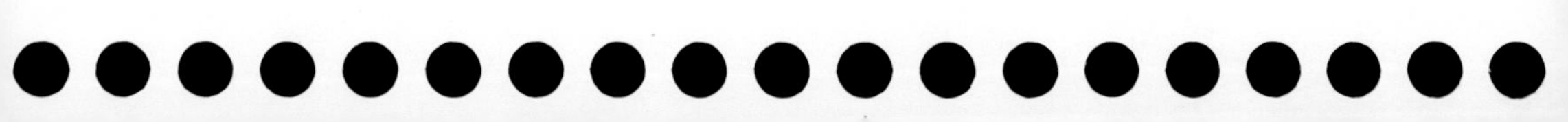

INSTRUMENT

Football Burnisher

FUNCTION

To smooth amalgam after condensing
To contour matrix band before placement
To perform initial carving of amalgam
(Also burnishes other restorative materials)

CHARACTERISTICS

Single or double ended

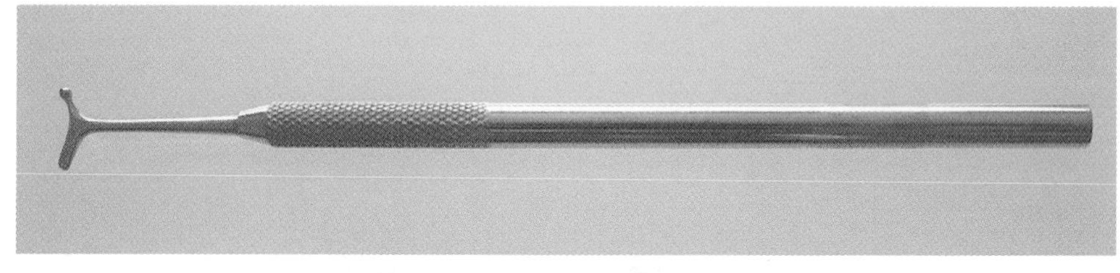

INSTRUMENT

T-Ball Burnisher

FUNCTION
To smooth amalgam after condensing
To contour matrix band before placement
To begin carving of amalgam
(Also burnishes other restorative materials)

CHARACTERISTICS
Single ended

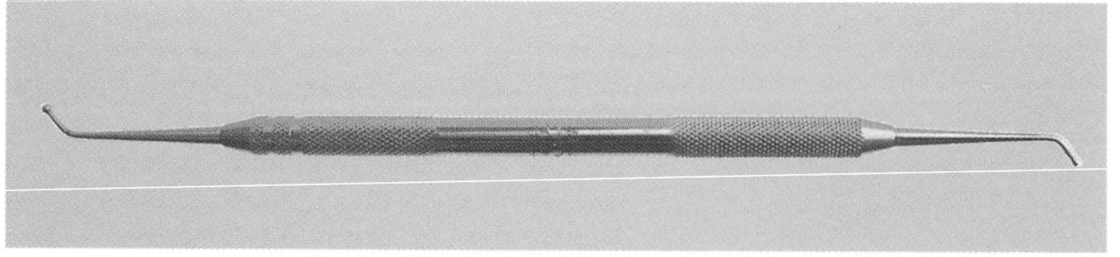

INSTRUMENT

Ball Burnisher

FUNCTION To smooth amalgam after condensing
To contour matrix band before placement
To perform initial carving of amalgam
(Also burnishes other restorative materials)

CHARACTERISTICS Single or double ended

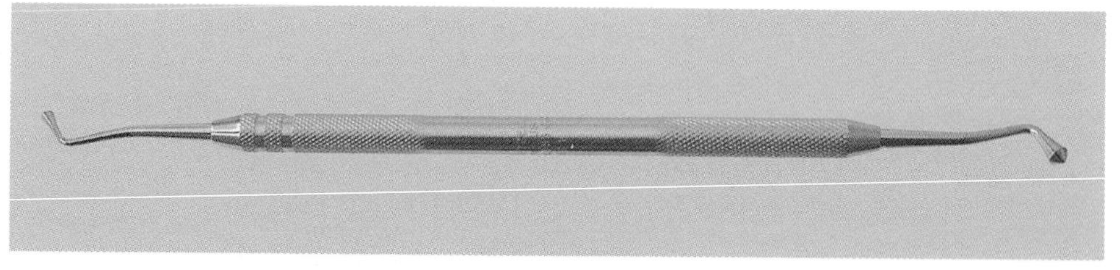

INSTRUMENT

Acorn Burnisher

FUNCTION To smooth amalgam after condensing
To perform initial carving of amalgam
(Also burnishes other restorative materials)

CHARACTERISTICS Single or double ended

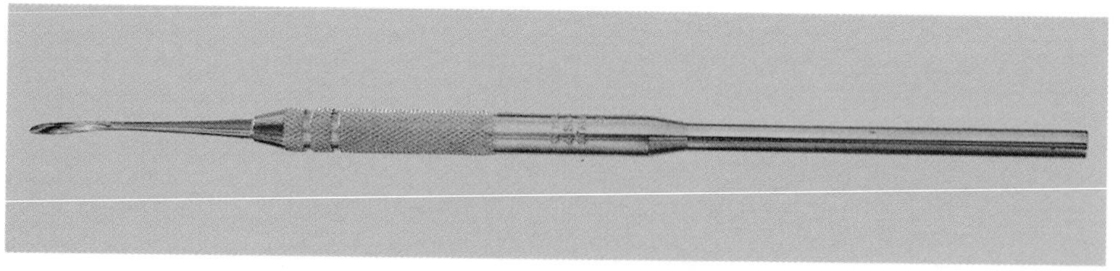

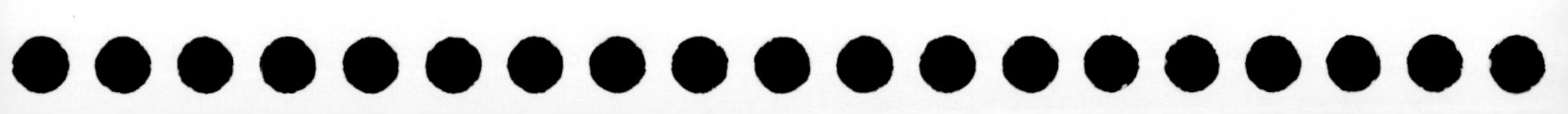

INSTRUMENT

Beavertail Burnisher

FUNCTION

To smooth amalgam after condensing
To perform initial carving of amalgam
To invert dental dam
(Also burnishes other restorative materials)

CHARACTERISTICS

Single or double ended

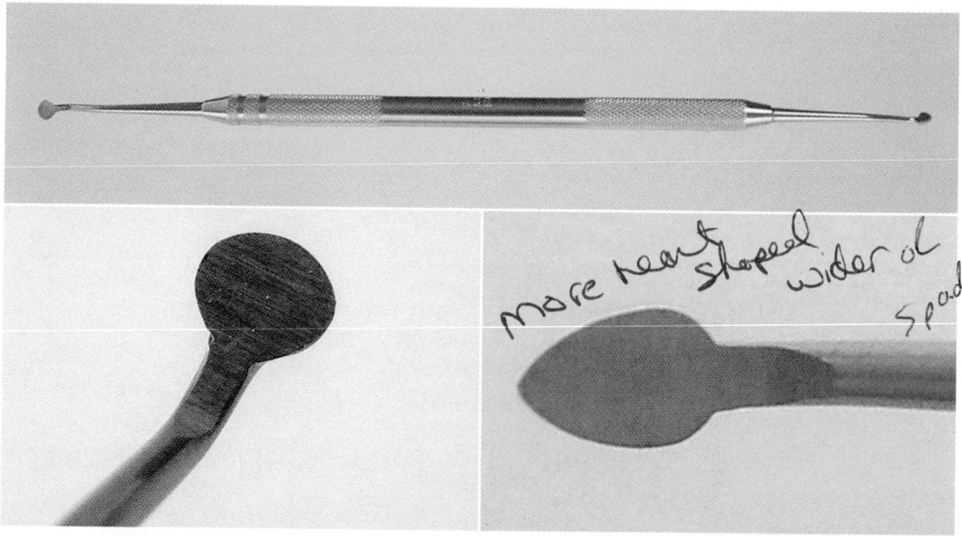
More heart shaped wider ol spade

INSTRUMENT

Tanner Carver

FUNCTION To carve occlusal anatomy into amalgam restorations (Also carves other restorative materials)

CHARACTERISTICS Double ended—Two ends shaped differently
Ends shaped differently from those of discoid-cleoid carver

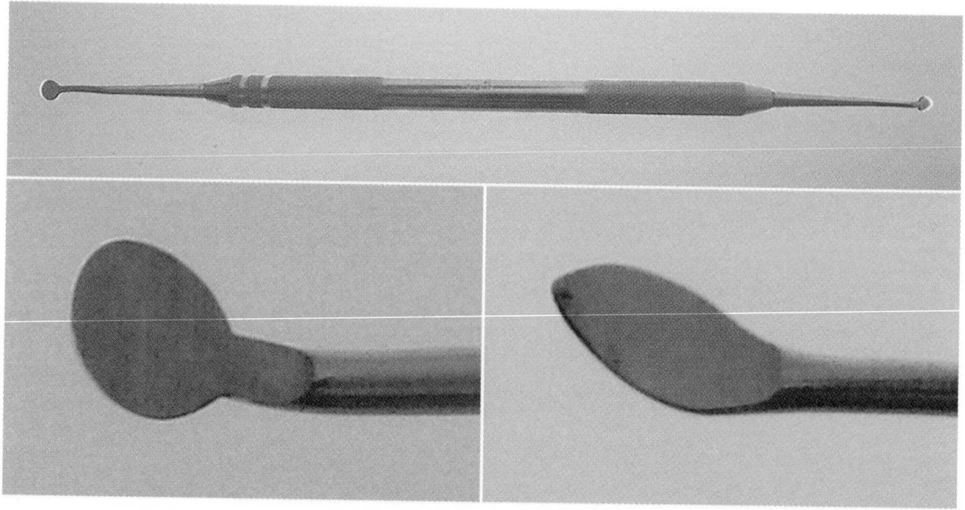

Discoid-Cleoid Carver

FUNCTION To carve occlusal anatomy into amalgam restorations (Also carves other restorative materials)

CHARACTERISTICS Double ended—Two ends shaped differently:

- Discoid end—Disc shaped
- Cleoid end—Pointed

Ends shaped differently from those of Tanner carver

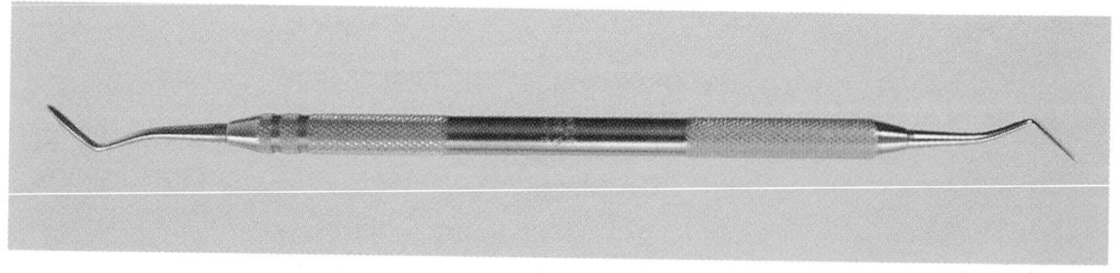

Hollenback Carver

FUNCTION To contour and carve occlusal and interproximal anatomy in amalgam restorations
(Also carves other restorative materials)

CHARACTERISTICS Double ended—Ends protrude at different angles

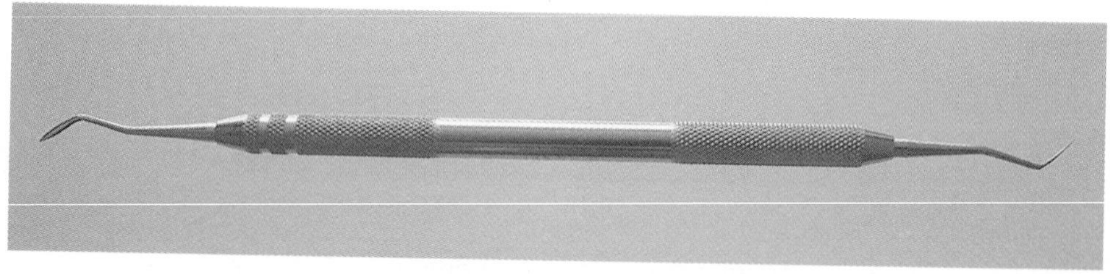

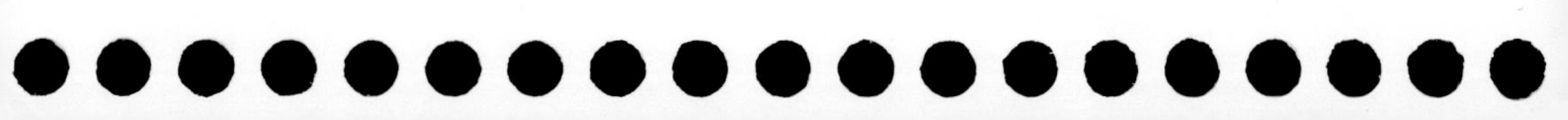

INSTRUMENT

Half-Hollenback Carver

FUNCTION To contour and carve occlusal and interproximal anatomy in amalgam restorations
(Also carves other restorative materials)

CHARACTERISTICS Half the size of Hollenback carver
Double ended—Ends protrude at different angles

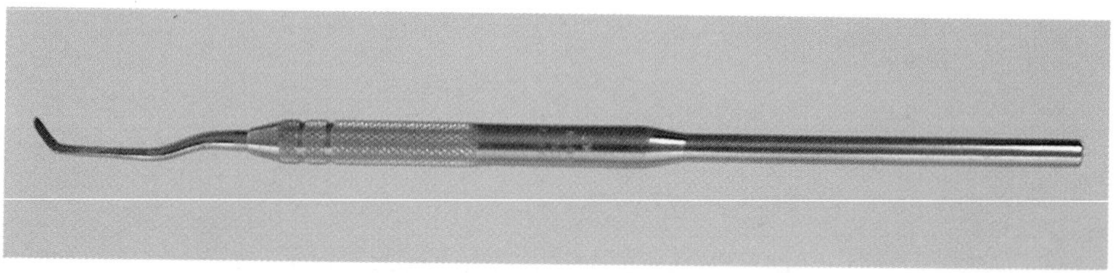

Gold Carving Knife

FUNCTION

To trim interproximal amalgam restoration, recreating contour of proximal wall
(Also carves other restorative materials)

CHARACTERISTICS

Single or double ended
Removes flash composite material from interproximal areas
Variety of designs

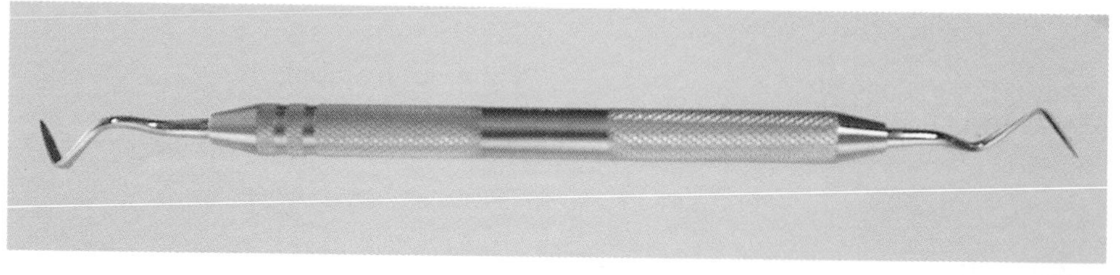

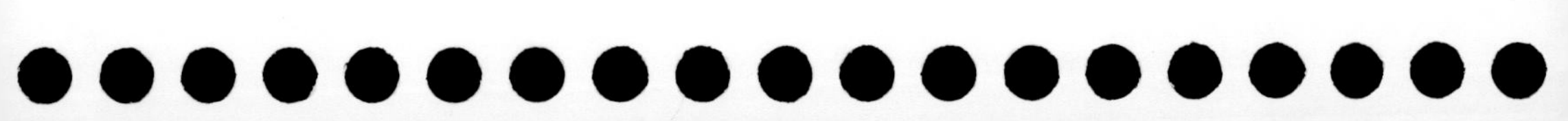

INSTRUMENT

Interproximal Carving Knife

FUNCTION

To trim interproximal amalgam restoration, recreating contour of proximal wall
(Also carves other restorative materials)

CHARACTERISTICS

Single or double ended
Removes flash composite material from interproximal areas
Variety of designs

194

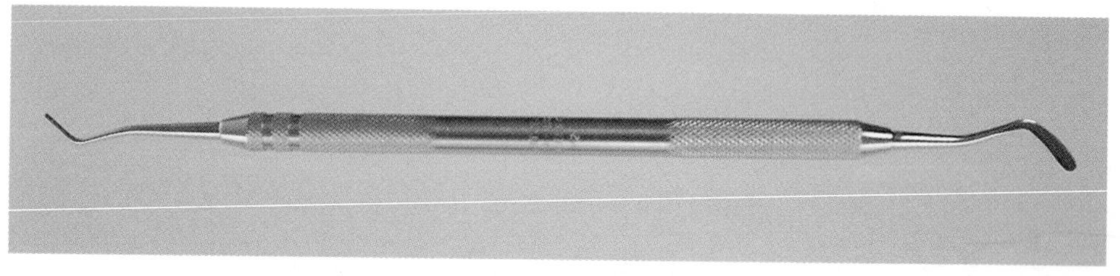

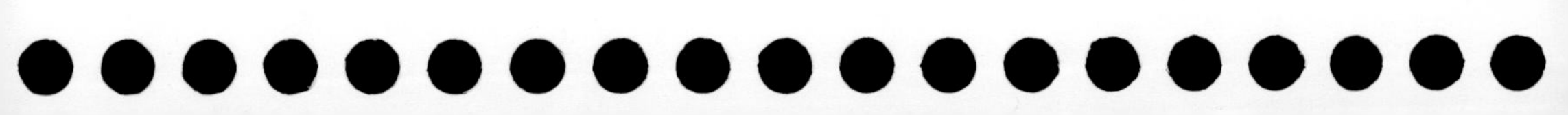

INSTRUMENT

Woodson

FUNCTION

To carry and place temporary restorative material for cavity preparation (paddle end)
To condense restorative material (plugger end)

CHARACTERISTICS

Double ended
Range of sizes
Plugger end available in variety of sizes
Paddle end available in different angles, sizes

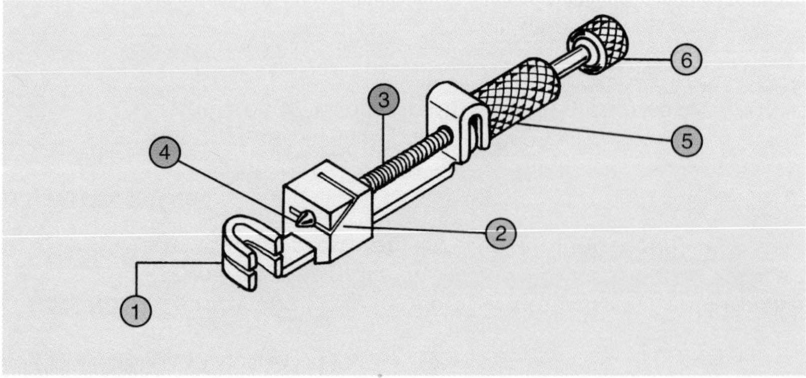

Tofflemire/Matrix Band Retainer

FUNCTION To maintain stability of matrix band during condensation of restorative material for class II preparation (used with amalgam, composite, and build-up materials)

CHARACTERISTICS Parts

① **Guide slots:** Straight slot; right and left slots for right or left quadrant
② **Diagonal slot:** Slides up and down on spindle; matrix band is placed in slot and spindle secures band in place; open slots are placed toward gingiva
③ **Spindle:** Holds matrix band in retainer
④ **Spindle pin:** Stabilizes band in holder
⑤ **Inner knob:** Adjusts size or loop of matrix band to fit around tooth and loosens band for removal
⑥ **Outer knob:** Positioned at end of spindle that tightens or loosens matrix band in retainer

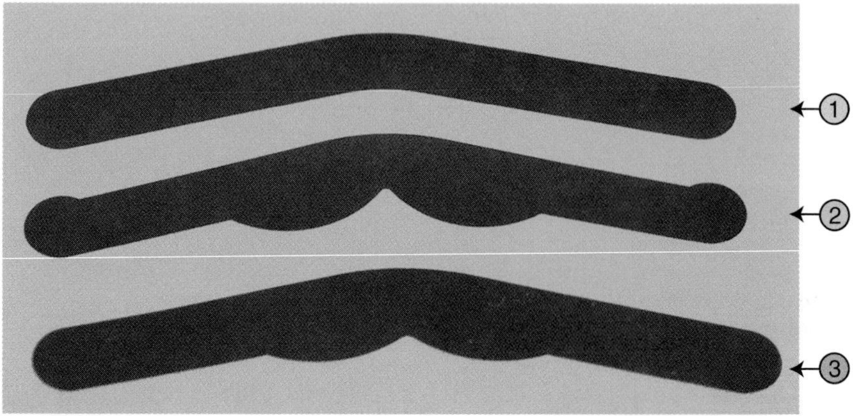

1
2
3

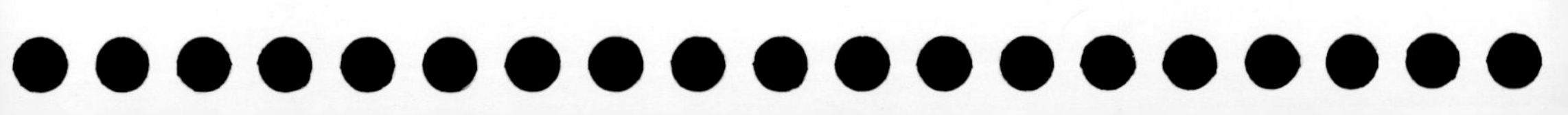

Matrix Bands

FUNCTION To replace missing proximal wall or walls of cavity preparation for condensation of restorative material (for class II preparations)

CHARACTERISTICS Variety of sizes, shapes, and thicknesses
Bands designed for specific teeth:

① Universal band—For all posterior teeth except larger teeth
② Premolar band—For premolars
③ Molar band—For larger molars

Pediatric band available for primary teeth

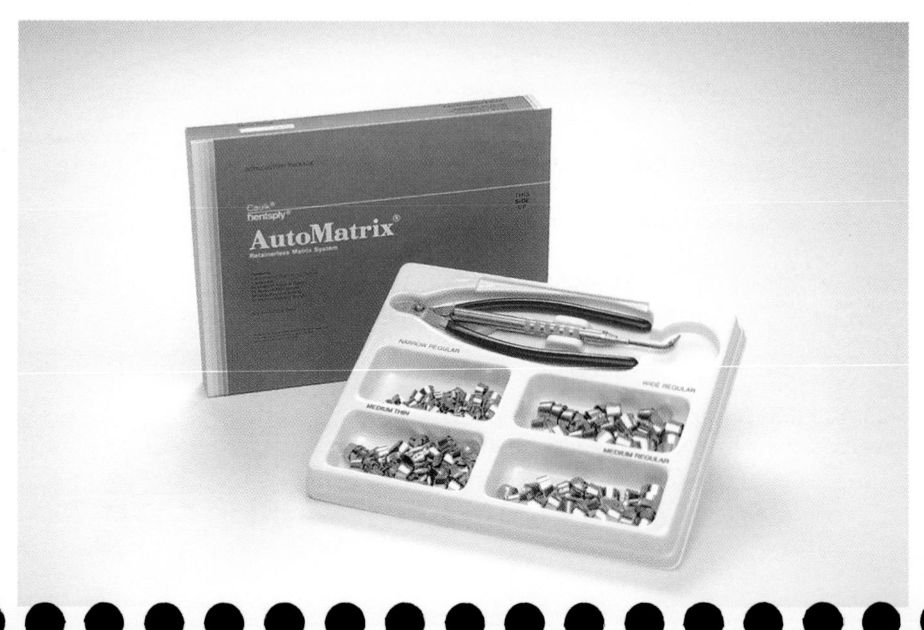

Caulk®
Dentsply®
THIS SIDE UP
AutoMatrix®
Retainerless Matrix System
NARROW REGULAR
WIDE REGULAR
MEDIUM THIN
MEDIUM REGULAR

AutoMatrix System

FUNCTION To replace missing proximal wall or walls of cavity preparation for condensation of restorative material (for class II preparations)

CHARACTERISTICS Alternative matrix band system
Variety of sizes and shapes
Bands designed for specific teeth:

- Universal band—For all posterior teeth except larger teeth
- Molar band—For larger molars
- Premolar band—For premolars
- Clear bands—For composite restorations
- Pediatric band—For primary teeth

PRACTICE NOTES

1. Bands are placed on the tooth and tightened with a tightening wrench.
2. Tightening wrench is also used to loosen bands.
3. Removing pliers are used to remove bands.

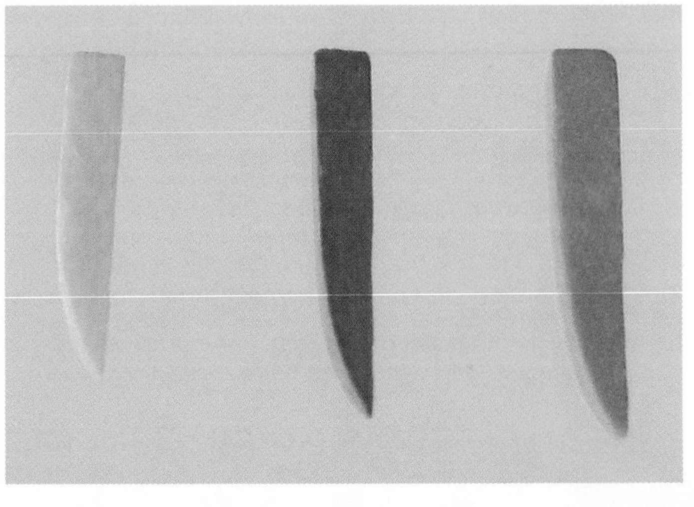

Wooden Wedges

FUNCTION To hold matrix band in place along gingival margin of class II preparation

CHARACTERISTICS Wood or plastic
Triangular, round, or anatomical shapes
Placed in gingival embrasure area
Variety of sizes and shapes available to accommodate embrasure area

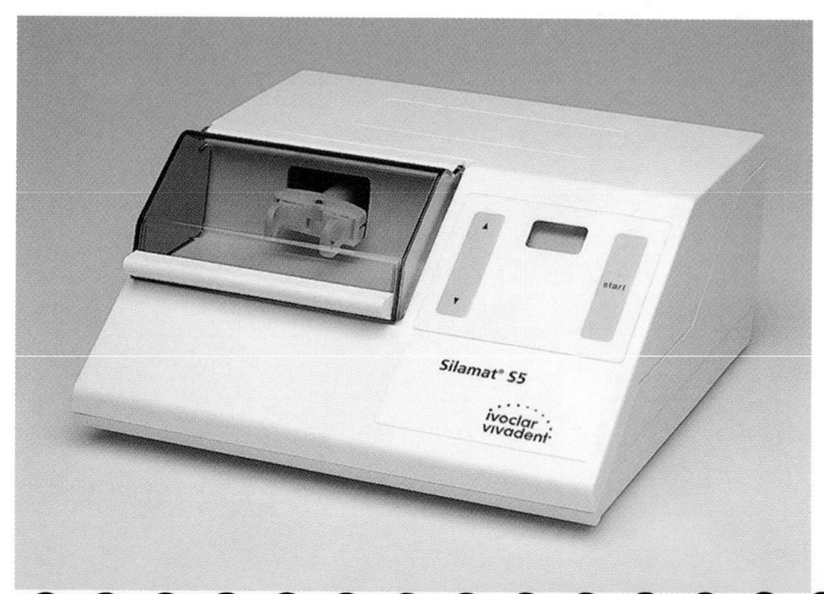
start
Silamat® S5
ivoclar
vivadent

Amalgamator

FUNCTION

To mix alloy and mercury into amalgam and other restorative materials

To mix cements

CHARACTERISTICS

Preloaded capsules contain alloy, mercury, and pestle to aid mixing.

- Various types of capsules are available; they are activated manually by twisting or pushing or using the activator.

Thin membrane separates materials until mixing occurs.

PRACTICE NOTES

1. The process of mixing is called *amalgamation* or *trituration*.
2. The mixing time recommended by the manufacturer should be used.

INSTRUMENT

Amalgam Well

FUNCTION To hold amalgam before it is placed in preparation
To hold amalgam while loading amalgam carrier

CHARACTERISTICS Metal, plastic, or glass

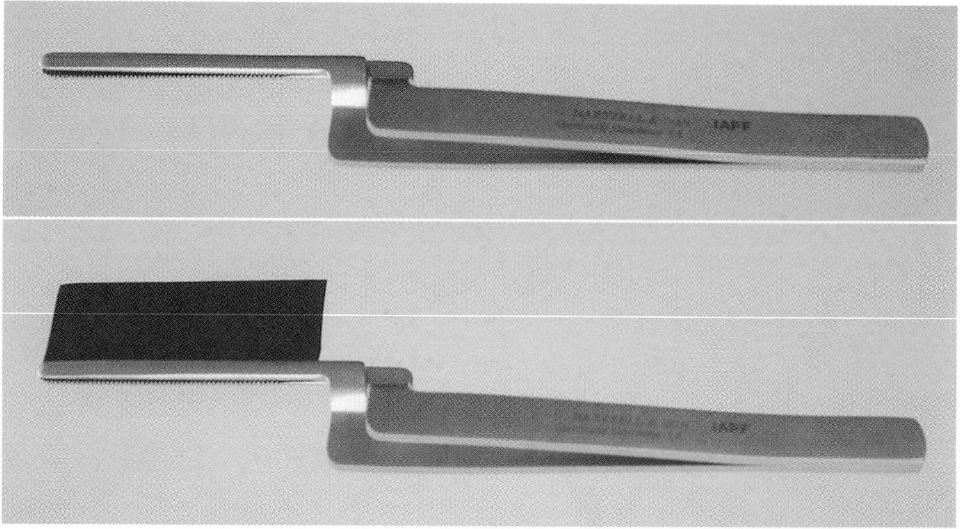

INSTRUMENT

Articulating Paper Holder

FUNCTION

To hold articulating paper in place
To check centric and lateral occlusion

CHARACTERISTICS

Articulating paper is blue or red.
Paper varies from thin to thick.

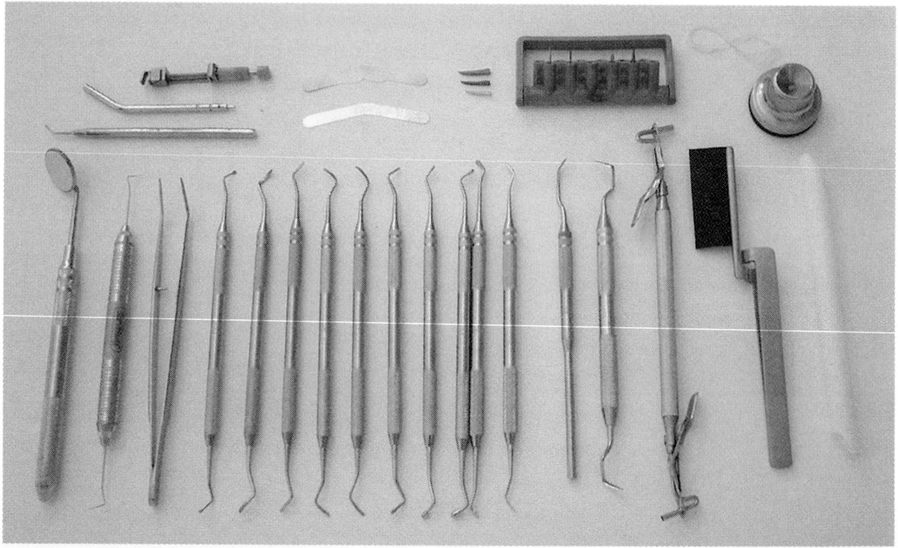

TRAY SETUP

Amalgam

TOP ROW (FROM LEFT TO RIGHT)

Tofflemire/matrix band retainer, air/water syringe tip, liner applicator, molar matrix band, universal matrix band, wedges, burs in bur block, dental floss, amalgam well

BOTTOM ROW (FROM LEFT TO RIGHT)

Mouth mirror, explorer, cotton forceps (pliers), small spoon excavator, large spoon excavator, enamel hatchet, mesial gingival margin trimmer, distal gingival margin trimmer, small condenser, large condenser, acorn burnisher, Tanner carver, half-Hollenback carver, gold carving knife, interproximal carving knife, amalgam carrier, articulating paper holder and articulating paper, high-velocity (volume) evacuation tip (HVE)

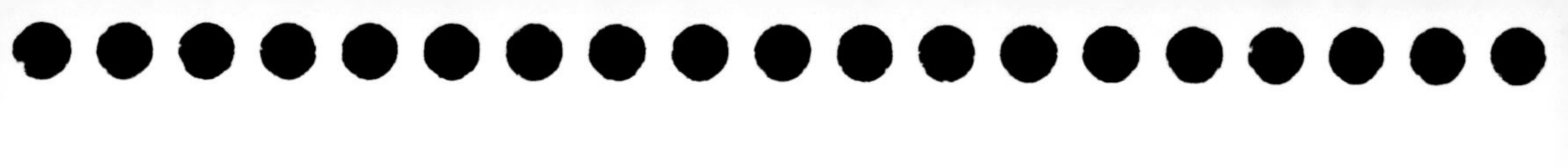

CHAPTER 9

Composite Instruments

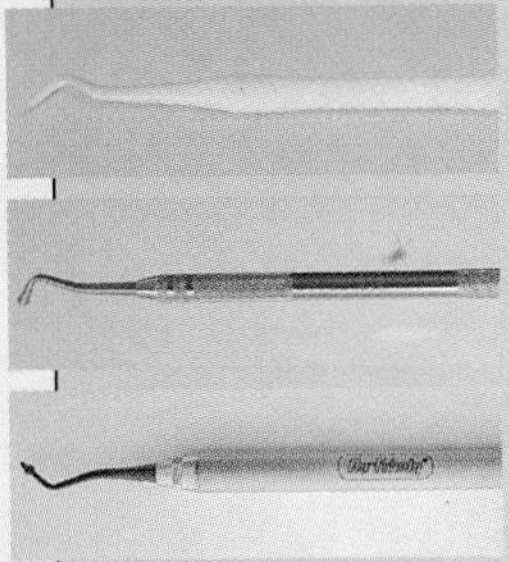

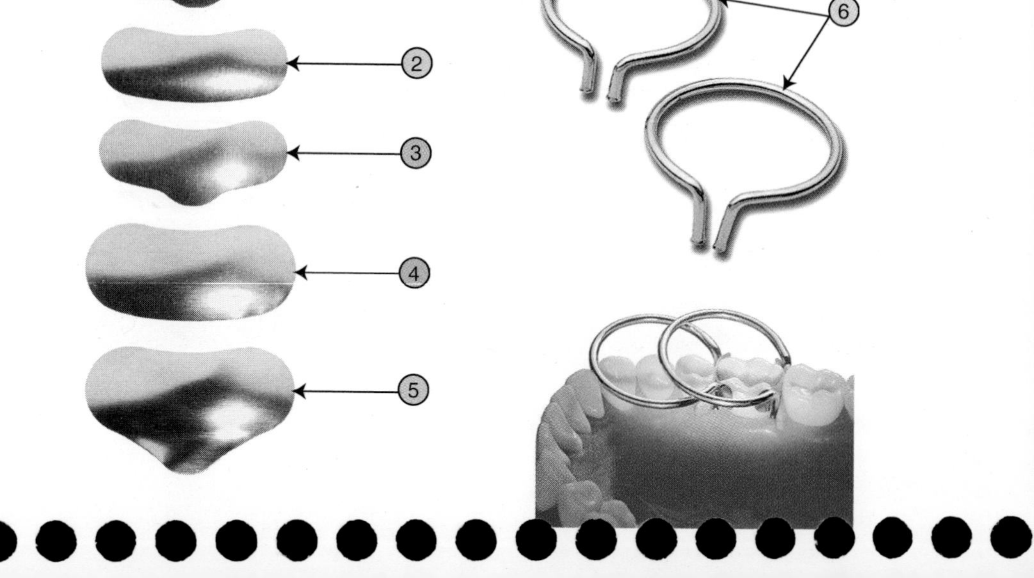
1
2
3
4
5
6

INSTRUMENT

Sectional Matrix System

FUNCTION To replace missing proximal wall of cavity preparation for placement of composite material (for class II restorations)

CHARACTERISTICS Variety of sizes and shapes to accommodate restoration:

① Pediatric band—Primary molar
② Small band—Bicuspid, small molar
③ Extended small band—Bicuspid, molar, with deep cervical restoration
④ Standard band—Molar restoration
⑤ Large band—Deep cervical restoration
⑥ Tension rings—Different sizes to accommodate restoration

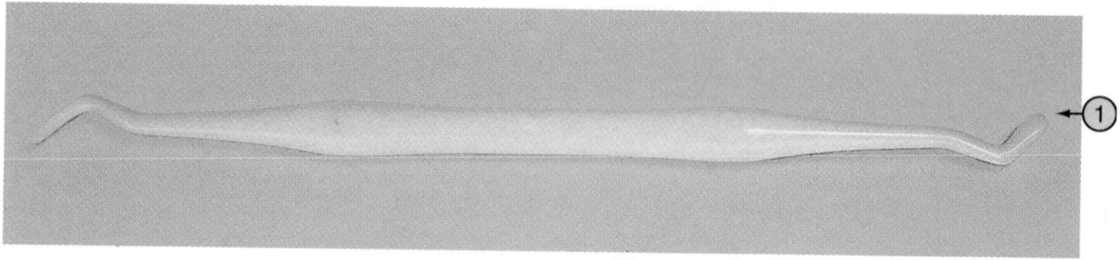

1

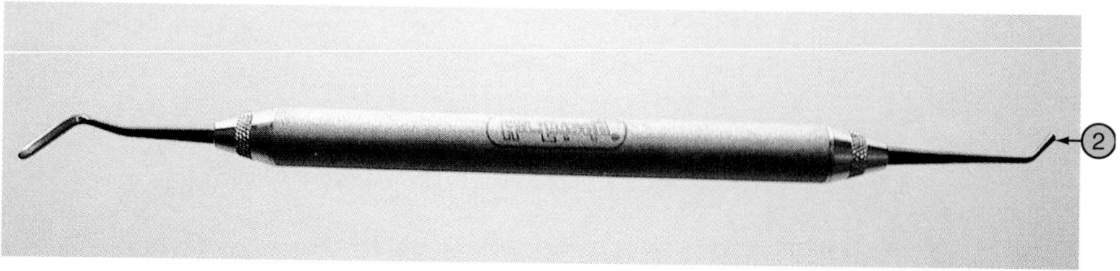

2

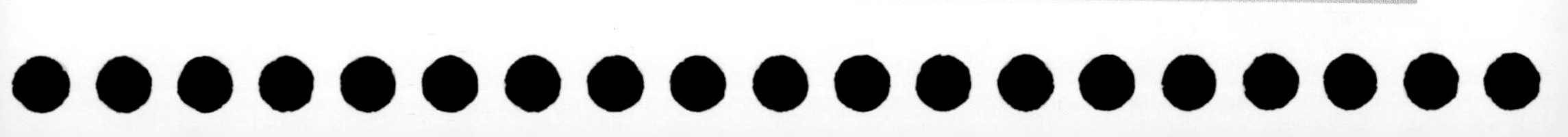

Composite Placement Instrument

FUNCTION

To carry composite material for cavity preparation
To place and condense composite material in cavity preparation
To carve composite material in cavity preparation

CHARACTERISTICS

Double ended

- Different angles on ends
- Ends shaped differently, one to accommodate initial placement of material, the other to contour and carve material

Metal or plastic:

① Plastic composite instrument
② Metal composite instrument

Variety of sizes, shapes, and angles

Hu-Friedy®

1

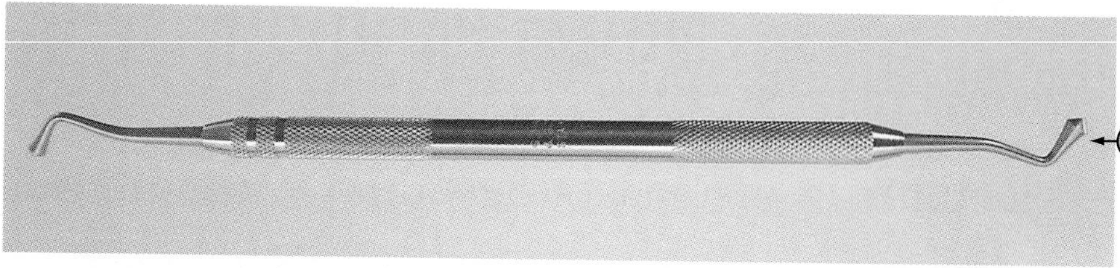

2

Composite Burnisher

FUNCTION To form occlusal anatomy in composite restorations
To achieve final contouring of anatomy, pits, fissures, and grooves

CHARACTERISTICS Double ended—Different angle on either end

① Composite burnisher
Titanium nitride coating—Creates hard, smooth, nonstick surface that resists scratching, sticking, or discoloration of composite material

② Acorn burnisher for composite restorations
Gold titanium nitride coating—Creates hard, smooth, nonstick surface that resists scratching, sticking, or discoloration of composite material

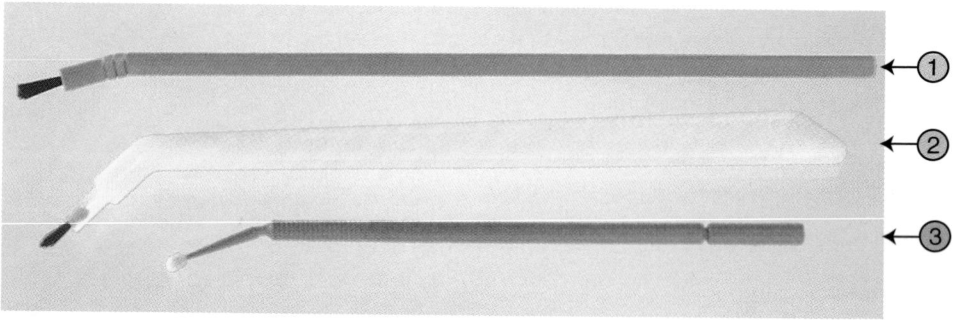

1

2

3

Applicator

FUNCTION To apply conditioning, primer, and bonding material to cavity preparation

CHARACTERISTICS Types:

① Disposable one-piece applicator—Several colors available for application of different materials; working end bends; various styles, sizes

② Two-piece applicator—Available with autoclavable handle and removable, disposable tip

③ Microbrush applicator—Disposable, various styles, sizes

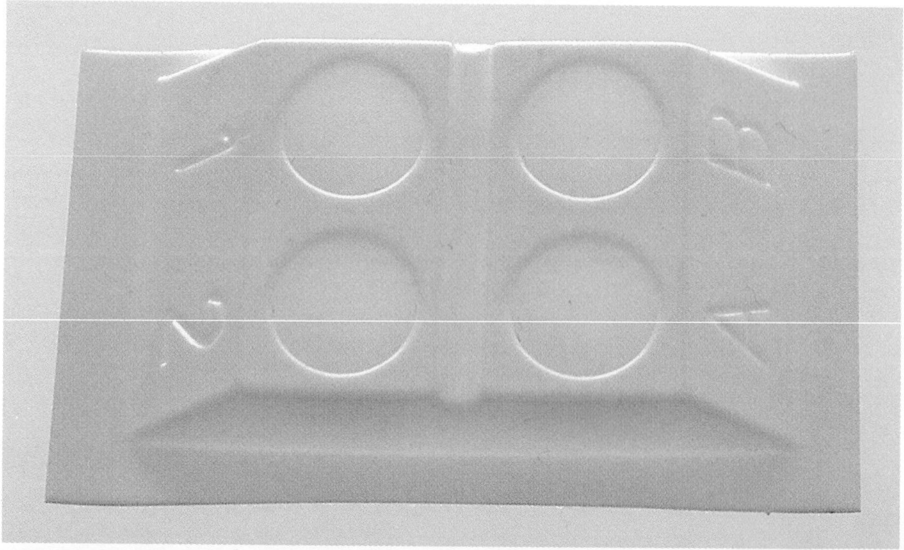

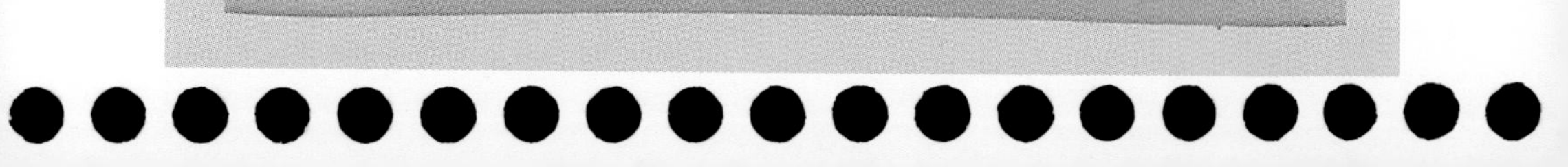

INSTRUMENT

Well for Composite Material

FUNCTION To hold material: etchant, bonding, and composite

CHARACTERISTICS Disposable or autoclavable
Labels on each well—Designate different materials

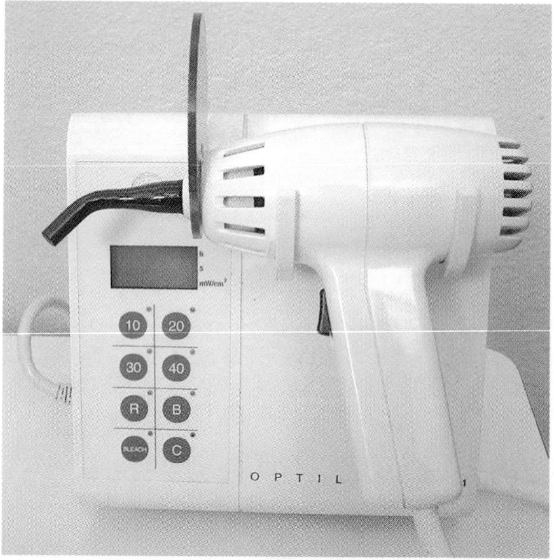
h
s
mW/cm²
10
20
30
40
R
B
BLEACH
C
O P T I L

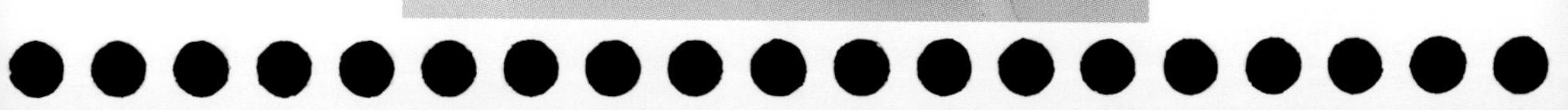

Curing Light

FUNCTION To harden light-cured materials: bonding, composite, sealants, build-up material

CHARACTERISTICS Various styles available—Electric or battery operated

PRACTICE NOTES

1. The material must be cured in increments of 2 mm or less to ensure complete setting.
2. A testing device should be used to check the accuracy of the curing light.

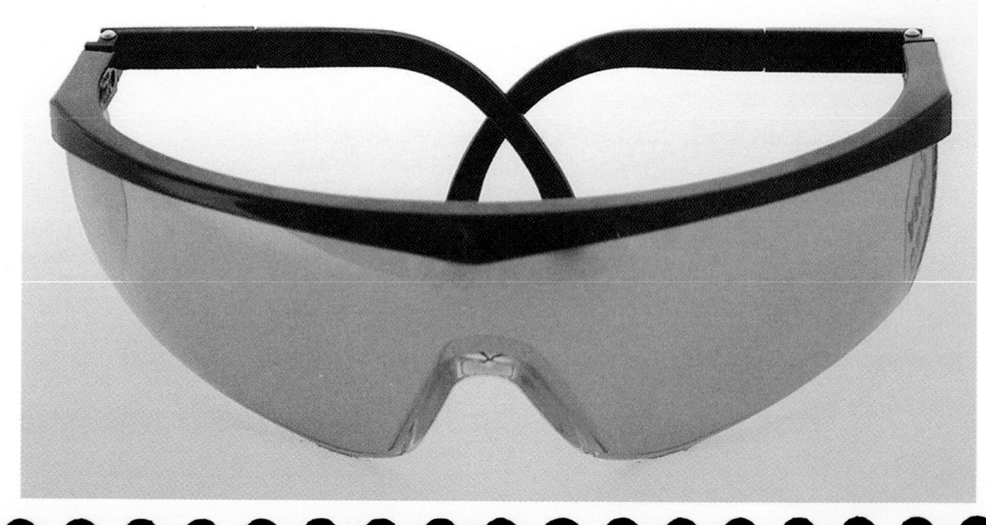

INSTRUMENT

Protective Shield for Curing Light

FUNCTION To protect operator's and assistant's eyes during curing stage of light-cured material

CHARACTERISTICS Orange color—Blocks harmful light to operator's and assistant's eyes
Protective shields—Available on curing light and paddle shield

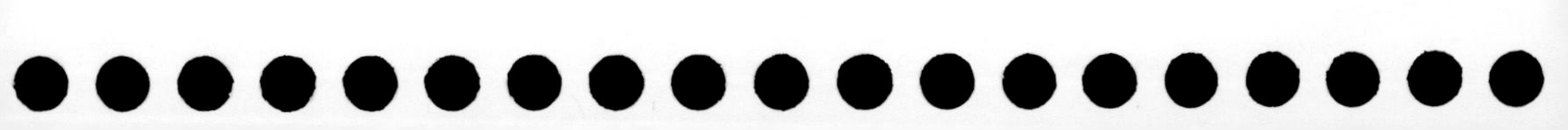

INSTRUMENT

Finishing Strip

FUNCTION To finish and smooth interproximal surface of restoration

CHARACTERISTICS Abrasive textures (i.e., sandpaper, synthetic material)
Different grit consistencies
No abrasive material in center of strip—To avoid removal of tooth structure

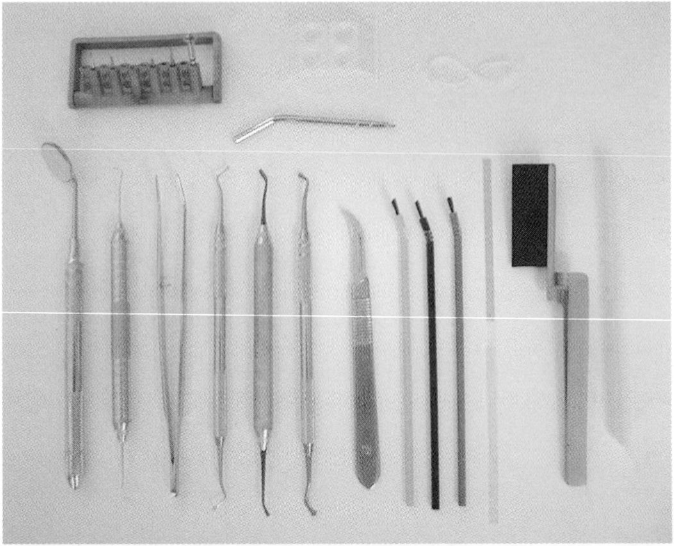

Composite Procedure

TOP ROW (FROM LEFT TO RIGHT)

Burs in bur holder, well for composite material, air/water syringe tip, dental floss

BOTTOM ROW (FROM LEFT TO RIGHT)

Mouth mirror, explorer, cotton forceps (pliers), spoon excavator, composite placement instrument, composite burnisher, scalpel and no. 12 blade, etchant and bonding applicator tips, composite finishing strip, articulating paper holder and articulating paper, high-velocity (volume) evacuation tip (HVE)

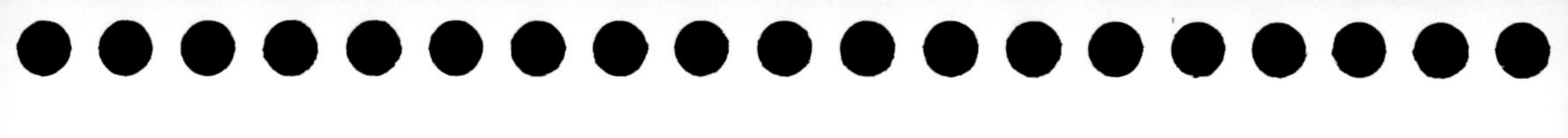

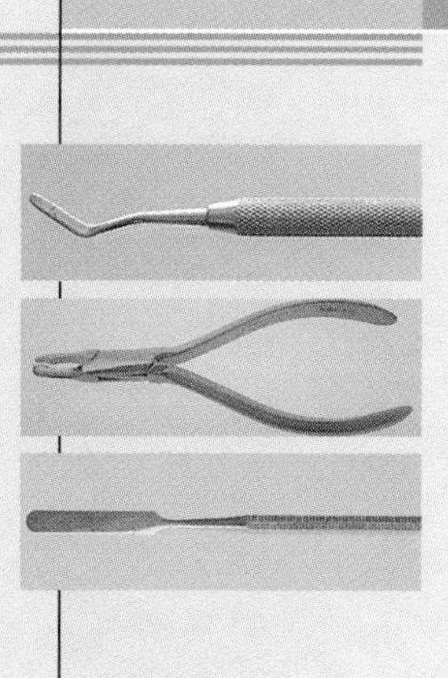

CHAPTER 10

Crown and Bridge Instruments

234

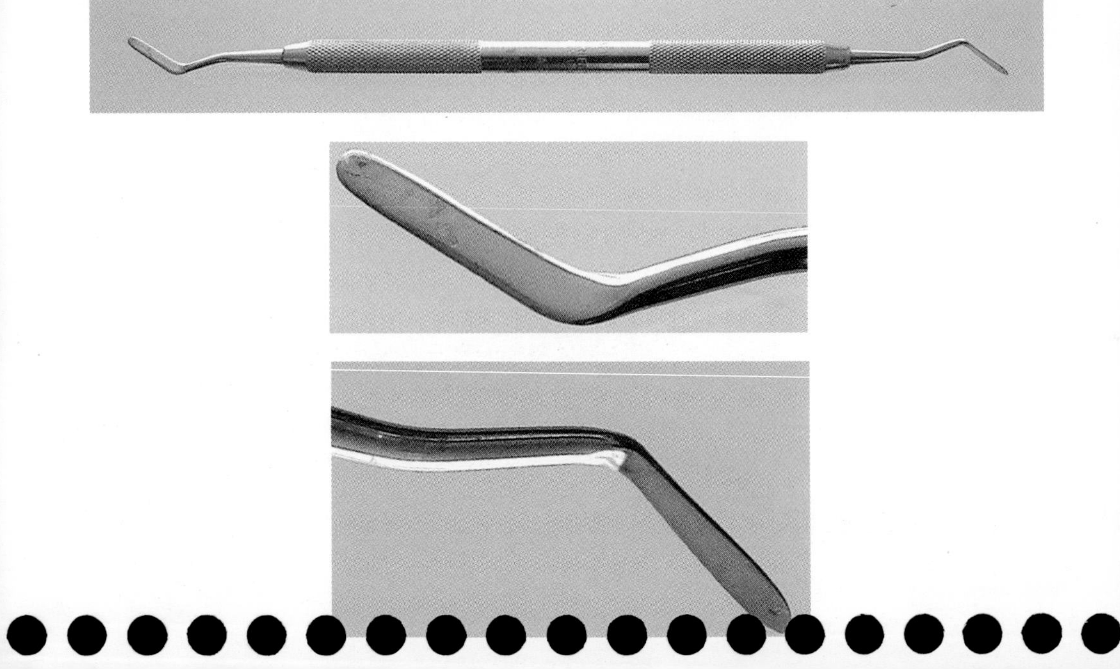

Gingival Retraction Cord Instrument

FUNCTION To place gingival retraction cord in sulcus area while preparing tooth for crown and/or before final impressions

CHARACTERISTICS Smooth or serrated edges
Double ended—Different angle on each end
Variety of styles

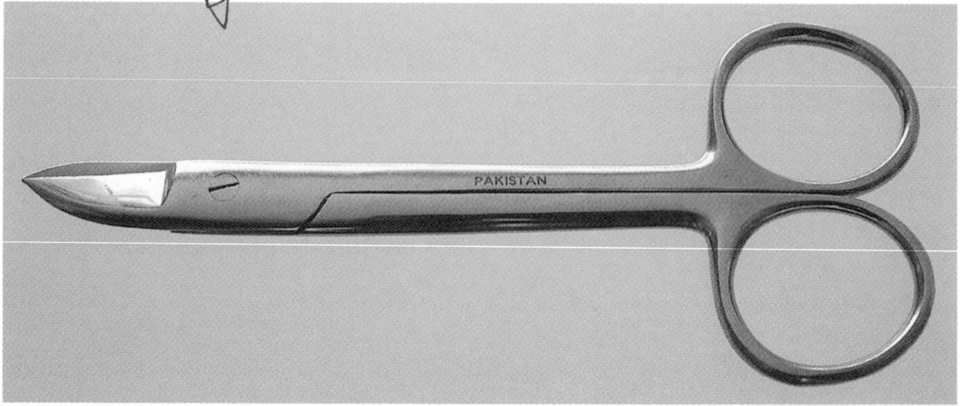

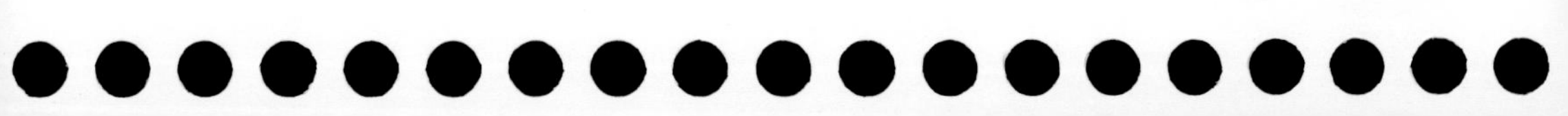

Crown and Bridge Scissors

FUNCTION

To trim aluminum temporary crowns on gingival side
To trim custom temporary crowns
To cut gingival retraction cord
To trim matrix bands

CHARACTERISTICS

Available with straight or curved, narrow or wide cutting edges
Variety of sizes

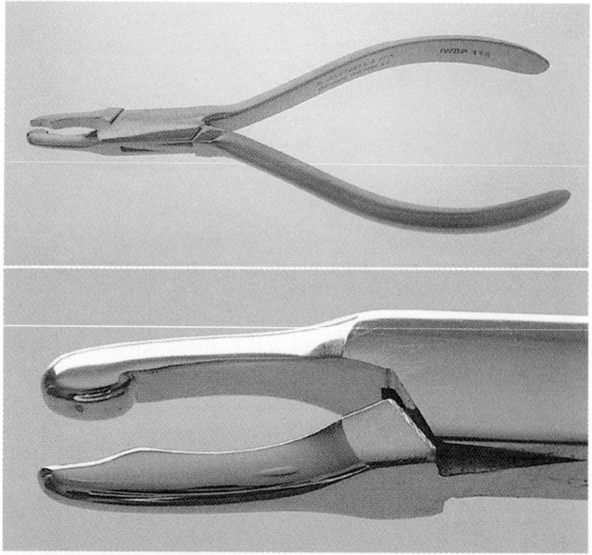

INSTRUMENT

Contouring Pliers

FUNCTION To crimp and contour marginal edge of temporary crown or stainless steel crown

CHARACTERISTICS Commonly used type: Johnson
Range of sizes available

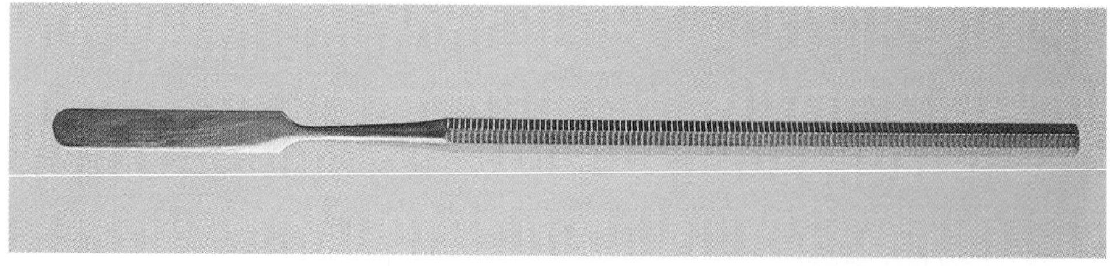

INSTRUMENT

Flexible Mixing Spatula

FUNCTION To mix dental materials

CHARACTERISTICS Flexible metal to allow proper manipulation
Range of sizes available

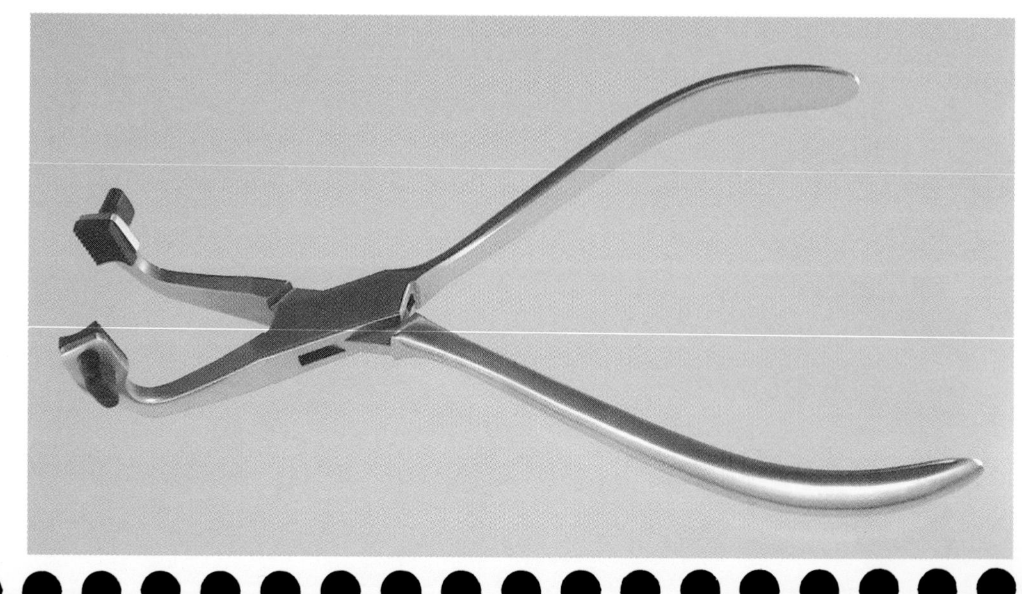

Provisional Crown–Removing Forceps

FUNCTION To remove provisional crown from tooth

CHARACTERISTICS Range of sizes available

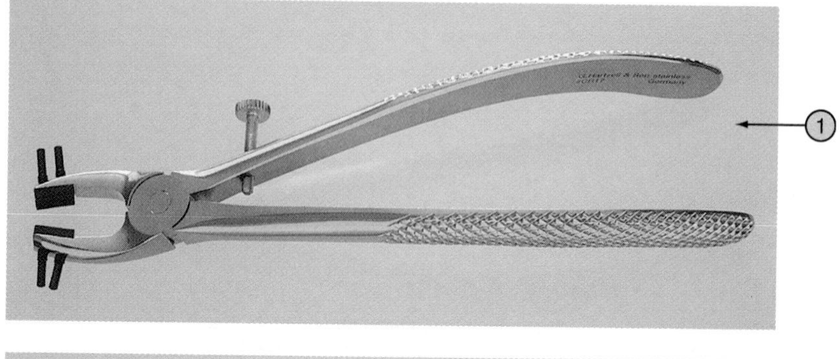
1

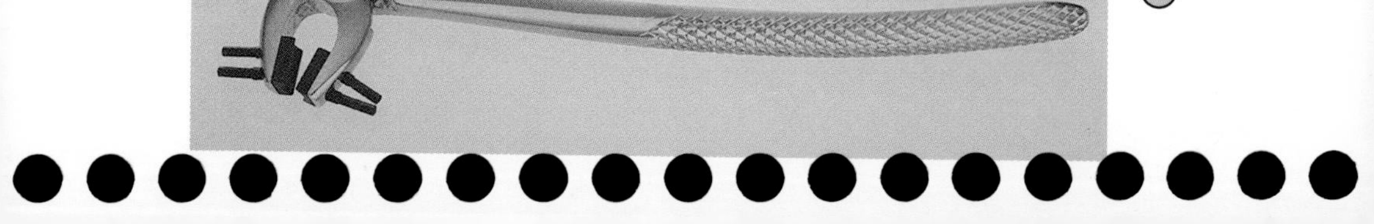
2

Trial Crown Remover

FUNCTION

To remove permanent crown from tooth during try-in phase
To remove provisional crown

CHARACTERISTICS

Types:

① Maxillary crown remover
② Mandibular crown remover

Replaceable pads—Provide nonslipping, tight grip

INSTRUMENT

Wooden Bite Stick

FUNCTION To seat permanent crown while patient bites in centric occlusion

CHARACTERISTICS Soft wood
Range of sizes available

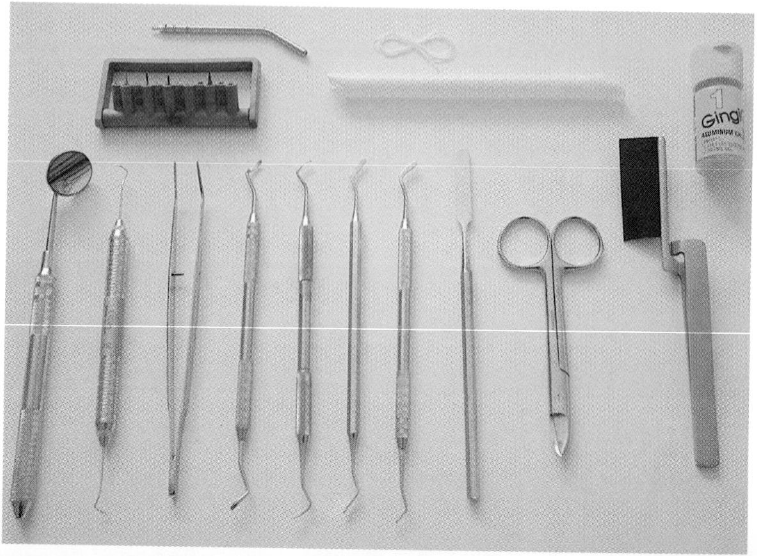

TRAY SETUP

Crown and Bridge Preparation

TOP ROW (FROM LEFT TO RIGHT)

Burs in bur block, air/water syringe tip, high-velocity (volume) evacuation tip (HVE), dental floss, gingival retraction cord

BOTTOM ROW (FROM LEFT TO RIGHT)

Mouth mirror, explorer, cotton forceps (pliers), spoon excavator, curette, gingival retraction cord instrument, Woodson, flexible cement mixing spatula, crown and bridge scissors, articulating paper holder with articulating paper

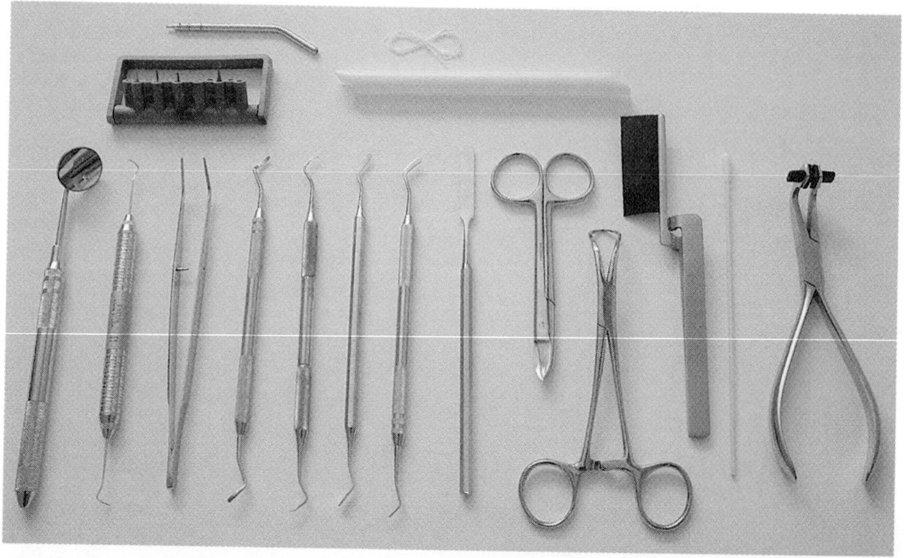

Crown and Bridge Cementation

TOP ROW (FROM LEFT TO RIGHT)

Burs in bur block, air/water syringe tip, high-velocity (volume) evacuation tip (HVE), dental floss

BOTTOM ROW (FROM LEFT TO RIGHT)

Mouth mirror, explorer, cotton forceps (pliers), spoon excavator, curette, gingival retraction cord instrument, Woodson, flexible cement mixing spatula, crown and bridge scissors, provisional crown–removing forceps, articulating paper holder with articulating paper, cotton swab for bite stick, trial crown remover

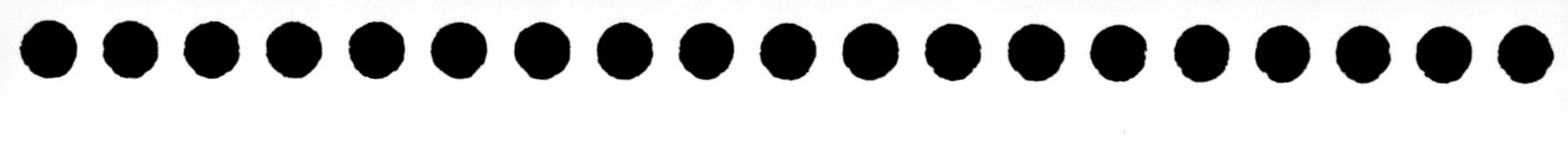

CHAPTER 11

Endodontic Instruments

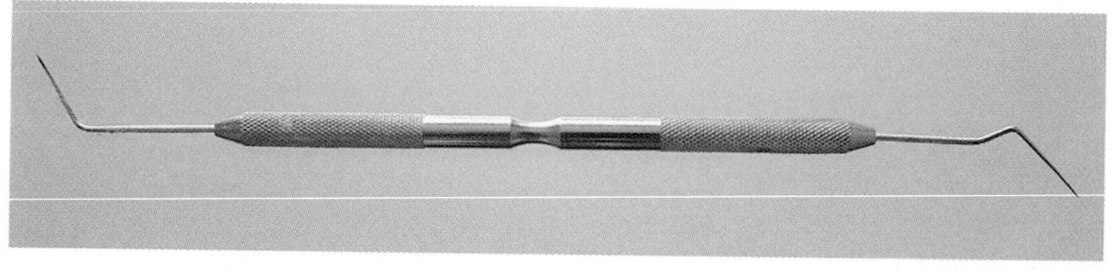

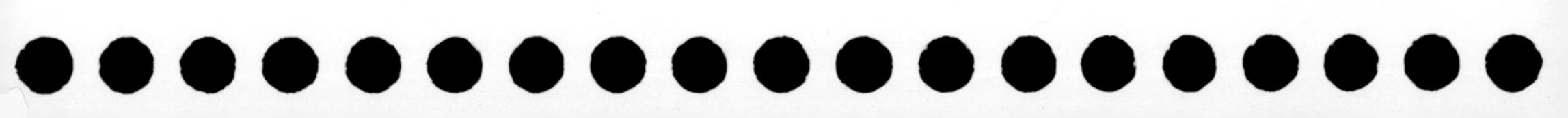

INSTRUMENT

Endodontic Explorer

FUNCTION To locate opening of small canal orifices for endodontic procedure

CHARACTERISTICS Double ended

- Working end—Longer than regular explorer to reach opening of canals

Endodontic long-shank spoon excavator

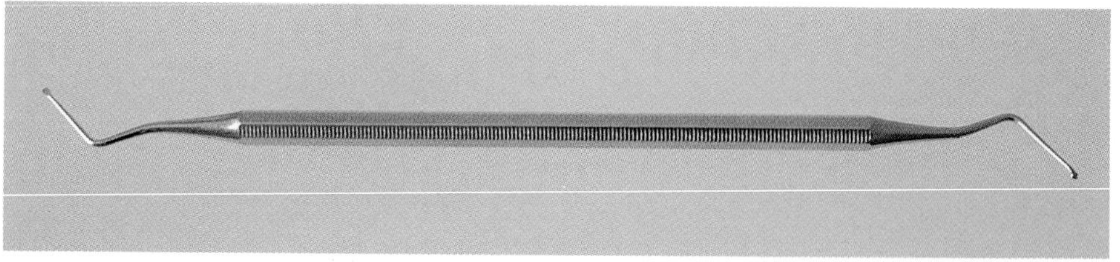

INSTRUMENT

Endodontic Long-Shank Spoon Excavator

FUNCTION To curet inside of tooth to base of pulp chamber

CHARACTERISTICS Long shank to reach deep into cavity preparation
Double ended
Range of sizes available

Endodontic Locking Forceps (pliers)

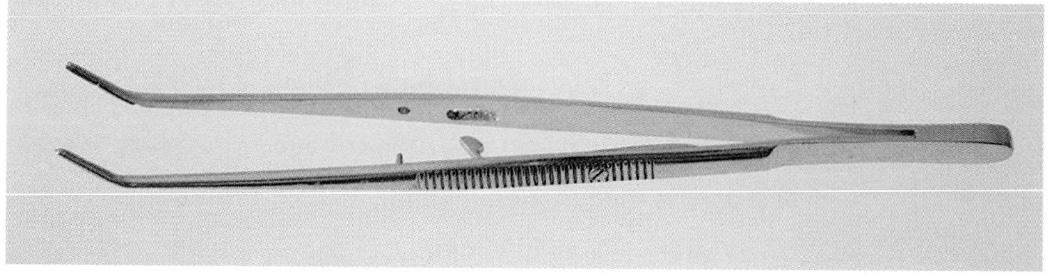

INSTRUMENT

Endodontic Locking Forceps (Pliers)

FUNCTION To grasp and lock material for transfer into and out of oral cavity

CHARACTERISTICS Similar to regular cotton forceps except for locking mechanism to secure material

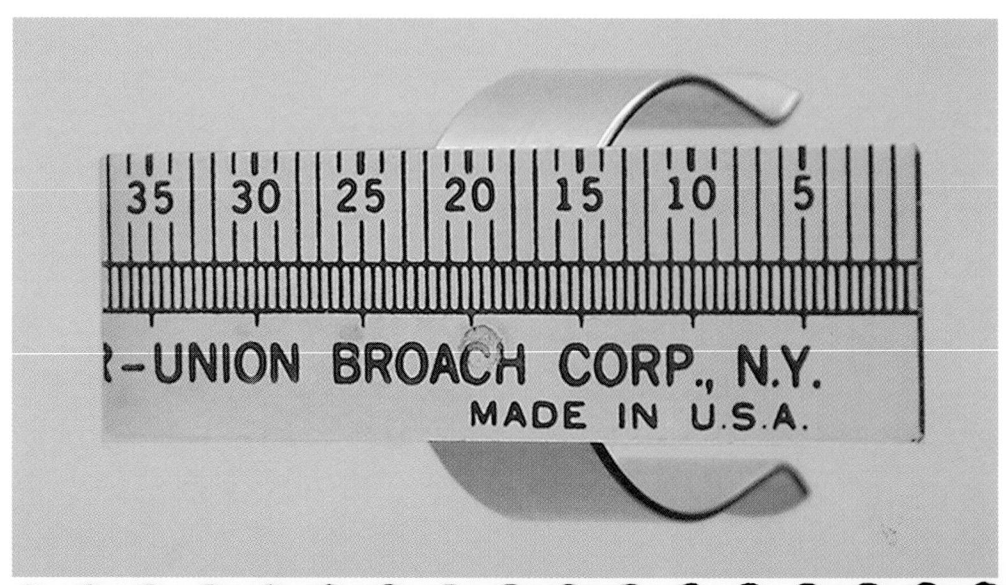
35 30 25 20 15 10 5
-UNION BROACH CORP., N.Y.
MADE IN U.S.A.

INSTRUMENT

Endodontic Millimeter Ruler

FUNCTION To measure files, reamers, other instruments, and materials in millimeter increments

CHARACTERISTICS Variety of designs

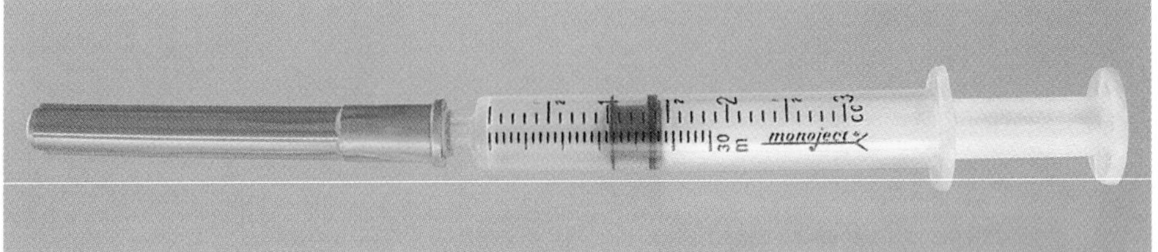

monoject
cc
30
m
1
2
3

Endodontic Irrigating Syringe

FUNCTION To carry and dispense irrigating solution into canal for cleansing during debridement of canal

CHARACTERISTICS Disposable

Broach remove pulp

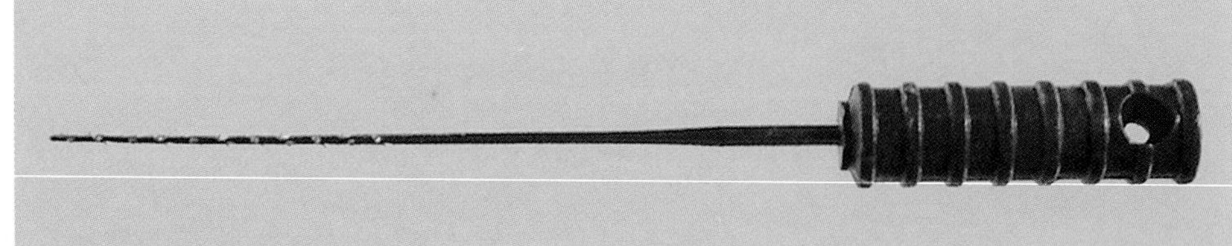

INSTRUMENT

Broach

FUNCTION To remove pulp tissue from canal

CHARACTERISTICS Working end—Barbed wire protrusions on shaft grab and remove vital or nonvital pulp fibers
Handles—Color coded according to size
Range of sizes—Diameter increases with size
Discarded after each use

K-files (Drill)

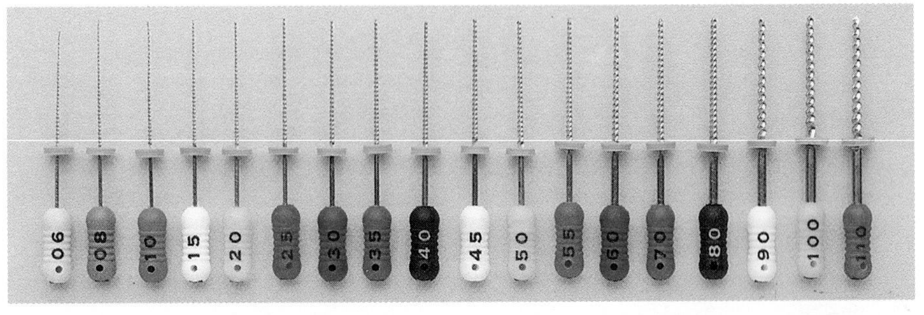

Root Canal File—K Type

FUNCTION

To clean inside walls of canal
To contour inner walls of canal

CHARACTERISTICS

Twisted design (more twists per millimeter than reamer)
Used with push-pull motion
Handles—Color coded according to size
Range of sizes—To accommodate width of canal (diameter increases with size)
Available in different lengths
Examples: 21 mm, 25 mm, 31 mm

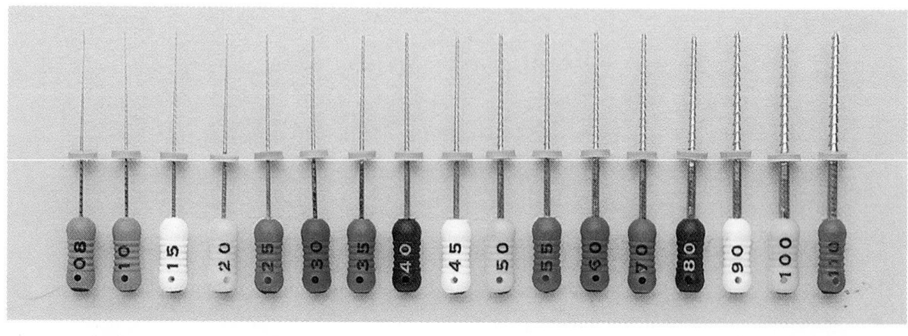

08
10
15
20
25
30
35
40
45
50
55
60
70
80
90
100

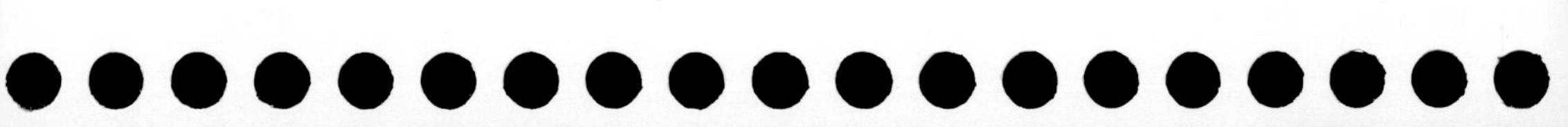

INSTRUMENT

Root Canal File—Hedstrom

FUNCTION

To clean inside walls of canal
To enlarge and smooth inner walls of canal

CHARACTERISTICS

Triangular cutting edge
Handles—Color coded according to size
Range of sizes—To accommodate width of canal (diameter increases with size)
Available in different lengths
Examples: 21 mm, 25 mm, 31 mm

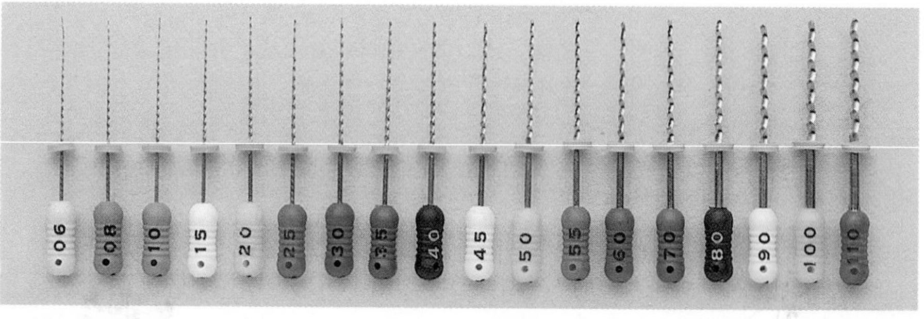
06
08
10
15
20
25
30
35
40
45
50
55
60
70
80
90
100
110

Reamer

FUNCTION

To cut and smooth dentinal walls of canal
To enlarge inner walls of canal

CHARACTERISTICS

Twisted triangular cutting edge (similar to K- type file, but cutting edge is farther apart, has fewer twists per millimeter)
Used with twisting motion
Handles—Color coded according to size
Range of sizes—To accommodate width of canal (diameter increases with size)
Available in different lengths
Examples: 21 mm, 25 mm, 31 mm

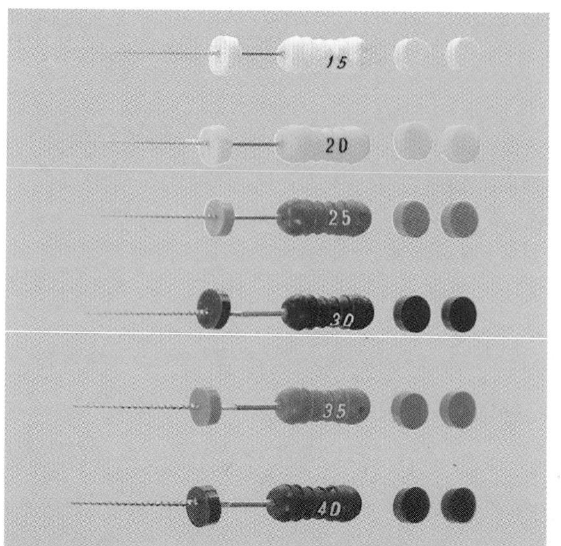
15
20
25
30
35
40

Endodontic Stoppers

FUNCTION To place on file or reamer to help determine length of canal

CHARACTERISTICS Files or reamers are measured from stopper to apex of root to determine length of canal. (Radiographs also help determine length.)

PRACTICE NOTES

1. Stoppers are color coded to correspond to a particular file or reamer, or a single color of stopper is used for all files or reamers.

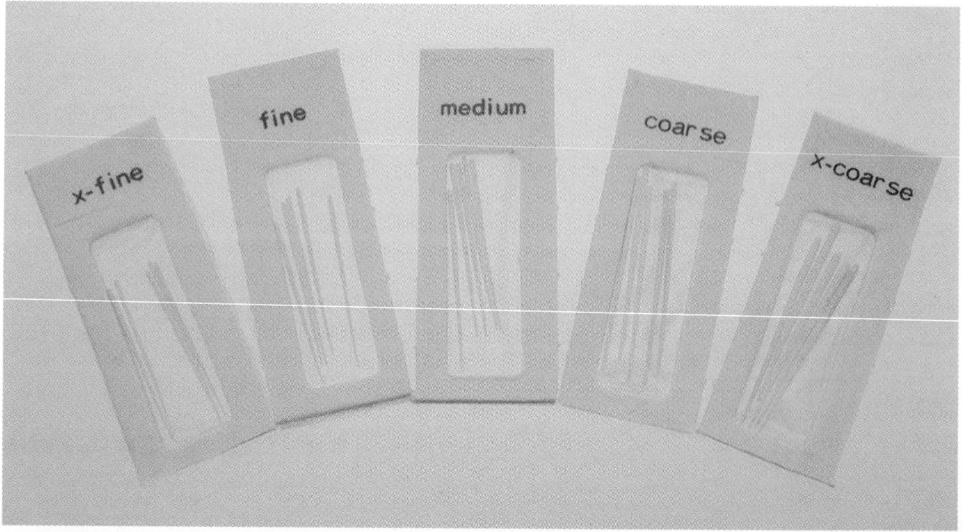

x-fine
fine
medium
coarse
x-coarse

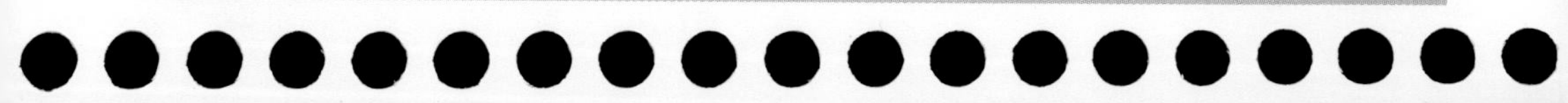

INSTRUMENT

Sterile Absorbent Paper Points

FUNCTION To dry pulp chambers of canal (new points are inserted repeatedly until pulp chamber is completely dry)

CHARACTERISTICS Size of point corresponds to width of canal
Range of sizes available

PRACTICE NOTE

1. The length of the point is measured to ensure that it corresponds to the length of the canal.

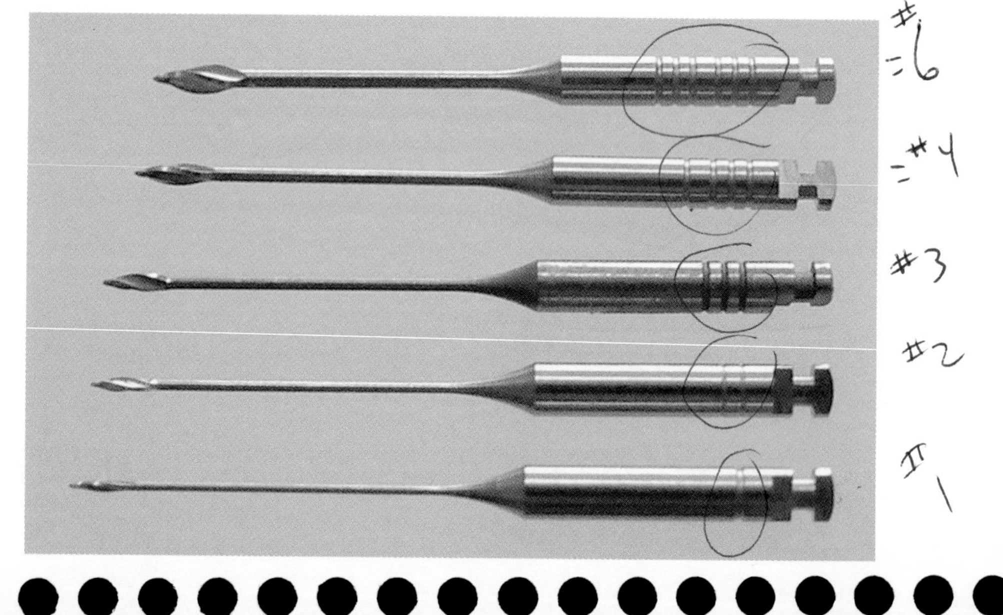

INSTRUMENT

Gates Glidden Bur or Drill

FUNCTION

To enlarge walls of pulp chamber
To open canal orifice

CHARACTERISTICS

Long-shank bur
Elliptical or flame-shaped cutting edge
Latch type—Used with slow-speed contra-angle handpiece (air driven or electric)
Range of sizes—Size identified by number of grooves on shank
Two lengths—Shorter for posterior teeth, longer for anterior teeth

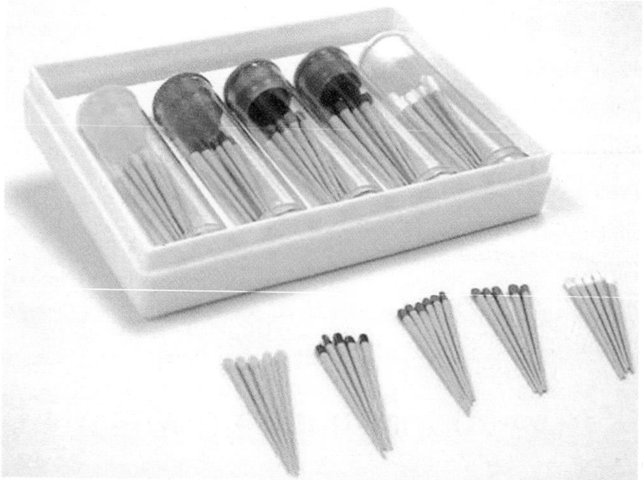

INSTRUMENT

Gutta-Percha

FUNCTION To fill pulp chamber after completion of canal preparation

CHARACTERISTICS Solid at room temperature, becomes soft and pliable when heated
May be heated in a cartridge and then dispensed into canal
Range of sizes—To correspond to size of canal

PRACTICE NOTE

1. Sealer, a cement material, is used with gutta-percha for final sealing of the canal.

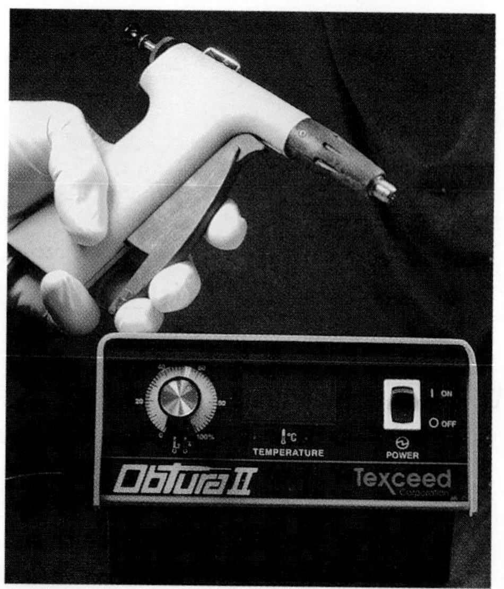
ON
OFF
TEMPERATURE
POWER
Obtura II
Texceed
Corporation

Gutta-Percha Warming Unit

FUNCTION

To heat gutta-percha outside the mouth before use

To inject heated gutta-percha in thermoplastic state into prepared canals

CHARACTERISTICS

Gutta-percha pellets—Used to load unit

Delivery system—Needle attaches to gun delivering gutta-percha into canal

PRACTICE NOTE

1. Temperature of the gutta-percha in the unit can be adjusted to control the viscosity of the material.

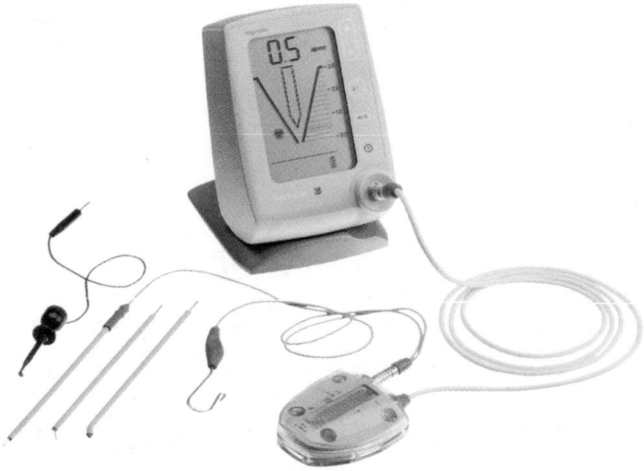

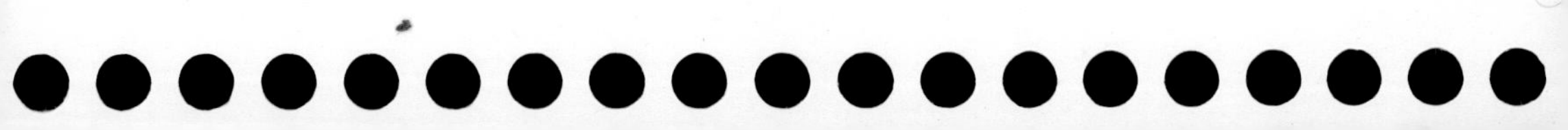

INSTRUMENT

Electronic Apex Locator

FUNCTION To electronically measure length of canal to apex of tooth

CHARACTERISTICS Attaches to file or reamer and is placed in canal using dry or wet environment
Length readout—Tone or digital

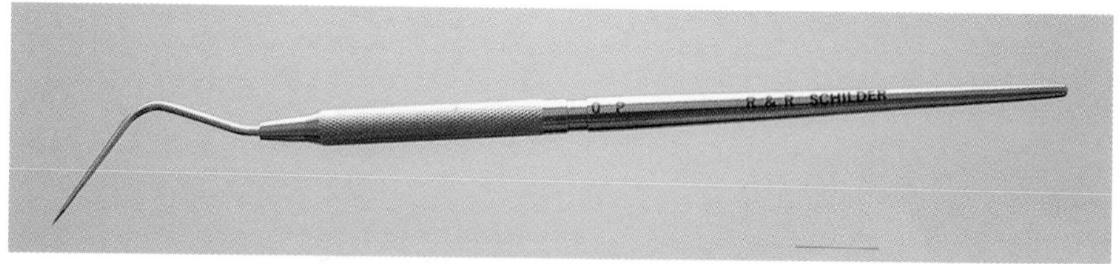
0 P
R & R SCHILDER

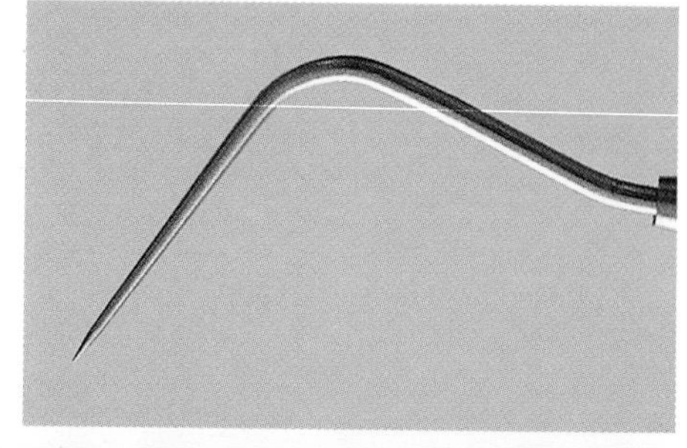

INSTRUMENT

Endodontic Spreader

FUNCTION To help condense gutta-percha laterally in canal
To use for final filling of canal

CHARACTERISTICS Pointed tip
Working end—Has rings in millimeter increments
Two handle styles—Conventional, finger spreader
Range of sizes—To correspond to size of canal

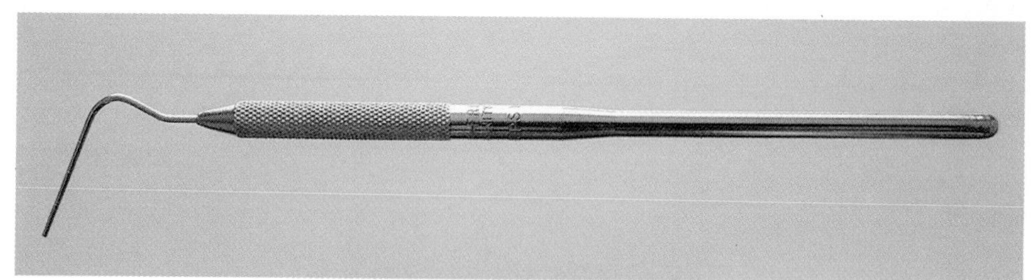

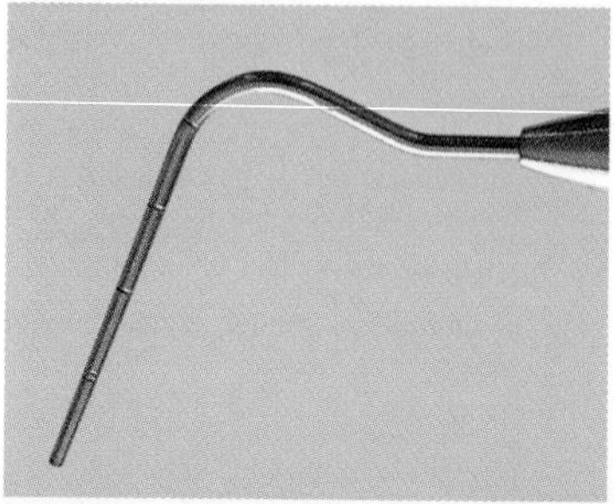

INSTRUMENT

Endodontic Plugger

FUNCTION

To help condense gutta-percha vertically in canal
To use for final filling of canal

CHARACTERISTICS

Flat tip
Working end—Has rings in millimeter increments
Two handle styles—Conventional, finger spreader
Range of sizes—To correspond to size of canal

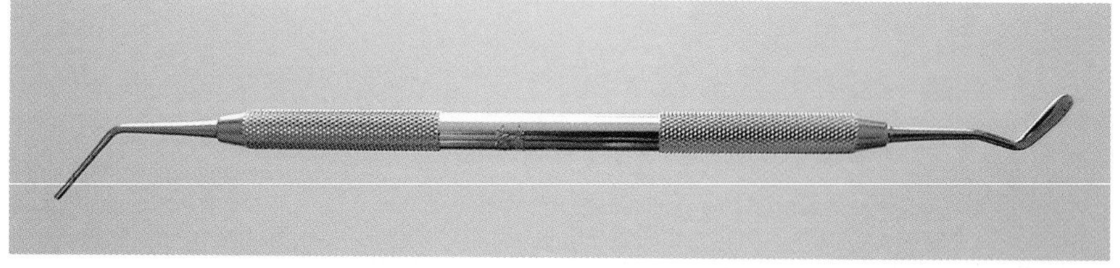

INSTRUMENT

Glick Instrument

FUNCTION

To condense gutta-percha into endodontically prepared teeth (using plugger end)
To sever excess gutta-percha (using heated plugger end)
To carry and place material into tooth (using paddle end)

CHARACTERISTICS

Double ended

- Plugger end—May have rings in millimeter increments

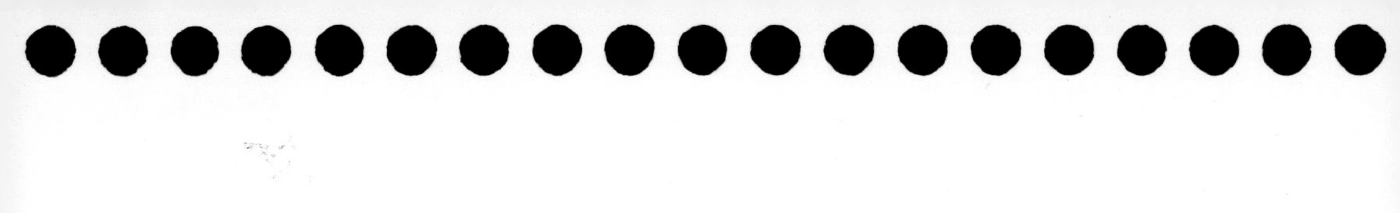

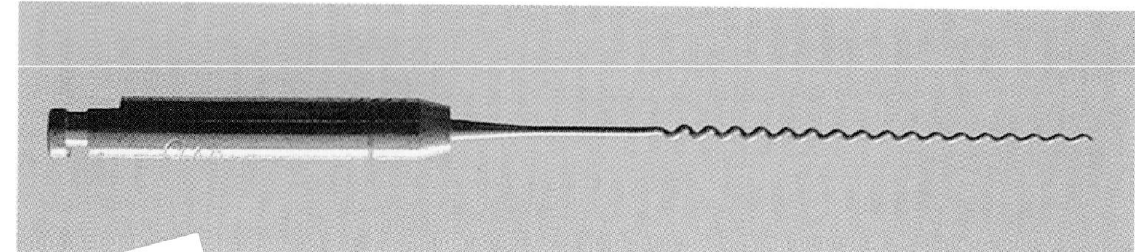

INSTRUMENT

Lentulo Spiral

FUNCTION To place endodontic sealer or cement in canal for final seal before placement of gutta-percha

CHARACTERISTICS Latch type—Used with slow-speed contra-angle handpiece (air driven or electric)

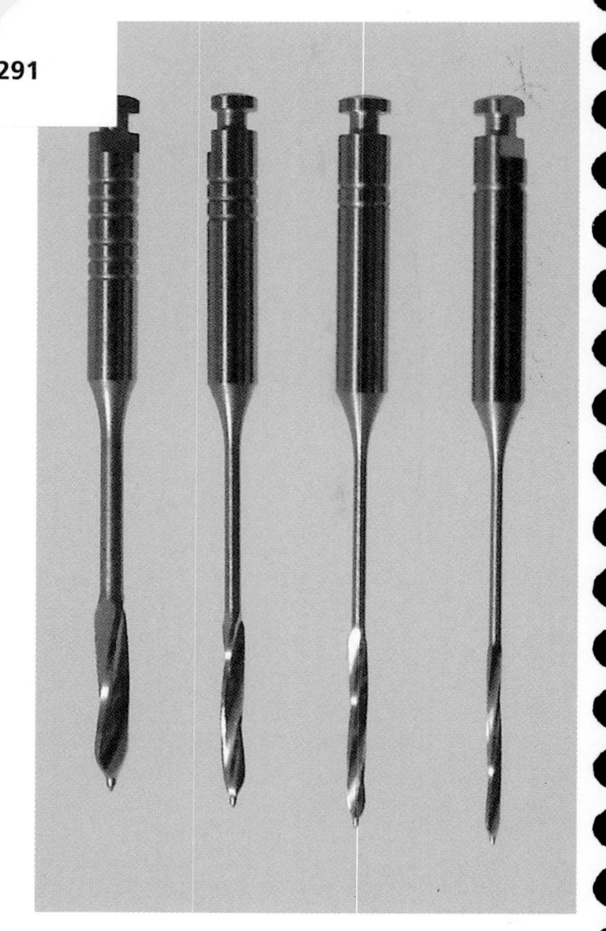

Peso File

FUNCTION

To prepare canal for endodontic post
To remove portion of gutta-percha sealed in canal to make room for endodontic post

CHARACTERISTICS

Parallel cutting edges
Latch type—Used with slow-speed contra-angle handpiece (air driven or electric)
Range of sizes—Size identified by number of grooves on shank

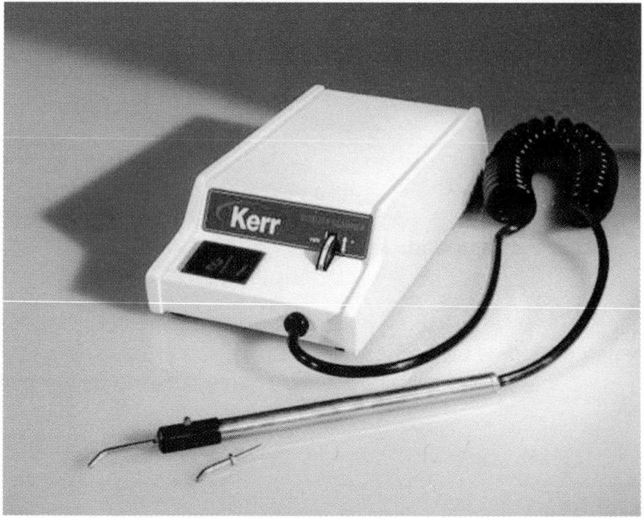

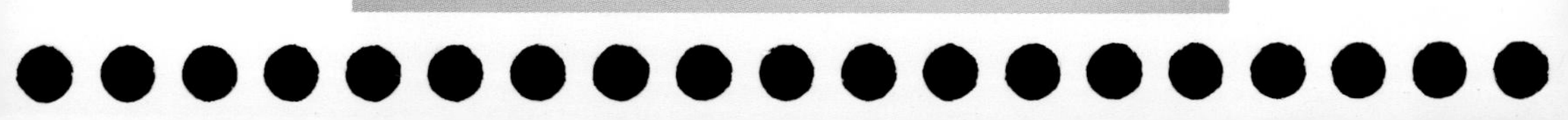

Vitalometer/Pulp Tester

FUNCTION To test vitality of pulp in teeth

CHARACTERISTICS Two types—Electronic, digital (digital readout)
Electric or battery operated

PRACTICE NOTES

1. The tester sends an impulse of electric current to the pulp, causing a reaction.
2. The current is increased by small increments until the patient indicates feeling a sensation.
3. Toothpaste is applied to the tip of the electrode to conduct electricity.
4. The tip is placed on the coronal part (facial or lingual) of a natural tooth
5. Each individual root/pulp on the tooth is tested.

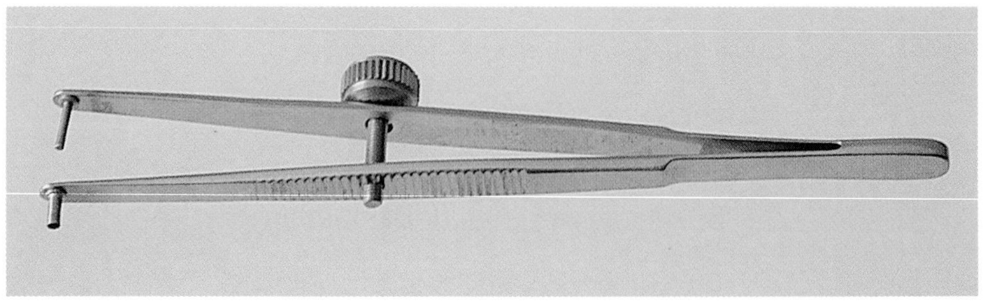

INSTRUMENT

Micro Retro Amalgam Carrier

FUNCTION To carry amalgam to surgical site of apicoectomy

CHARACTERISTICS Very small—To accommodate retro fills for apicoectomy

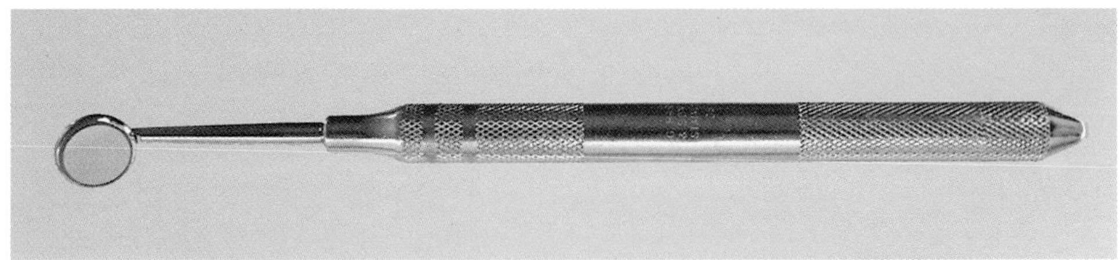

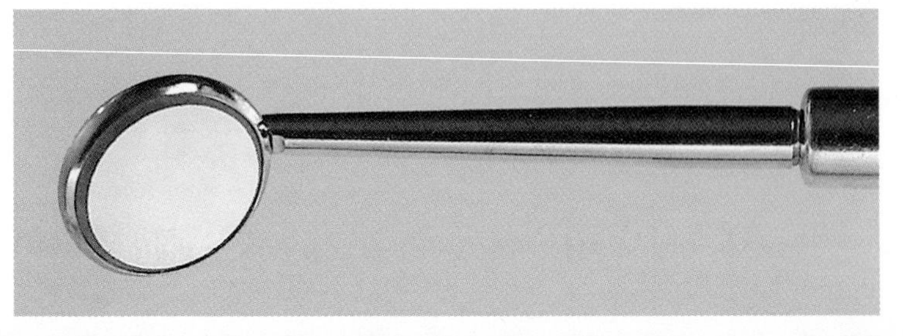

INSTRUMENT

Micro Retro Mouth Mirror

FUNCTION To view surgical site of apicoectomy retro fill

CHARACTERISTICS Very small—To accommodate retro fills for apicoectomy
Smaller sizes are available

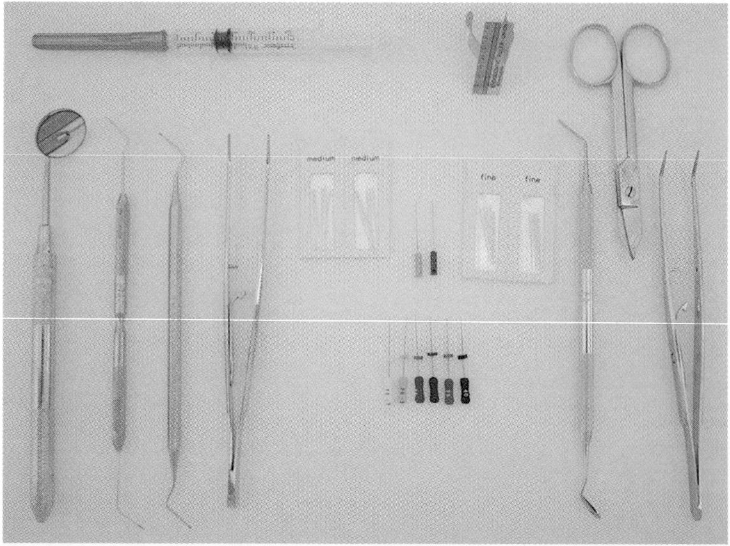

300

Opening a Tooth for Endodontic Therapy

TOP ROW (FROM LEFT TO RIGHT)

Irrigating disposable syringe, millimeter ruler with finger ring, crown and bridge scissors

BOTTOM ROW (FROM LEFT TO RIGHT)

Mouth mirror, endodontic explorer, endodontic long-shank spoon excavator, endodontic locking cotton forceps, medium absorbent sterile paper points, broaches, fine absorbent sterile paper points, files with color-coded rubber stops, Glick endodontic instrument, extra endodontic locking forceps

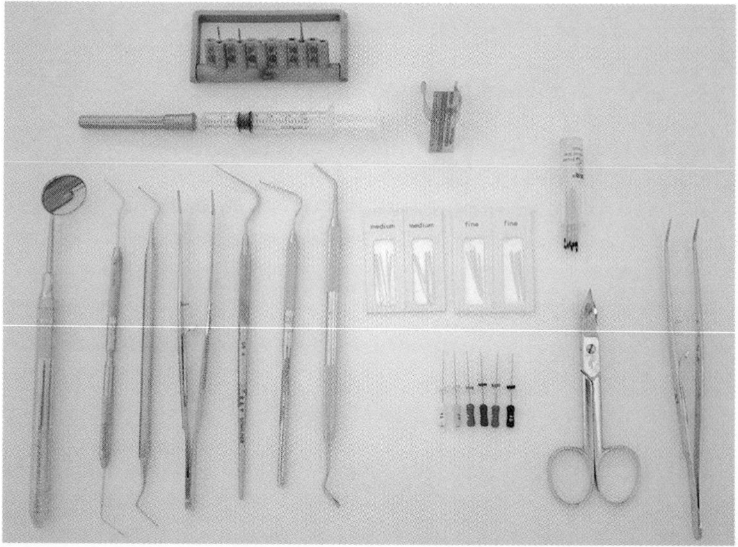
medium
medium
fine
fine

Sealing a Tooth for Endodontic Therapy

TOP ROW (FROM LEFT TO RIGHT)

Irrigating syringe, burs in bur block, millimeter ruler with finger ring

BOTTOM ROW (FROM LEFT TO RIGHT)

Mouth mirror, endodontic explorer, endodontic long-shank spoon excavator, endodontic locking cotton forceps, endodontic spreader, endodontic plugger, Glick instrument, medium and fine absorbent sterile paper points, files with color-coded rubber stops, gutta-percha, crown and bridge scissors, extra endodontic locking forceps

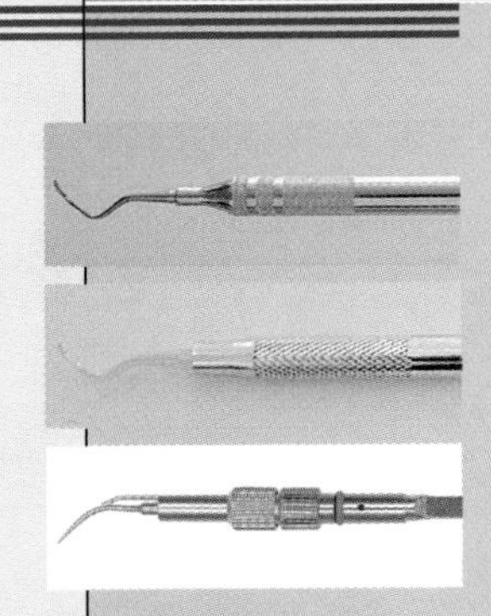

CHAPTER 12

Hygiene Instruments

1

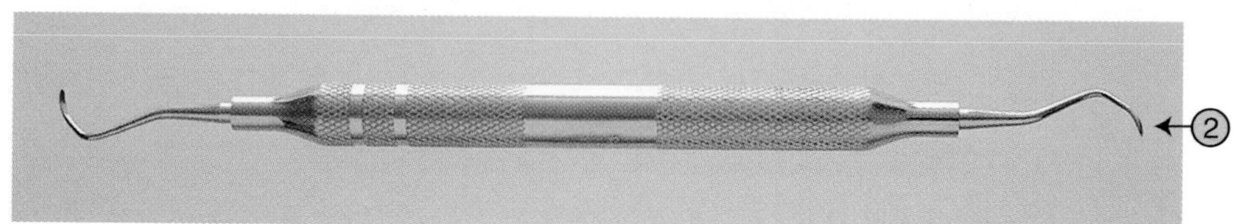
2

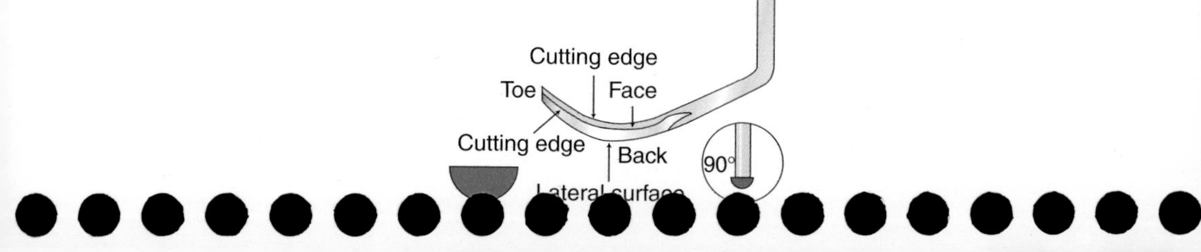
Cutting edge
Toe
Face
Cutting edge
Back
90°
Lateral surface

Universal Curettes (Curet)

FUNCTION

To scale and remove deposits and stains from teeth
To scale supragingival and subgingival surfaces
To remove soft tissue lining of periodontal pocket and root planning

CHARACTERISTICS

Blade—Two cutting edges, rounded toe
Back of blade—Rounded
Blade at 90-degree angle to lower shank
Flexible or rigid shank
Shank length—Varies to accommodate clinical crown of tooth
Single or double ended
Range of sizes
Curette named by designer:

① Barnhart 1/2
② Ratcliff 3/4

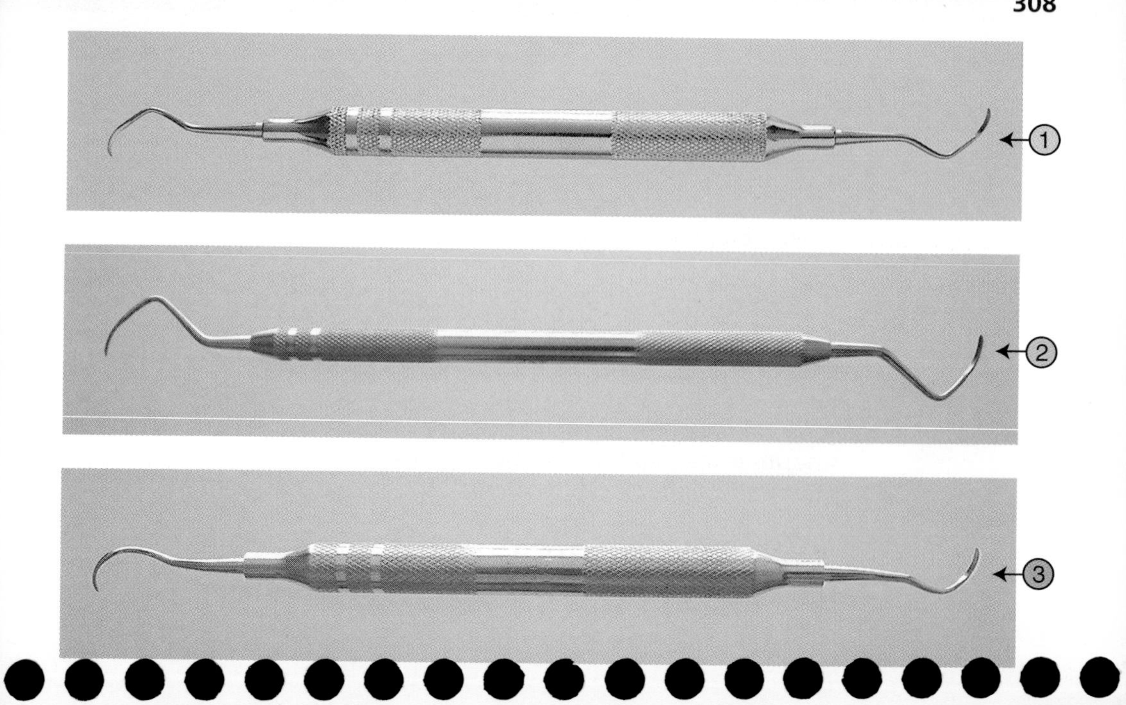
1
2
3

Universal Curettes (Curet)

FUNCTION

To scale and remove deposits and stains from teeth
To scale supragingival and subgingival surfaces
To remove soft tissue lining of periodontal pocket and root planning

CHARACTERISTICS

Blade—Two cutting edges, rounded toe
Back of blade—Rounded
Blade at 90-degree angle to lower shank
Flexible or rigid shank
Shank length—Varies to accommodate clinical crown of tooth
Single or double ended
Range of sizes
Curette named by designer:

1. UC/Rule $^{5}/_{6}$
2. Loma Linda $^{11}/_{12}$
3. McCall $^{17}/_{18}$

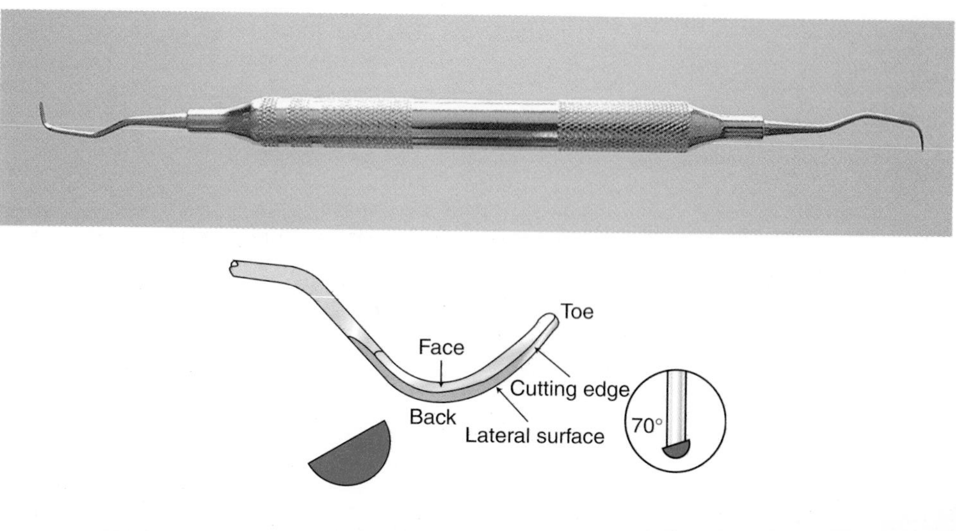
Toe
Face
Cutting edge
Back
Lateral surface
70°

Area-Specific Curettes—Anterior

FUNCTION

To scale and remove deposits from subgingival surfaces of anterior teeth

To use for root planning, periodontal debridement, and soft tissue curettage

CHARACTERISTICS

Two cutting edges (only lower cutting edge is used)

Blade—Rounded back and toe

Blade at 70-degree angle to lower shank

Blade types—Standard, rigid, extra rigid

Curvature of blade designed to adapt to specific teeth and surfaces: centrals, laterals, cuspids, mesial, distal, facial, lingual

Range of sizes available

$\frac{1}{2}$, $\frac{3}{4}$, $\frac{5}{6}$

Curette named by designer

Examples: Gracey, Kramer-Nevins, Turgeon

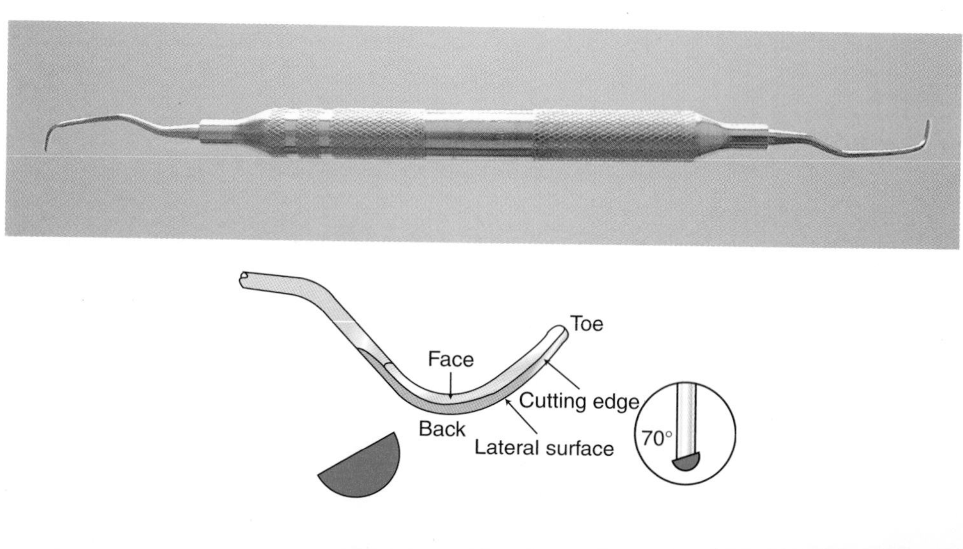
Toe
Face
Cutting edge
Back
Lateral surface
70°

Area-Specific Curettes—Posterior

FUNCTION

To scale and remove deposits from subgingival surfaces of posterior teeth

To use for root planning, periodontal debridement, and soft tissue curettage

CHARACTERISTICS

Two cutting edges (only lower cutting edge is used)

Blade—Rounded back and toe

Blade at 70-degree angle to lower shank

Blade types—Standard, rigid, extra rigid

Curvature of blade designed to adapt to specific teeth and surfaces: premolars, molars, mesial, distal, buccal, lingual

Range of size, shape, and bends in shank

Two bends in shank *Examples:* 7/8, 9/10

Three bends in shank *Examples:* 11/12, 13/14, 15/16, 17/18

Curette named by designer

Examples: Gracey, Kramer-Nevins, Turgeon

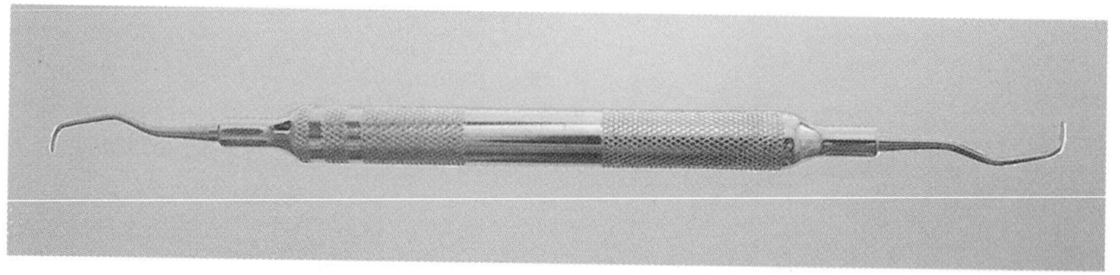

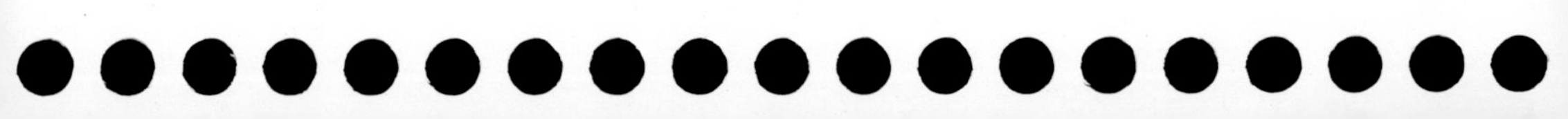

Extended Area-Specific Curettes—Anterior

FUNCTION To scale and remove deposits in deep periodontal pockets (5 mm or deeper)

CHARACTERISTICS
Two cutting edges (only lower cutting edge is used)
Blade at 70-degree angle to lower shank
Blade types—Standard, rigid, extra rigid
Curvature of blade designed to adapt to anteriors
Terminal shank redesigned—3 mm longer than standard area-specific curette

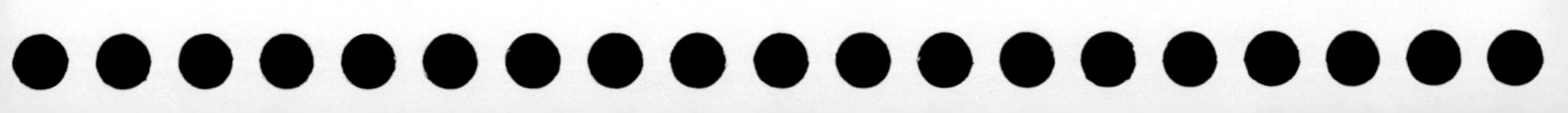

Extended Area-Specific Curettes—Anterior (continued)

CHARACTERISTICS **(continued)**

Range of sizes
Manufacturer's trademark name usually follows $1/2$, $3/4$, $5/6$ numbering system
Commonly used types: $3/4$, $5/6$
Double-ended curettes packaged in sets
Curettes named by designer
Example: Gracey $1/2$

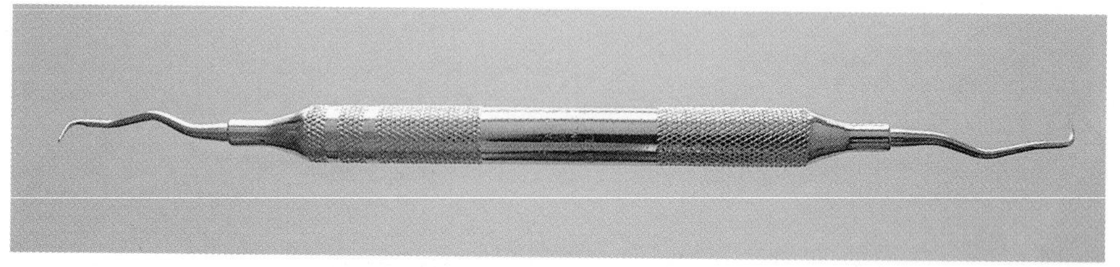

Extended Area-Specific Curettes—Posterior

FUNCTION To scale and remove deposits in deep periodontal pockets (5 mm or deeper)

CHARACTERISTICS Two cutting edges (only lower cutting edge is used)
Blade at 70-degree angle to lower shank
Blade types—Standard, rigid, extra rigid
Curvature of blade designed to adapt to premolars, molars
Terminal shank redesigned—3 mm longer than standard area-specific curette

INSTRUMENT

Extended Area-Specific Curettes—Posterior (continued)

CHARACTERISTICS **(continued)**

Range of sizes

Commonly used types: $^{11}/_{12}$, $^{13}/_{14}$, $^{15}/_{16}$, $^{17}/_{18}$

Double-ended curettes packaged in sets

Curettes named by designer

Examples:

Gracey $^{11}/_{12}$ Rigid

Gracey $^{11}/_{12}$

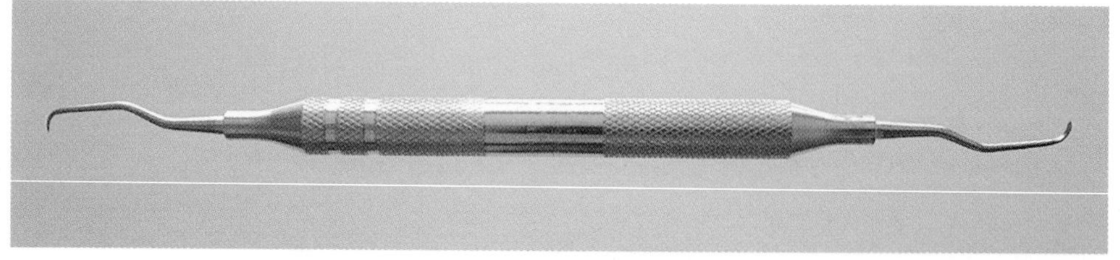

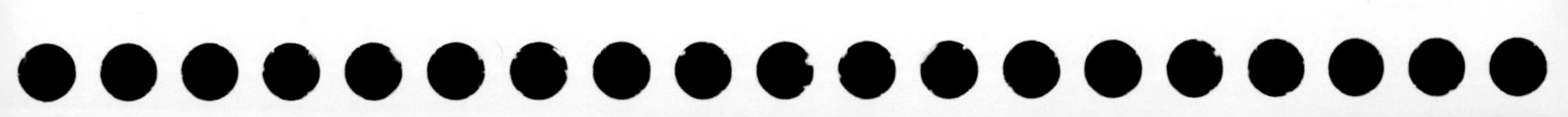

Mini Extended Area-Specific Curettes—Anterior

FUNCTION To scale in deep periodontal pockets (5 mm)

CHARACTERISTICS

Blade redesigned to be half the length of extended area-specific curette
Designed for narrow roots, pockets, or furcations
Two cutting edges (only lower cutting edge is used)
Blade at 70-degree angle to lower shank
Blade types—Standard, rigid, extra rigid
Curvature of blade designed to adapt to anteriors
Range of sizes
Manufacturer's trademark name usually follows $^1/_2$, $^3/_4$, $^5/_6$ numbering system
Curettes named by designer
Example: Gracey $^1/_2$

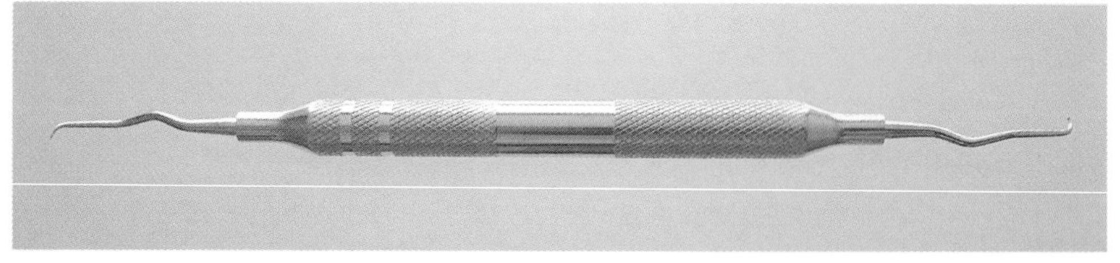

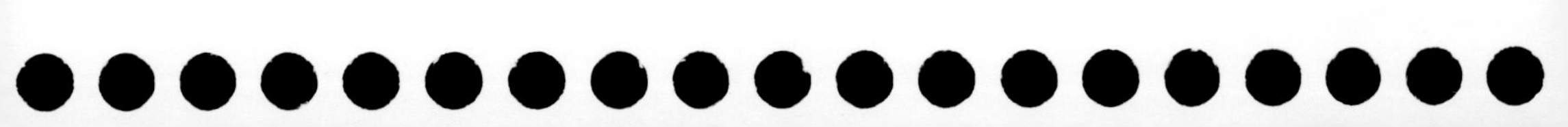

INSTRUMENT

Mini Extended Area-Specific Curettes—Posterior

FUNCTION To scale in deep periodontal pockets (5 mm)

CHARACTERISTICS Blade redesigned to be half the length of extended area-specific curette
Designed for narrow roots, pockets, or furcations
Two cutting edges (only lower cutting edge is used)
Blade at 70-degree angle to lower shank
Blade types—Standard, rigid, extra rigid
Curvature of blade designed to adapt to premolars, molars
Range of size, shape, and bends in shank available
Two bends in shank *Examples:* 7/8, 9/10
Three bends in shank *Examples:* 11/12, 13/14, 15/16, 17/18
Curettes named by designer
Example: Gracey 11/12, mini extender

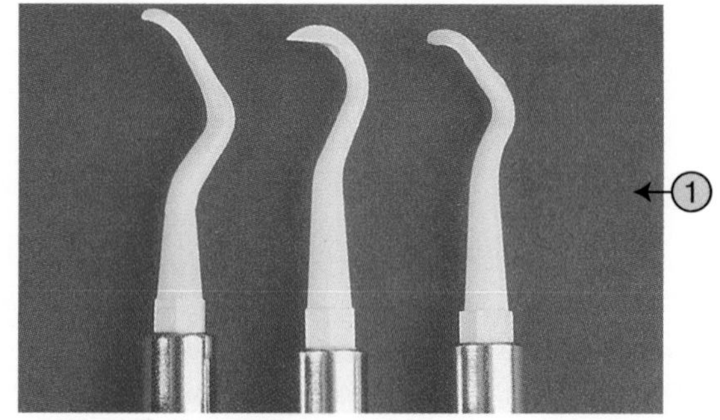
1
1 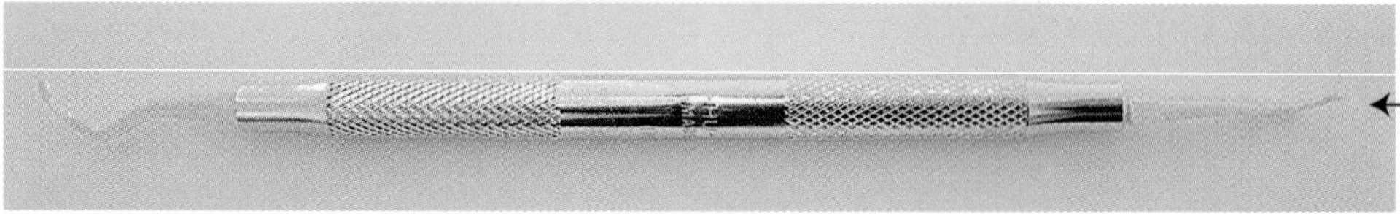
2

INSTRUMENT

Implant Scaler

FUNCTION To remove deposits and stains from surface of implant

CHARACTERISTICS Different designs allow scaling without scratching of titanium implants.
Some tips are made of Plasteel (a high-grade resin)
① Disposable tips (each tip should be sterilized before use)
② Titanium-coated scaler

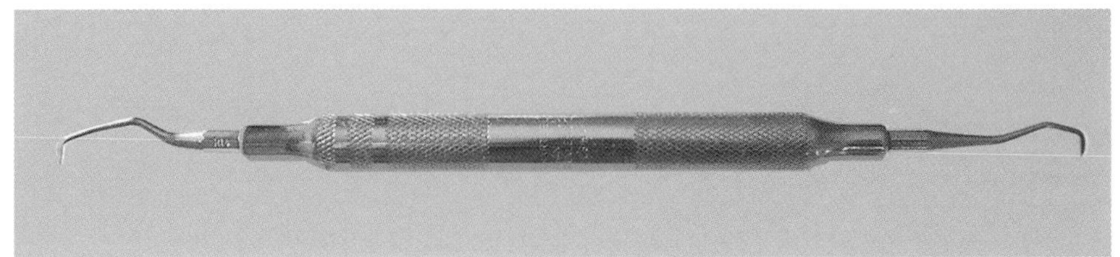

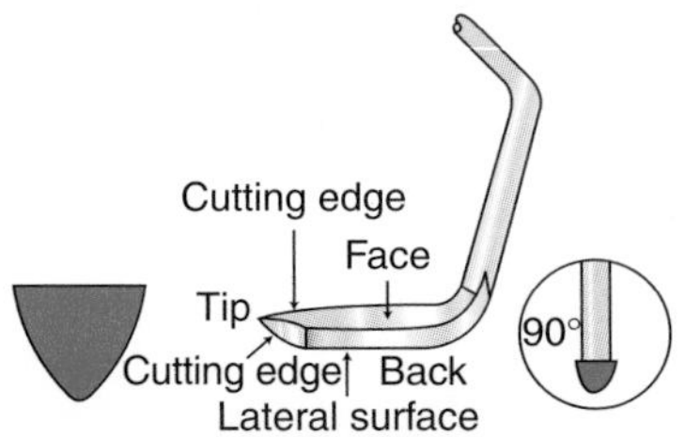
Cutting edge
Face
Tip
Cutting edge
Back
Lateral surface
90°

INSTRUMENT

Straight Sickle Scaler

FUNCTION To remove large amounts of deposits from supragingival surfaces

CHARACTERISTICS Two cutting edges on straight blade that ends in sharp point
Long, two bends in shank
Variety of sizes and angles
Single or double ended—Two ends may be shaped differently

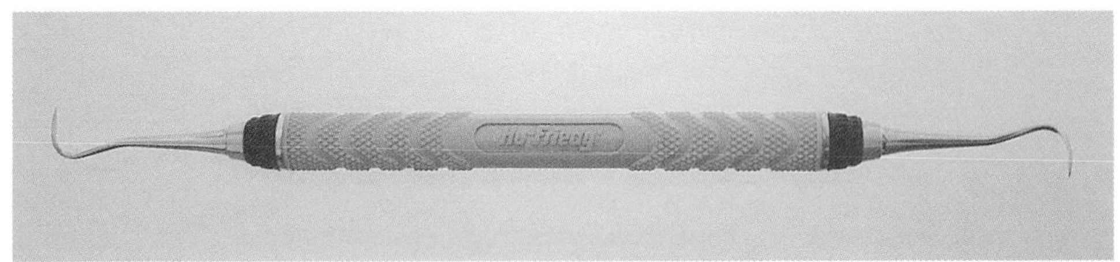

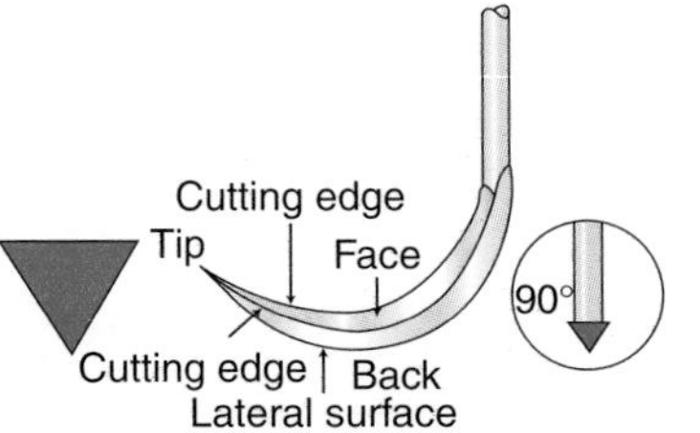
Cutting edge
Tip
Face
90°
Cutting edge
Back
Lateral surface

INSTRUMENT

Curved Sickle Scaler

FUNCTION To remove large amounts of deposits from supragingival surfaces

CHARACTERISTICS Two cutting edges on curved blade that ends in sharp point
Long, straight shank with one gentle bend
Variety of sizes and angles
Single or double ended—Two ends may be shaped differently

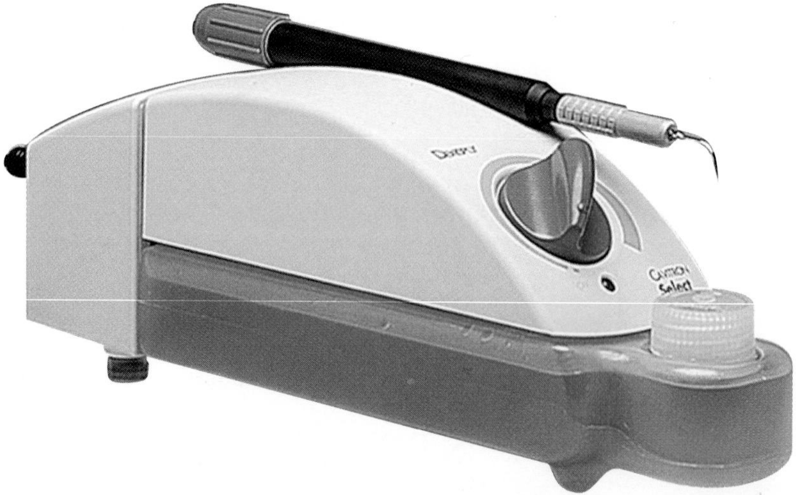

332

Ultrasonic Scaling Unit (Power Scaler)

FUNCTION To use with water-cooled ultrasonic tips vibrating at high frequency

CHARACTERISTICS Ultra-high frequency sound waves convert mechanical energy into vibrations (frequency ranges from 18 to 50 kHz).

Some units have self-contained water reservoirs *(shown)*.

Some units have an additional air/water/sodium bicarbonate slurry polishing system to remove extrinsic stains and dental plaque.

Variety of sizes and designs are available from several manufacturers.

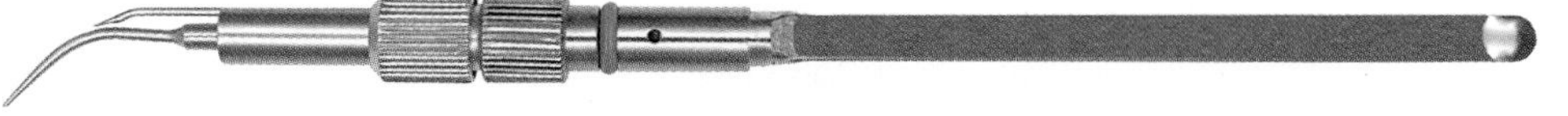

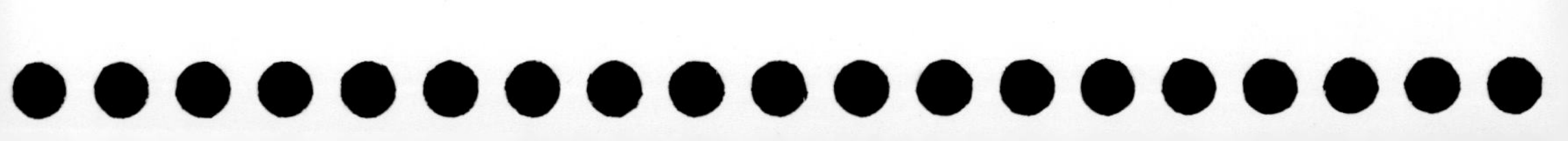

Ultrasonic Scaler Instrument Tip*—Supragingival

FUNCTION

To remove supragingival calculus on teeth
To remove bacterial plaque from periodontal pockets
To remove heavy debris and stains from teeth
To remove excess cement from orthodontic bands after cementation and after band removal

CHARACTERISTICS

Used with ultrasonic scaling unit
Available in different lengths (called *stacks*): 25 kHz or 30 kHz, depending on unit
Water-cooled inserts (water systems vary with internal or external water delivery)
Variety of shapes, sizes, and designs, depending on designated and varying grips
Example: Original Prophy
Tip style: Finely beveled external water delivery tube

*These tips are also known as *ultrasonic inserts.*

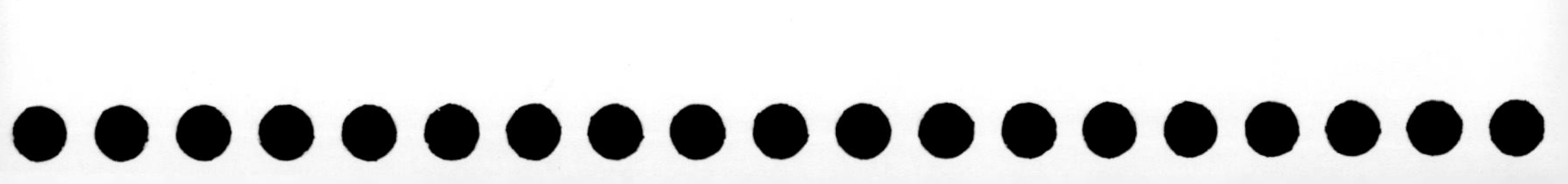

Ultrasonic Scaler Instrument Tip*—Subgingival

FUNCTION

To remove subgingival calculus on teeth
To remove bacterial plaque from periodontal pockets

CHARACTERISTICS

Used with ultrasonic scaling unit
Available in different lengths (called *stacks*): 25 kHz or 30 kHz, depending on unit
Water-cooled inserts (water systems vary with internal or external water delivery)
Variety of shapes, sizes, and designs, depending on designated area and varying grips
Example: After Five design
Tip style: Finely beveled external water delivery tube

*These tips are also known as *ultrasonic inserts*.

Hu-Friedy

Ultrasonic Scaler Instrument Tip*—Furcation

FUNCTION To remove bacterial plaque from furcation areas

CHARACTERISTICS Used with ultrasonic scaling unit
Available in different lengths (called *stacks*): 25 kHz or 30 kHz, depending on unit
Water-cooled inserts (water systems vary with internal or external water delivery)
Variety of shapes, sizes, and designs, depending on designated area and varying grips
Example: Furcation Plus design
Tip style: 0.8 mm ball end adapts to furcation, external water delivery tube

*These tips are also known as *ultrasonic inserts*.

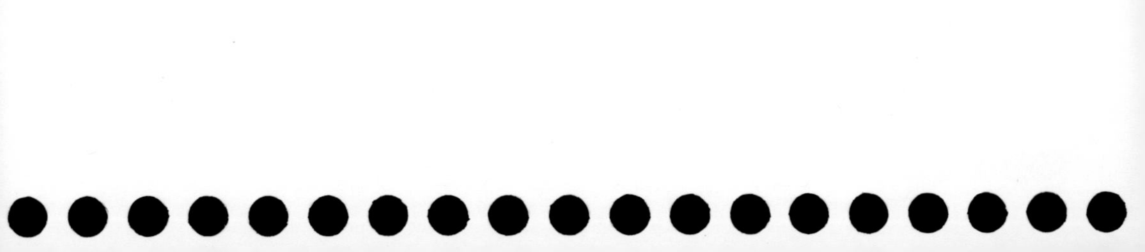

Ultrasonic Scaler Instrument Tip*—Universal

FUNCTION To remove bacterial plaque and general deposits

CHARACTERISTICS Used with ultrasonic scaling unit

Available in different lengths (called *stacks*): 25 kHz or 30 kHz, depending on unit

Water-cooled Inserts (water systems vary with internal or external water delivery)

Variety of shapes, sizes, and designs, depending on designated area and varying grips

Example: Streamline design

Tip style: Water delivered directly from base of tip, eliminating need for external water system; efficient at low settings

*These tips are also known as *ultrasonic inserts*.

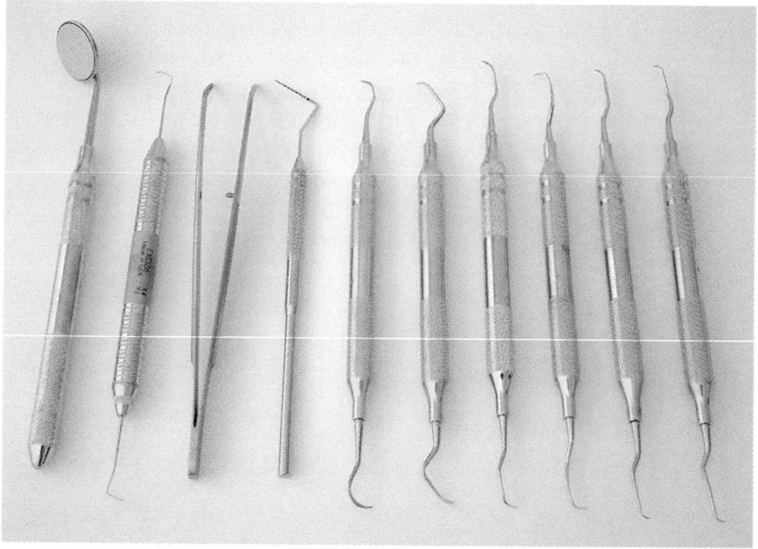

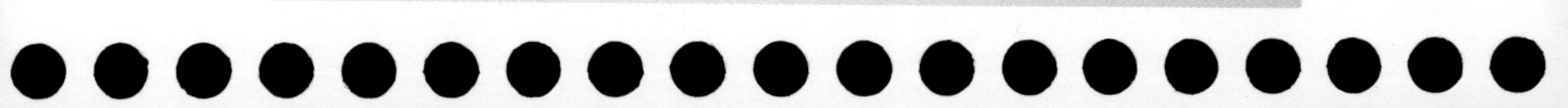

TRAY SETUP

Hygiene

FROM LEFT TO RIGHT

Mouth mirror, explorer, cotton forceps (pliers), periodontal probe, sickle curved/straight, 4L/4R universal posterior, $\frac{1}{2}$, $\frac{11}{12}$, $\frac{1}{2}$, mini-extended $\frac{1}{2}$

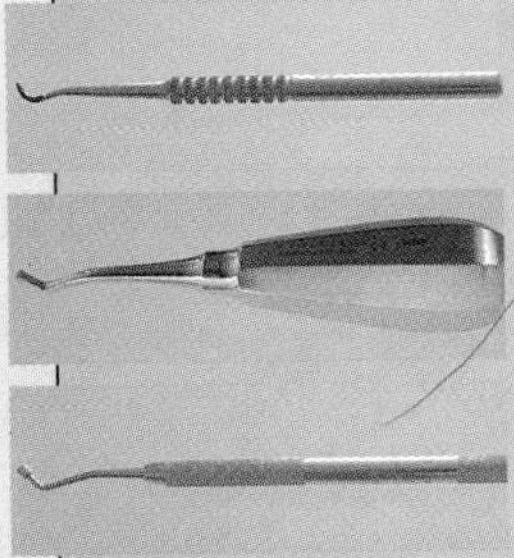

CHAPTER 13

Orthodontic Instruments

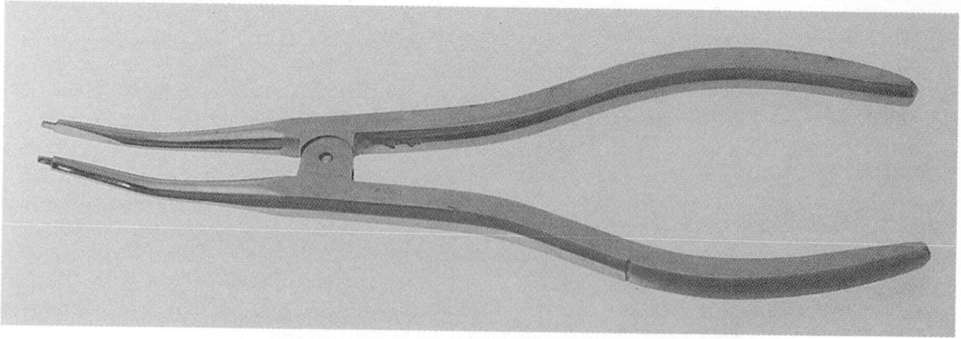

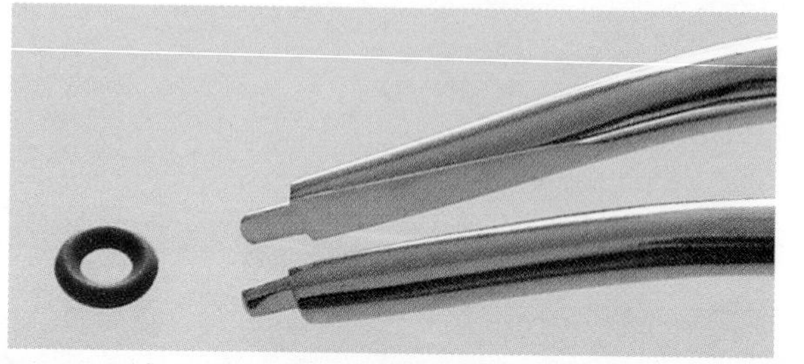

INSTRUMENT

Elastic Separating Pliers

FUNCTION To grip and place separators around contact area of tooth

CHARACTERISTICS Single ended

INSTRUMENT

Bracket Placement Card

FUNCTION To place each bracket and/or band on card according to tooth placement in mouth

CHARACTERISTICS Tape on card holds brackets in place before they are bonded to teeth.

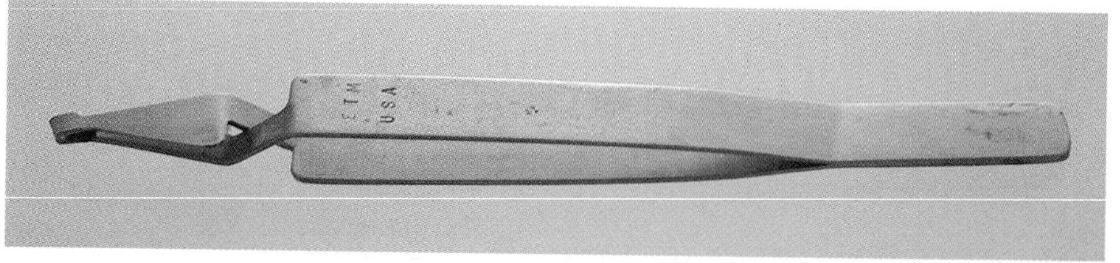
ETM
USA

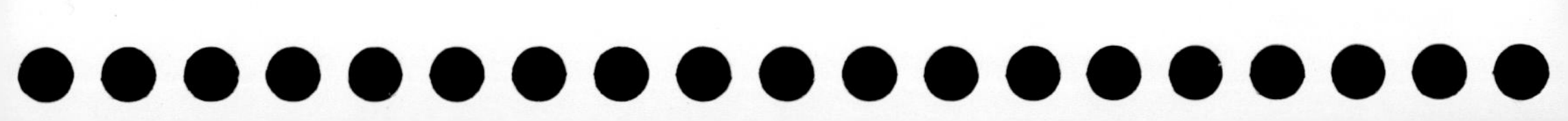

Bracket Placement Pliers

FUNCTION To hold and carry bracket by placing tip of pliers into slot of bracket
To place bracket on tooth for bonding

CHARACTERISTICS Range of sizes

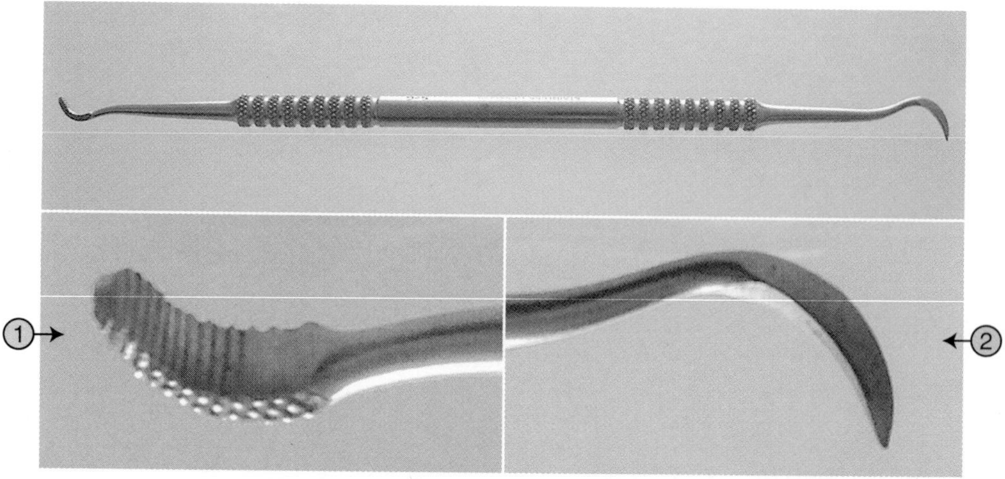

①

②

Orthodontic (Shure) Scaler

FUNCTION

To place brackets for bonding (both ends)
To remove separators (scaler end)
To remove elastic ligature ties (scaler end)
To remove excess cement or bonding material (scaler end)
To check for loose bands and brackets (both ends)

CHARACTERISTICS

Universal instrument used for several orthodontic functions:

- Single ended—Scaler or band seater
- Double ended—Band seater on one end ① and orthodontic scaler on opposite end ②

C. HARTZELL & SON
Germany stainless
CE
WBP

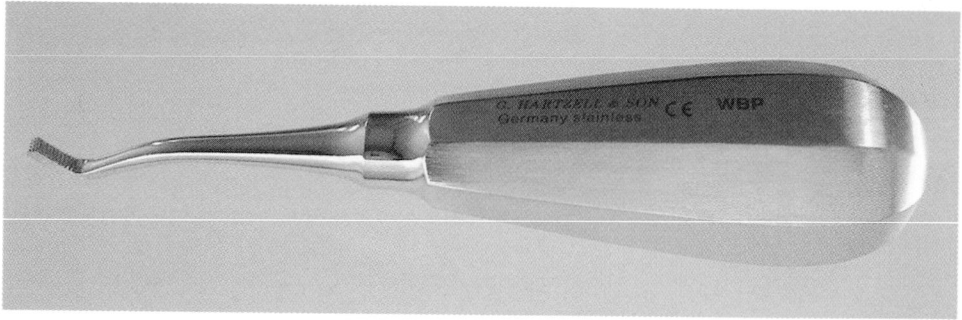

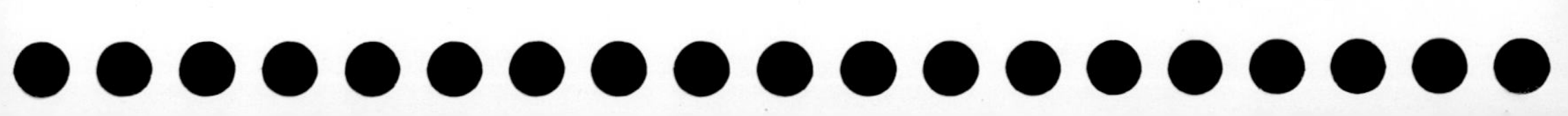

INSTRUMENT

Band Pusher

FUNCTION To push orthodontic bands into place during try-in and cementing phases

CHARACTERISTICS Single or double ended

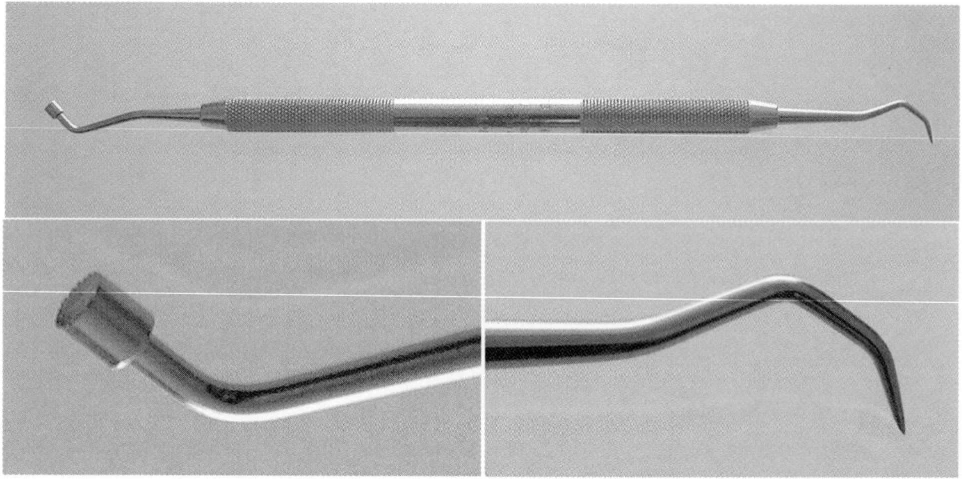

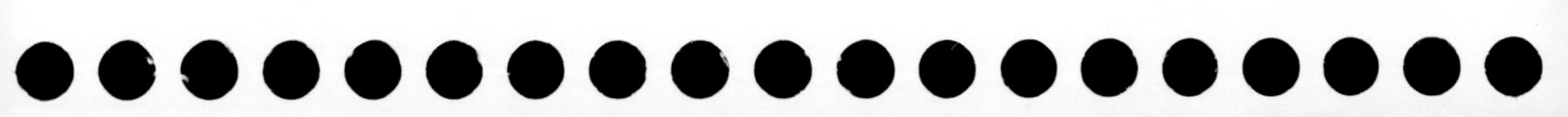

INSTRUMENT

Band Seater or Plugger with Scaler

FUNCTION To seat or place orthodontic bands during try-in and cementing phases
To remove excess material after cementation or bonding of bands

CHARACTERISTICS Double ended

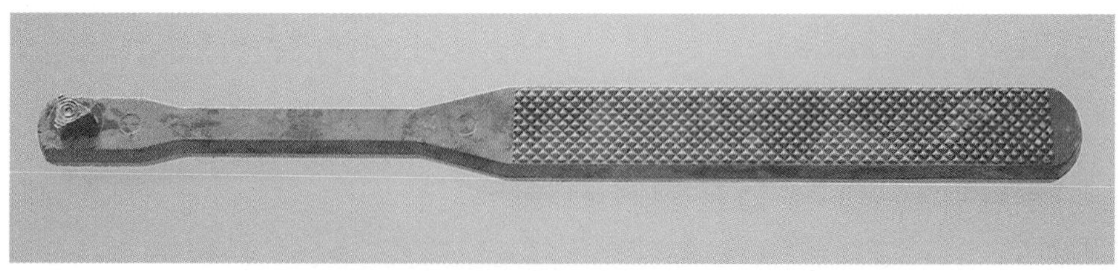

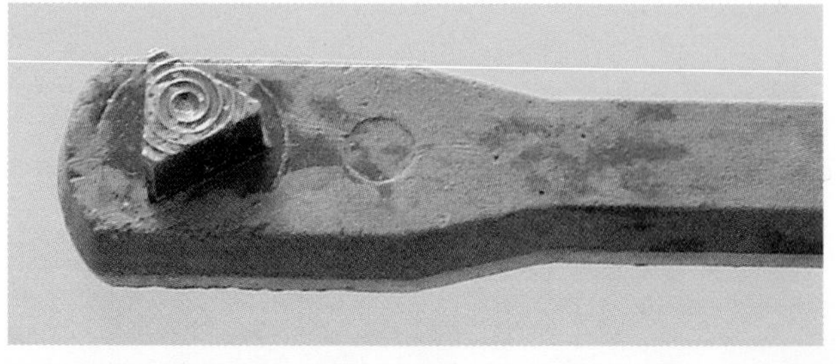

INSTRUMENT

Bite Stick

FUNCTION To assist seating or placing of orthodontic bands for try-in or cementing phase

CHARACTERISTICS Single ended

PRACTICE NOTE

1. The patient bites down on the end of the instrument to apply pressure to seat the band.

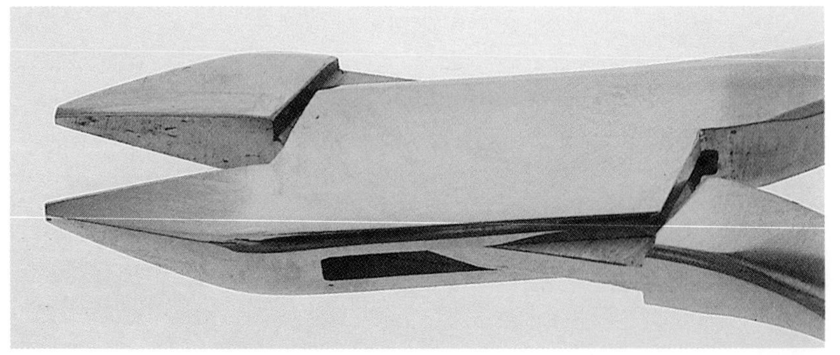

INSTRUMENT

Arch-Bending Pliers

FUNCTION To bend arch wires

CHARACTERISTICS Variety of styles, depending on type of arch wire used— Round, square, or rectangular

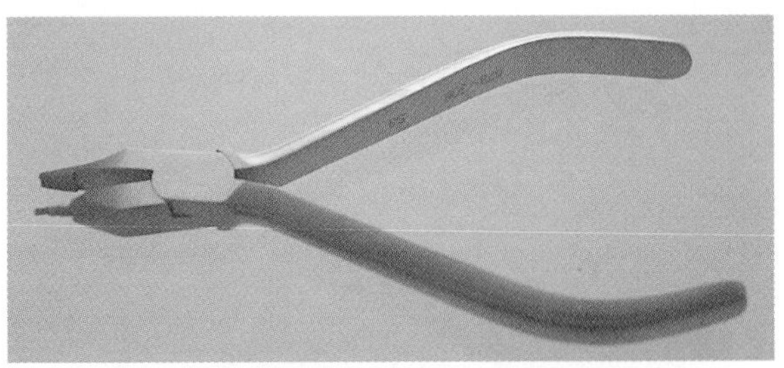

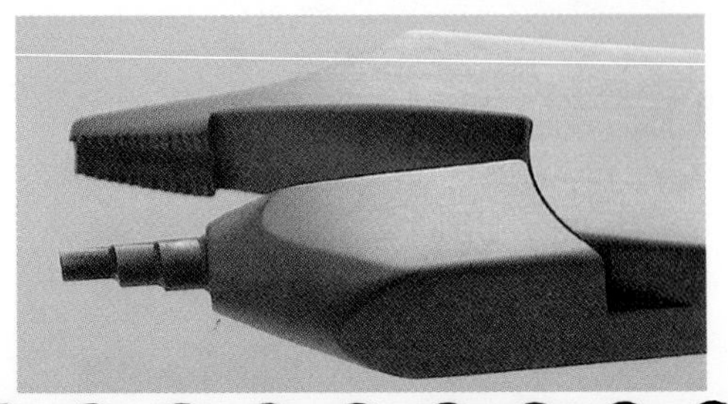

INSTRUMENT

Tweed Loop-Forming Pliers (Jarabek Pliers)

FUNCTION To bend and form loops in arch wire
To bend wires for removable appliances

CHARACTERISTICS Grooves in beak—Help to bend and form loops in wire
Variety of styles

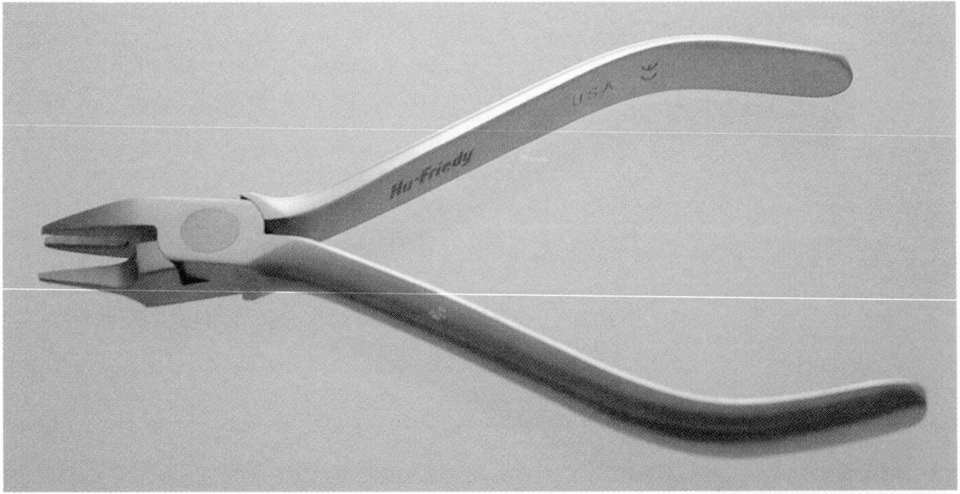

INSTRUMENT

Three-Prong Pliers

FUNCTION To contour and bend light wire

CHARACTERISTICS Range of sizes

INSTRUMENT

Bird Beak Pliers

FUNCTION To bend and form orthodontic wire

CHARACTERISTICS Versatile wire-bending pliers
Beaks on working end meet very precisely

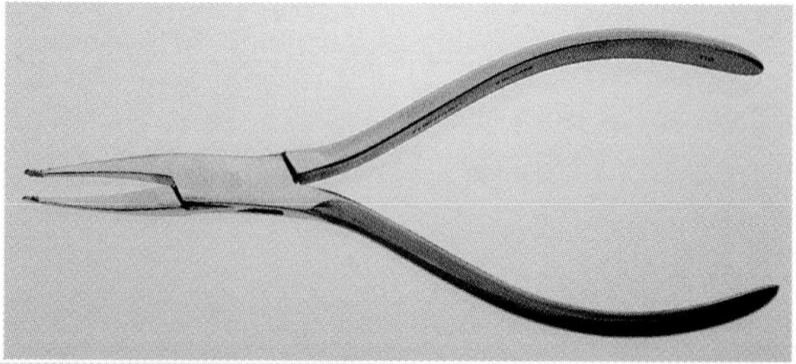

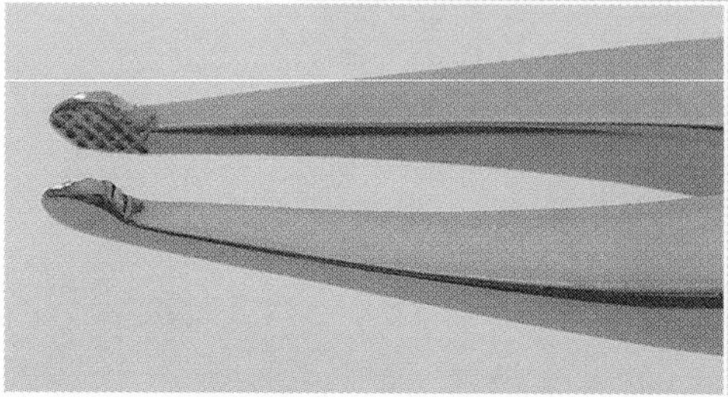

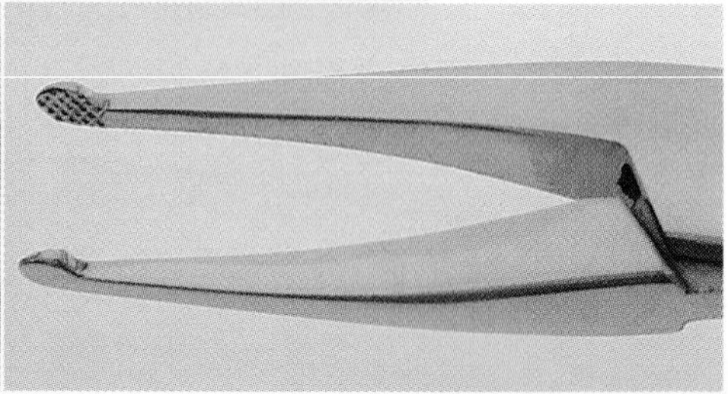

INSTRUMENT

How (or Howe) Pliers

FUNCTION

To place and remove arch wires
To check for loose bands

CHARACTERISTICS

All-purpose pliers for orthodontic procedures
Serrated tips for better grip on wire
Straight or curved beaks

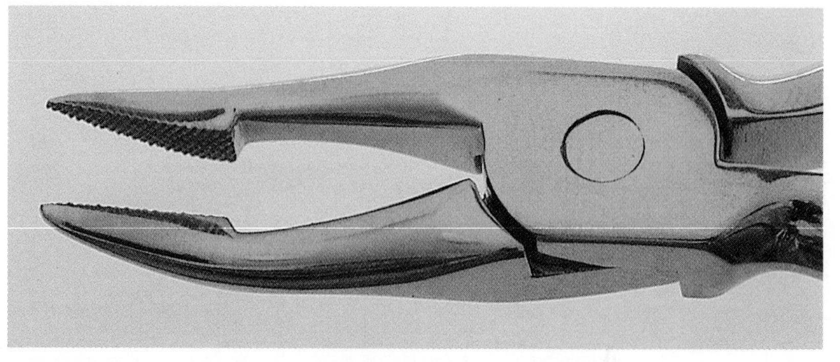

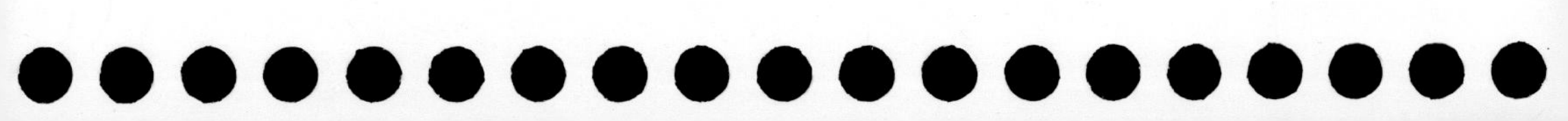

INSTRUMENT

Weingart Utility Pliers

FUNCTION

To place and remove arch wires
To aid a variety of functions for orthodontic procedures

CHARACTERISTICS

Working ends—Tapered, slim tips to allow pliers to fit between brackets for ease of arch wire placement

INSTRUMENT

Orthodontic Hemostat

FUNCTION To hold and place separators

To hold, place, and/or tie ligatures to arch wire

CHARACTERISTICS Multifunctional instrument for orthodontic procedures

Example: Mathieu pliers

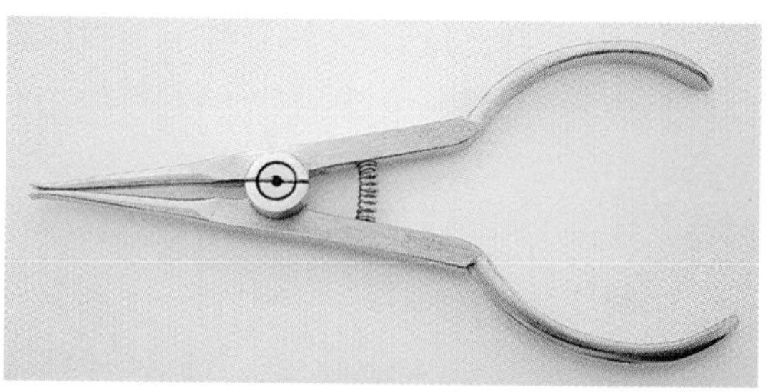

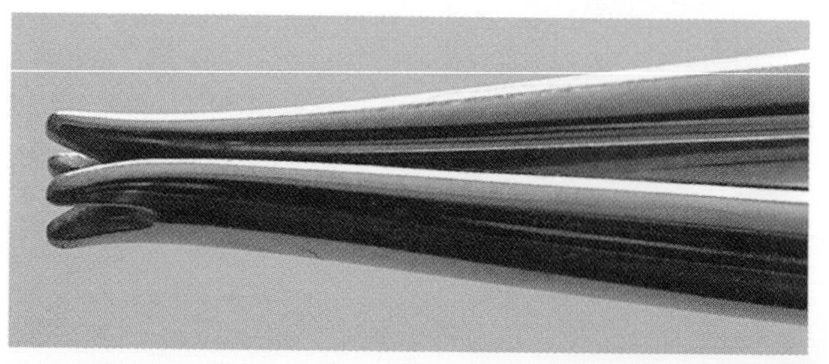

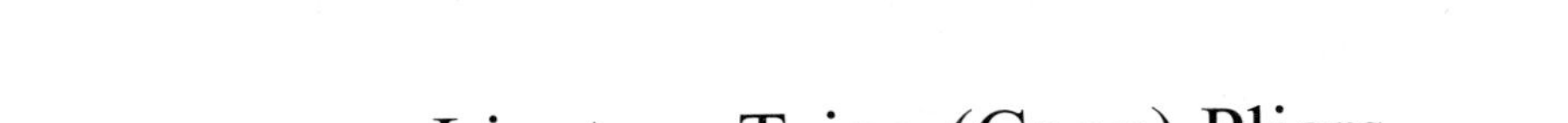

INSTRUMENT

Ligature-Tying (Coon) Pliers

FUNCTION To tie in ligature to arch wire

CHARACTERISTICS Channel on pliers—Locks wire ends in place as tips spread
Variety of styles

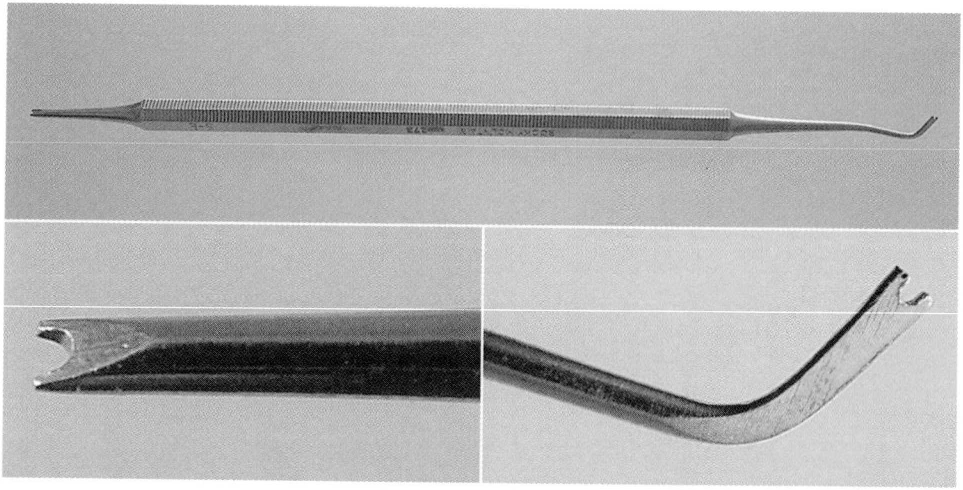

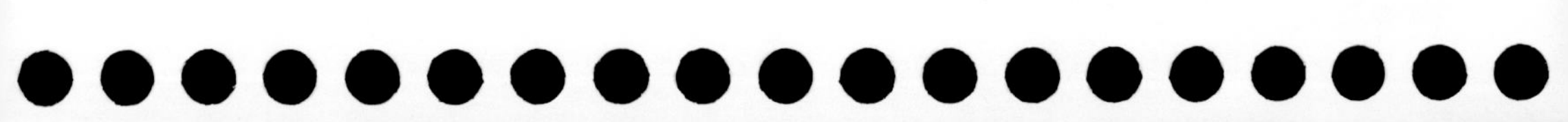

Ligature Director

FUNCTION To place ligature wire around brackets after it has been tied to arch wire

CHARACTERISTICS Single or double ended
Ends of instrument—Have notches to assist placement of ligature tie around brackets

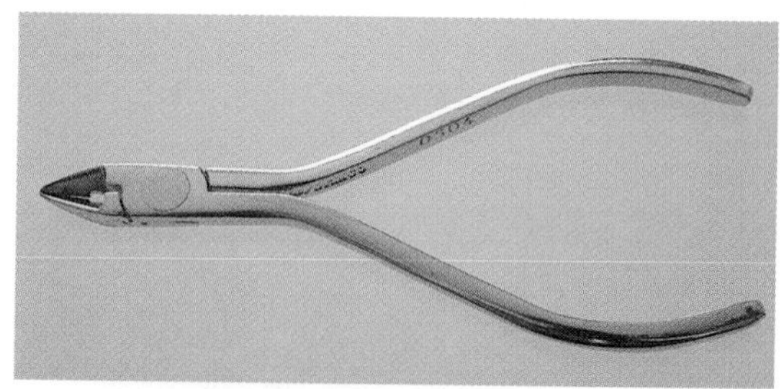

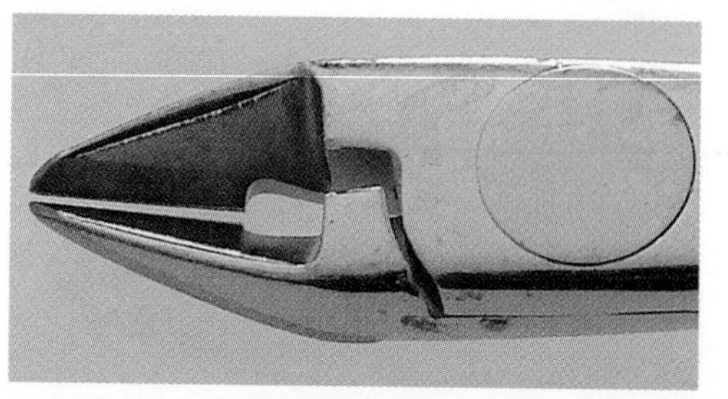

Ligature and Wire Cutters

FUNCTION To cut ligature after it has been tied to arch wire
To cut ligature tie to allow removal of arch wire

CHARACTERISTICS Range of sizes available

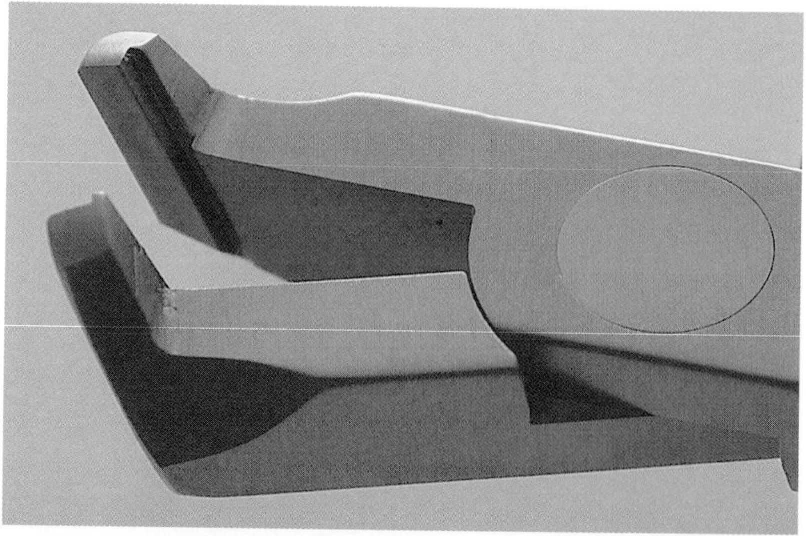

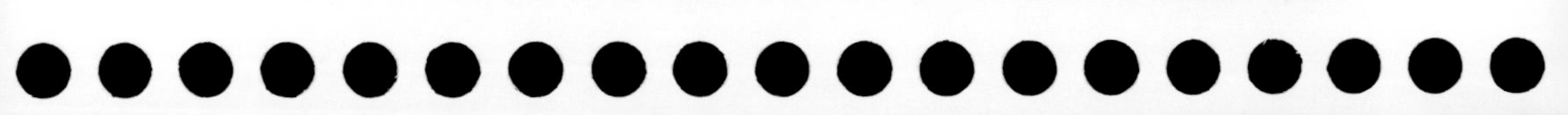

INSTRUMENT

Distal End–Cutting Pliers

FUNCTION To cut distal end of arch wire after placement in brackets and buccal tubes

CHARACTERISTICS Catch and hold excess wire after wire has been cut

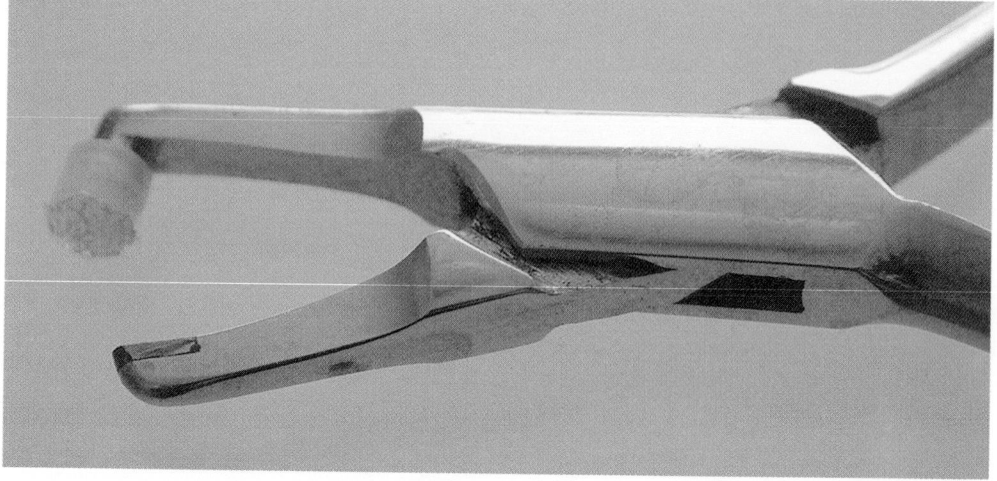

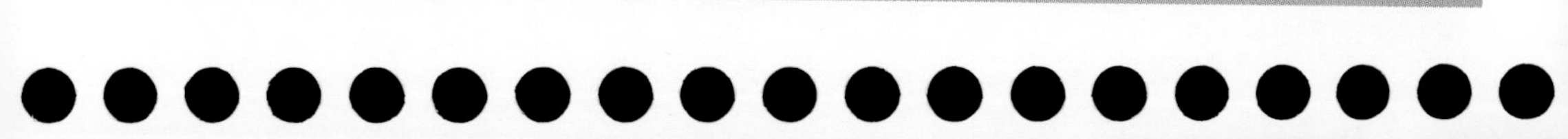

Posterior Band Remover

FUNCTION To remove orthodontic bands from teeth

CHARACTERISTICS Two beak types:

- One beak has round cover to place on occlusal surface of tooth to prevent damage during removal of band.
- Opposite beak is curved and is placed on gingival side of bracket to apply pressure and remove band from tooth.

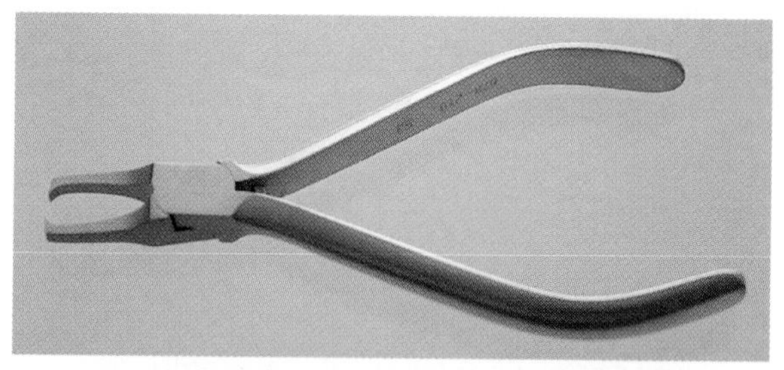

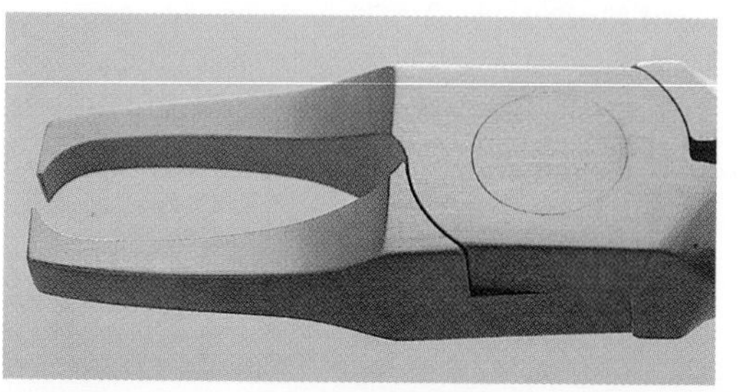

INSTRUMENT

Bracket Remover

FUNCTION To remove anterior or posterior brackets from teeth

CHARACTERISTICS Grasp bracket to remove it from tooth

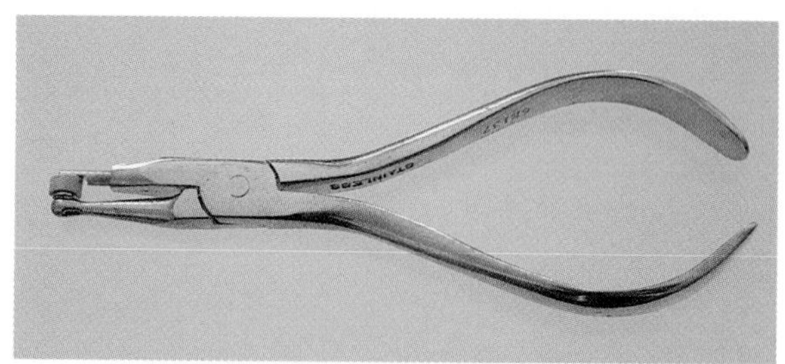
STAINLESS

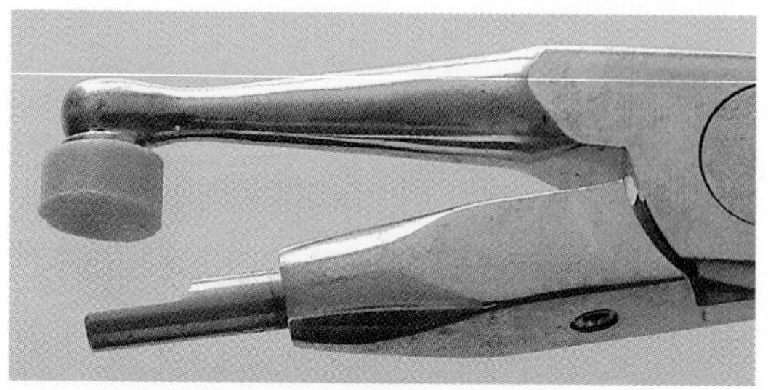

INSTRUMENT

Adhesive-Removing Pliers

FUNCTION To remove excess adhesive after debonding of brackets

CHARACTERISTICS Carbide-inserted tip on short beak
Plastic pad on round end (pad can be changed)

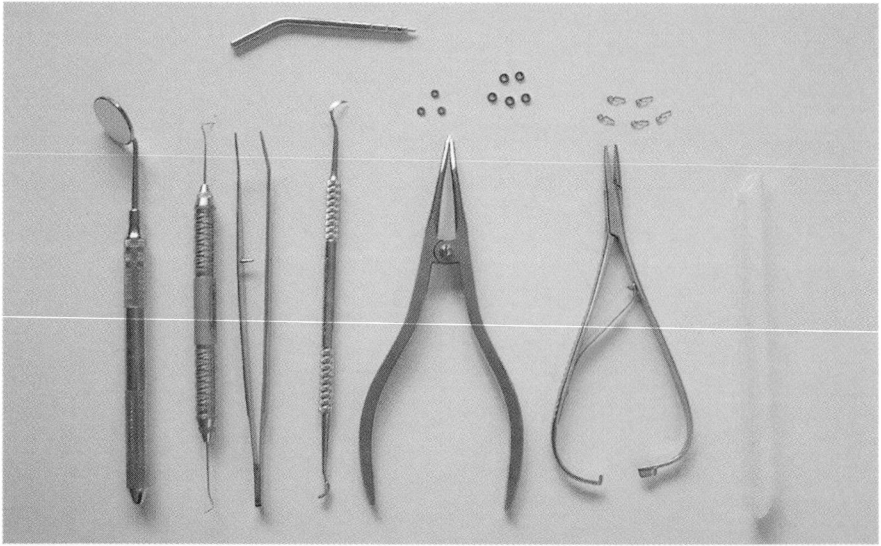

TRAY SETUP

Orthodontic Separating Procedure

TOP

Air/water syringe tip

BOTTOM (FROM LEFT TO RIGHT)

Mouth mirror, explorer, cotton forceps (pliers), orthodontic (Shure) scaler, elastic separating pliers, elastic separators, orthodontic hemostat (Mathieu pliers), spring coil separators, high-velocity (volume) evacuation disposable tip (HVE)

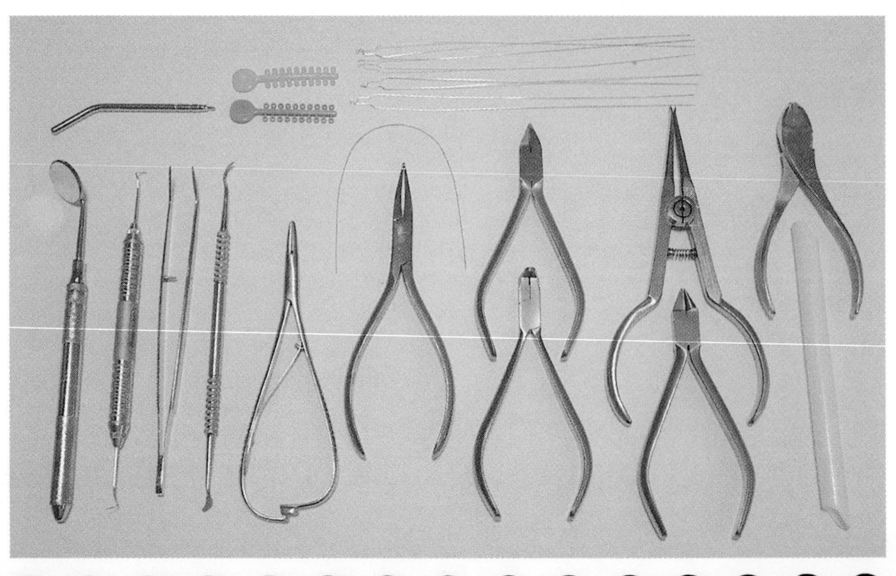

Orthodontic Tying-In Arch Wire

TOP (FROM LEFT TO RIGHT)

Air/water syringe tip, elastic ligatures, wire ligature ties

BOTTOM (FROM LEFT TO RIGHT)

Mouth mirror, explorer, cotton forceps, orthodontic (Shure) scaler, orthodontic hemostat (Mathieu pliers), preformed arch wire, How (or Howe) pliers, wire-bending pliers, distal end cutter, ligature-tying (Coon) pliers, bird beak pliers, wire cutters, high-velocity (volume) evacuation tip (HVE)

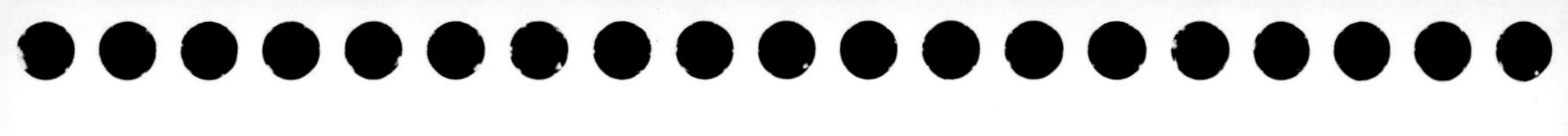

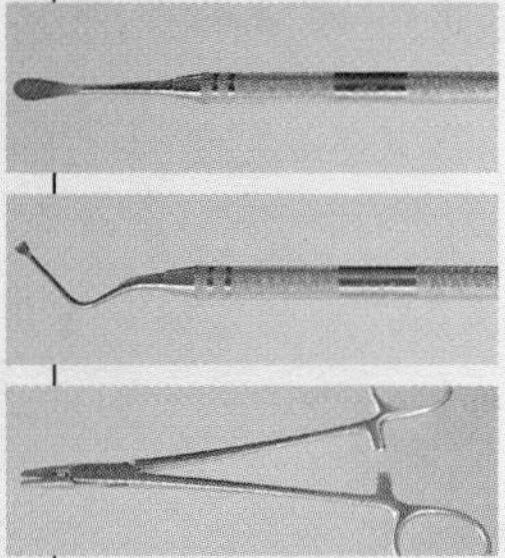

CHAPTER 14

Universal Surgical Instruments

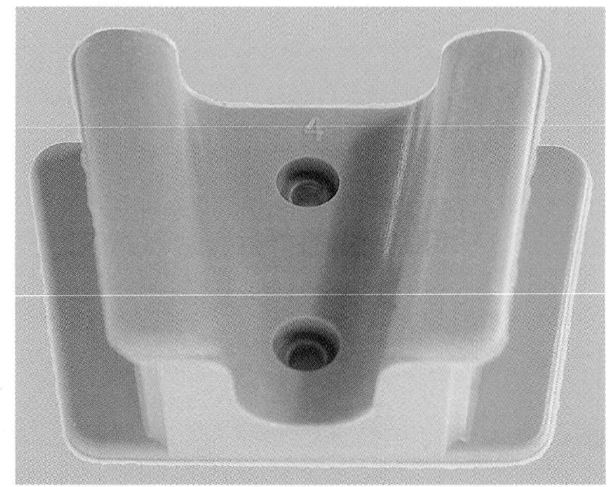
4

INSTRUMENT

Mouth Prop

FUNCTION To hold patient's mouth open during dental procedure

CHARACTERISTICS Placed in posterior part of mouth while patient bites down
Often used for sedated patients
Disposables available
Range of sizes—Pediatric to large adult

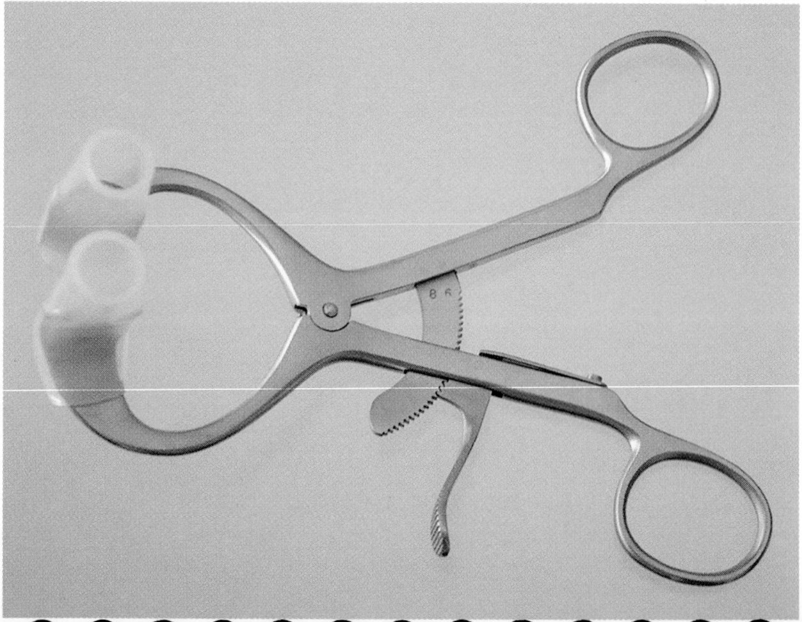

Mouth Gag

FUNCTION To hold patient's mouth open during dental procedure

CHARACTERISTICS Often used for sedated patients
Locking device
Range of sizes available

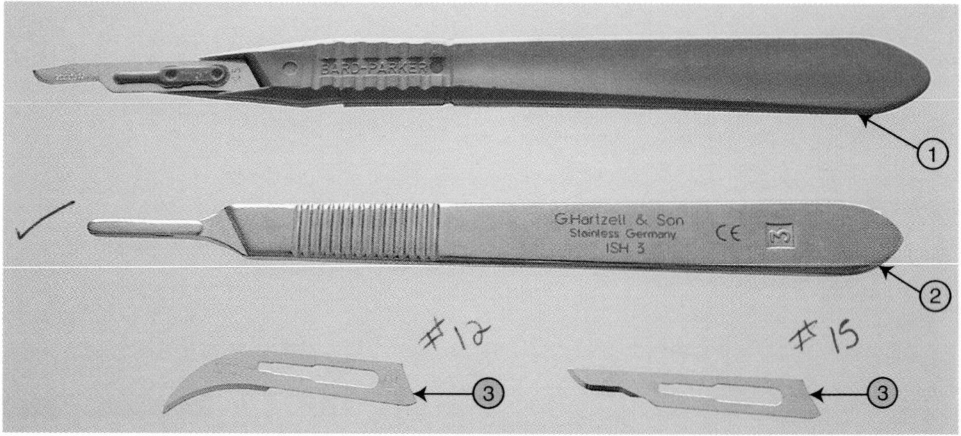
BARD-PARKER
1
G.Hartzell & Son
Stainless Germany
ISH 3
CE
3
2
#12
#15
3
3

Bard Parker handle

INSTRUMENT

Scalpel Handle with Blades

FUNCTION

To hold blade in place
To cut tissue with blade
To trim interproximal restorations

CHARACTERISTICS

Blades—Disposable, variety of shapes and sizes

1. Disposable handle/blade in one unit
2. Autoclavable handle
3. Commonly used blades: No. 12, no. 15

400

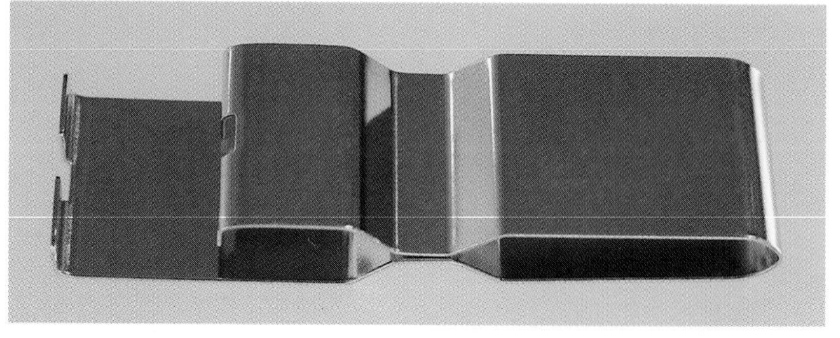

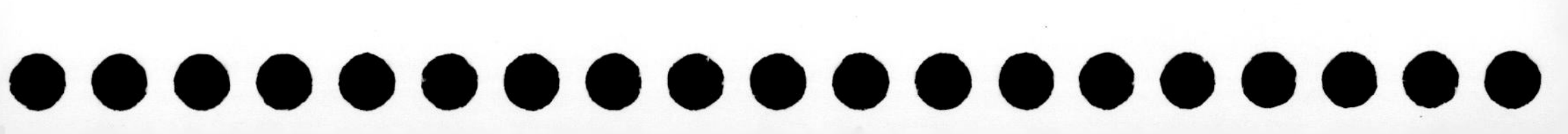

Scalpel Blade Remover

FUNCTION To remove blade from scalpel handle safely

CHARACTERISTICS Removes all sizes of blades
Autoclavable

PRACTICE NOTES

Steps for removing blade:

1) Insert blade with blade side up; align to notch.
2) Press down on blade remover.
3) Pull handle away from blade.

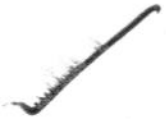

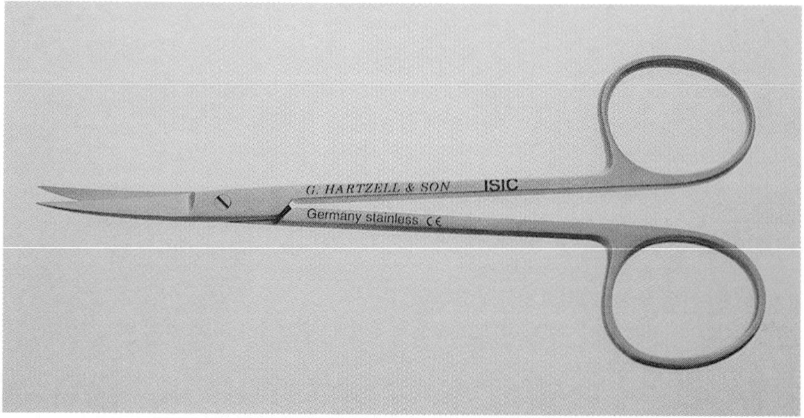
G. HARTZELL & SON
ISIC
Germany stainless CE

INSTRUMENT

Tissue Scissors

FUNCTION To cut tissue

CHARACTERISTICS Straight or curved
Variety of shapes and sizes
Variety of uses

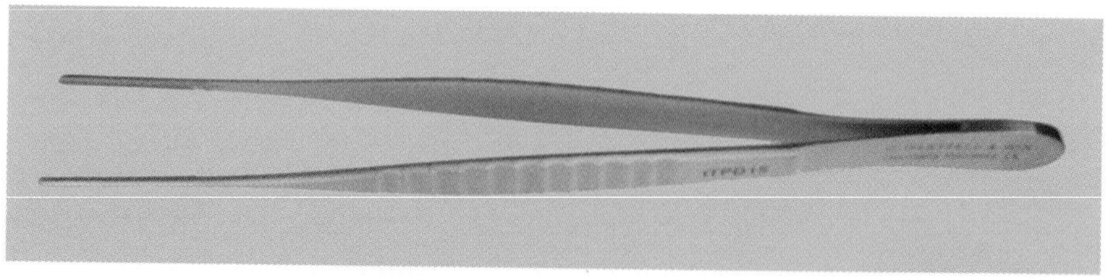

INSTRUMENT

Tissue Forceps

FUNCTION To hold tissue during surgical procedures

CHARACTERISTICS Serrated or rat-tooth tips
Range of sizes available

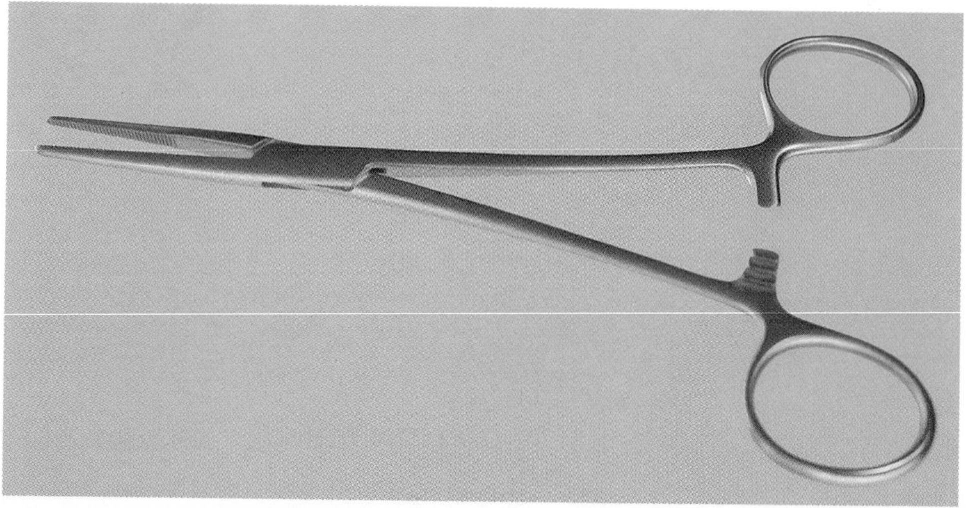

INSTRUMENT

Hemostat

FUNCTION To grasp tissue or bone fragments

CHARACTERISTICS Straight or curved
Working end—Serrated, locking
Variety of functions
Range of sizes available

Periosteal Elevator

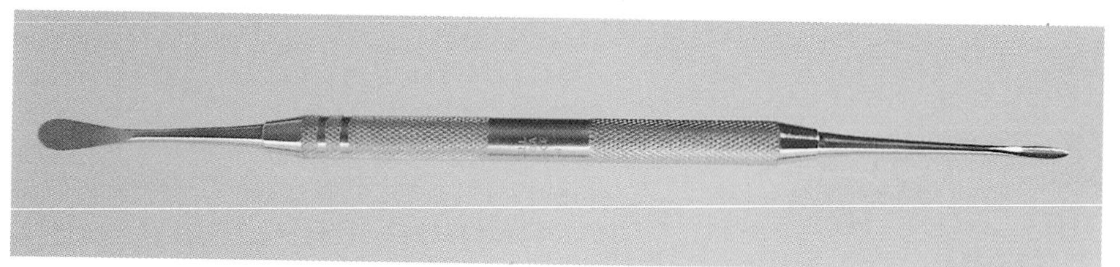

Periosteal Elevator

FUNCTION To separate tissue from tooth or bone
To hold tissue away from surgical site

CHARACTERISTICS Working end—Pointed or round
Range of sizes available

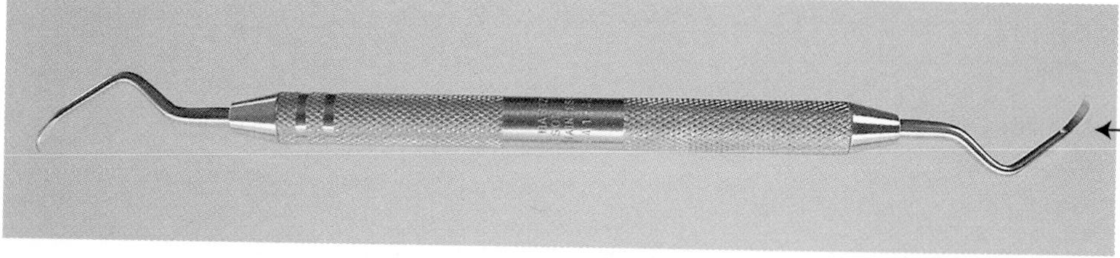

①

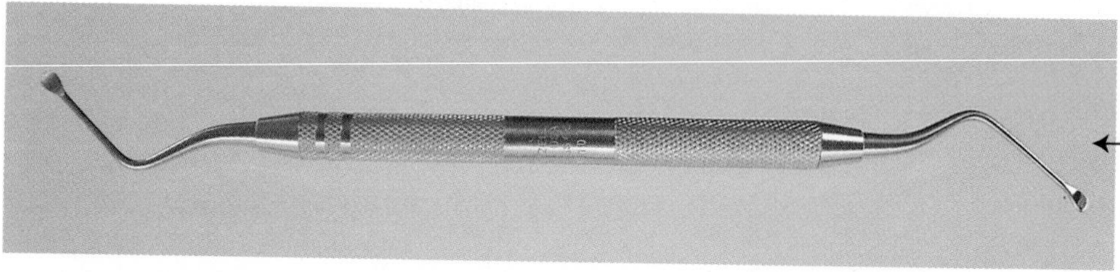

②

Surgical Curette

FUNCTION

To remove debris or granulation tissue from surgical site
To remove cyst from extraction site or surgical site
To perform gross tissue debridement

CHARACTERISTICS

Single or double ended
Variety of sizes and shapes

Examples:

① Commonly used type: Prichard
② Miller

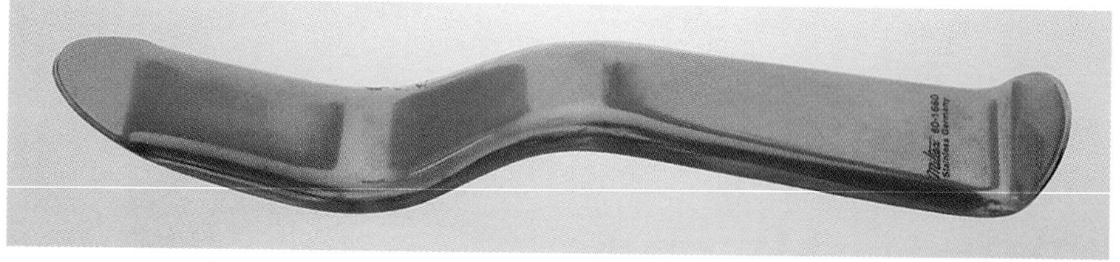
60-1660
Stainless Germany

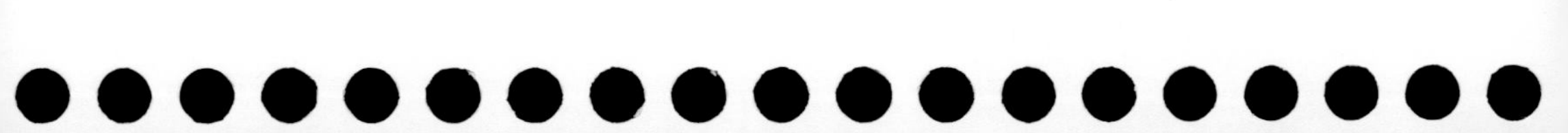

INSTRUMENT

Tongue and Cheek Retractor

FUNCTION To hold and retract tongue or cheek during surgery

CHARACTERISTICS Variety of styles and sizes
Example: Commonly used type: Minnesota

414

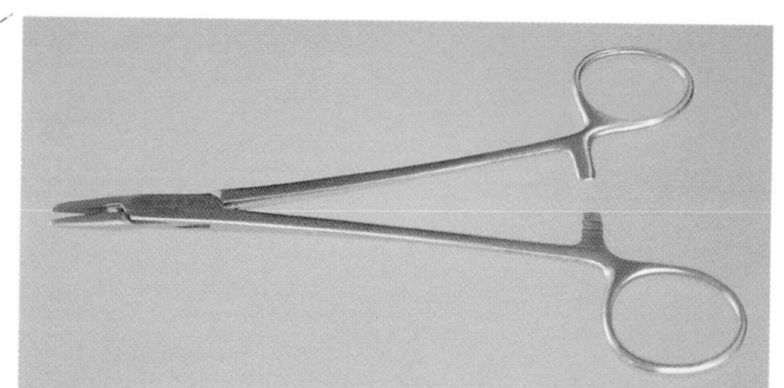

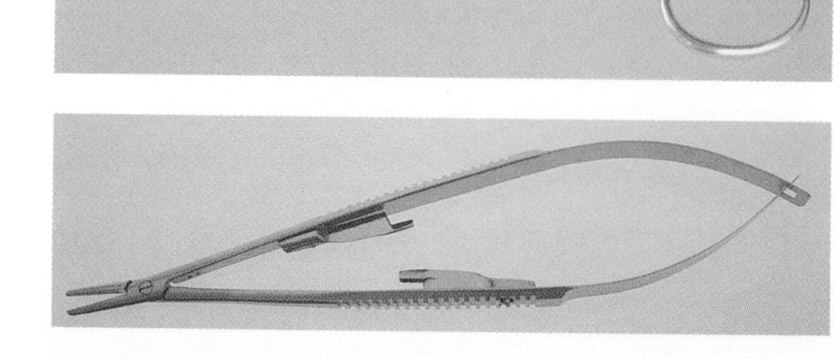

Needle Holder

FUNCTION To grasp and manipulate suture needle during use

CHARACTERISTICS Working end—Different lengths, curved or straight
Notched ends available (to accommodate needle)
Variety of styles
Range of sizes—Micro for microsurgery to large

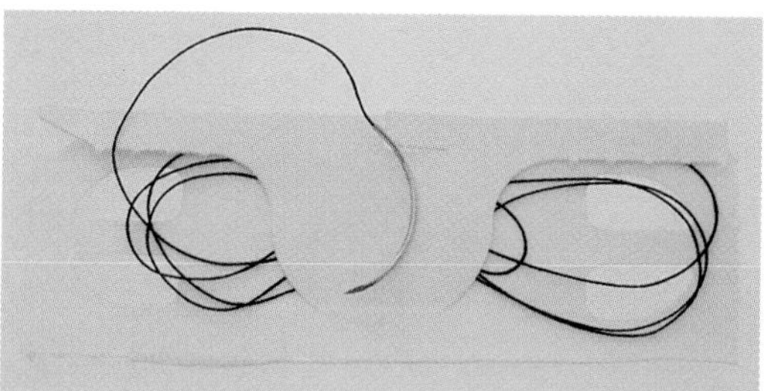

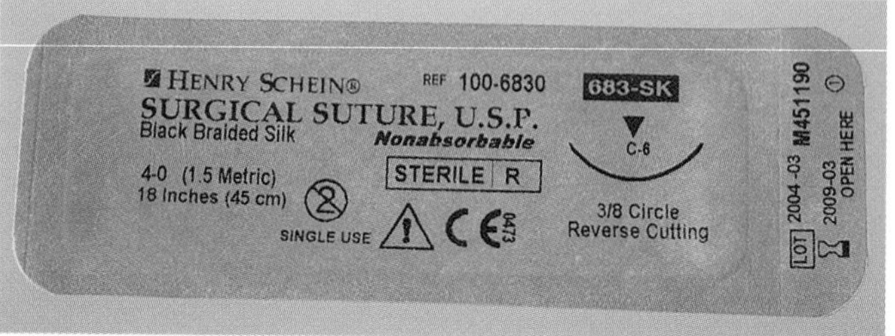
HENRY SCHEIN®
REF 100-6830
683-SK
SURGICAL SUTURE, U.S.P.
Black Braided Silk
Nonabsorbable
4-0 (1.5 Metric)
18 Inches (45 cm)
STERILE R
SINGLE USE
0473
C-6
3/8 Circle
Reverse Cutting
LOT 2004 -03 M451190
2009-03
OPEN HERE

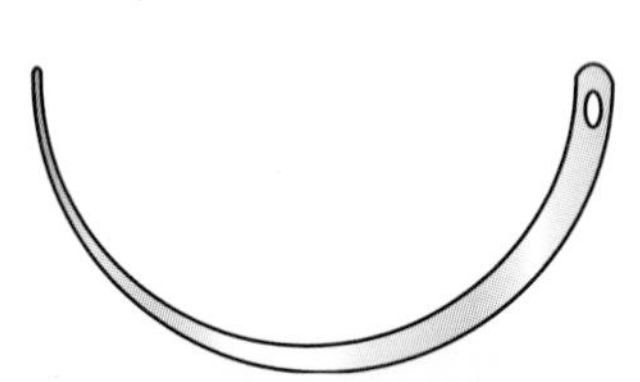

INSTRUMENT

Suture Needle and Sutures

FUNCTION To suture surgical site

CHARACTERISTICS Resorbable sutures—Gut plain, chromic gut, polyglycolic (PGA)
Nonresorbable sutures—Silk, nylon, polyester, polypropylene
Available in sterile package
Variety of suture needle sizes available with different sutures

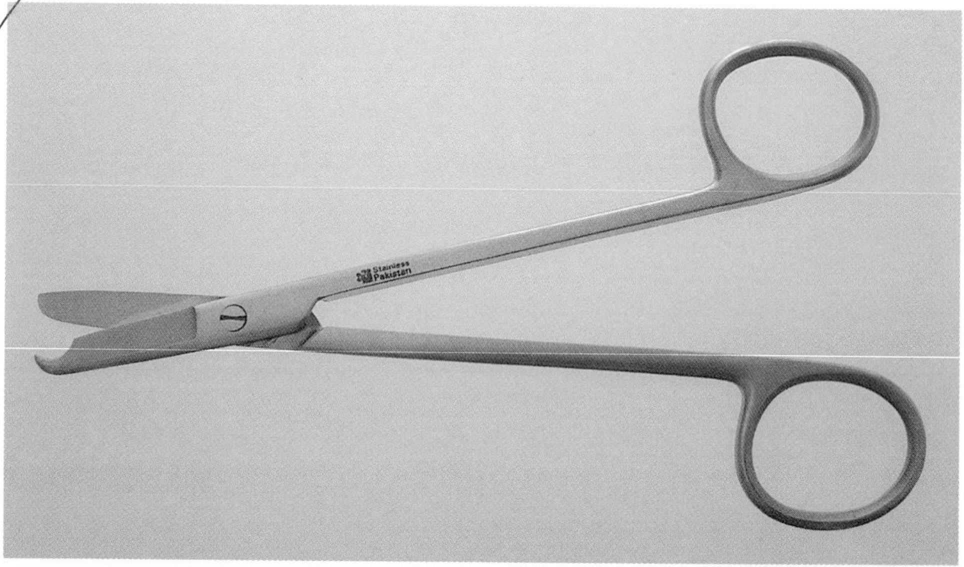

INSTRUMENT

Suture Scissors

FUNCTION To cut sutures

CHARACTERISTICS Cutting edges—Straight or angled
May have notch on end of cutting edge
Range of sizes

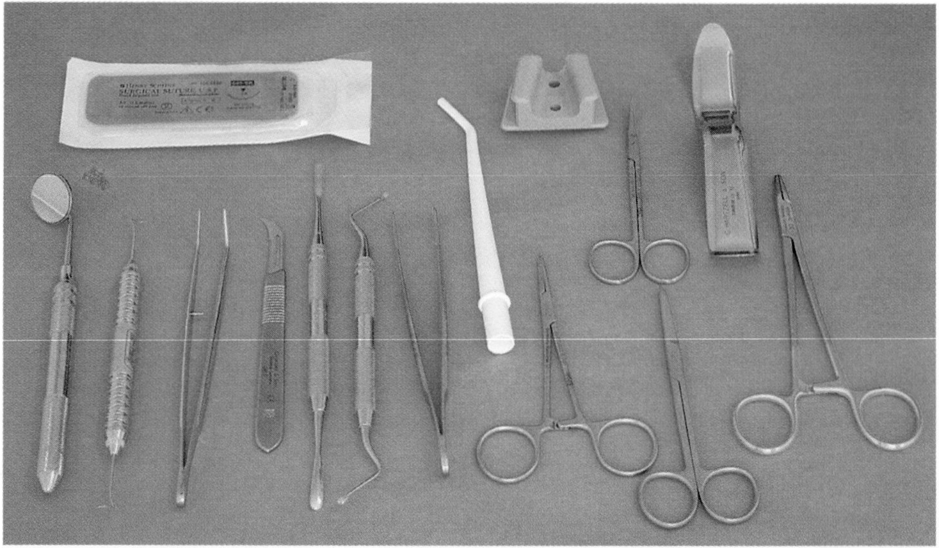

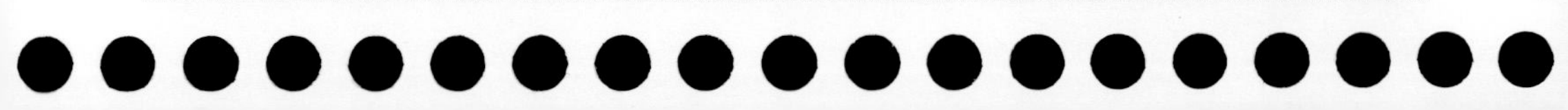

Universal Surgical Procedure

TOP ROW (FROM LEFT TO RIGHT)

Sutures, mouth prop

BOTTOM ROW (FROM LEFT TO RIGHT)

Mouth mirror, explorer, cotton forceps (pliers), scalpel with blade # 12, periosteal elevator, surgical curette (Prichard), tissue holder, surgical aspirator tip, hemostat, tissue scissors, suture scissors, tongue and check retractor, needle holder

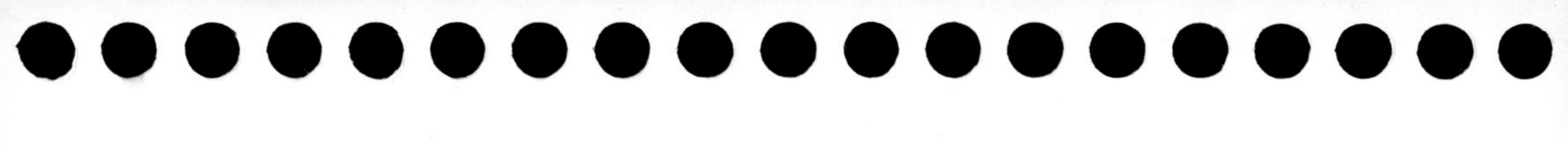

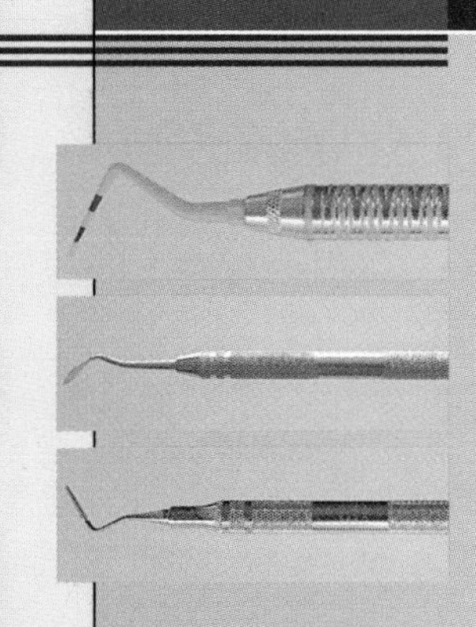

CHAPTER 15

Periodontal Instruments

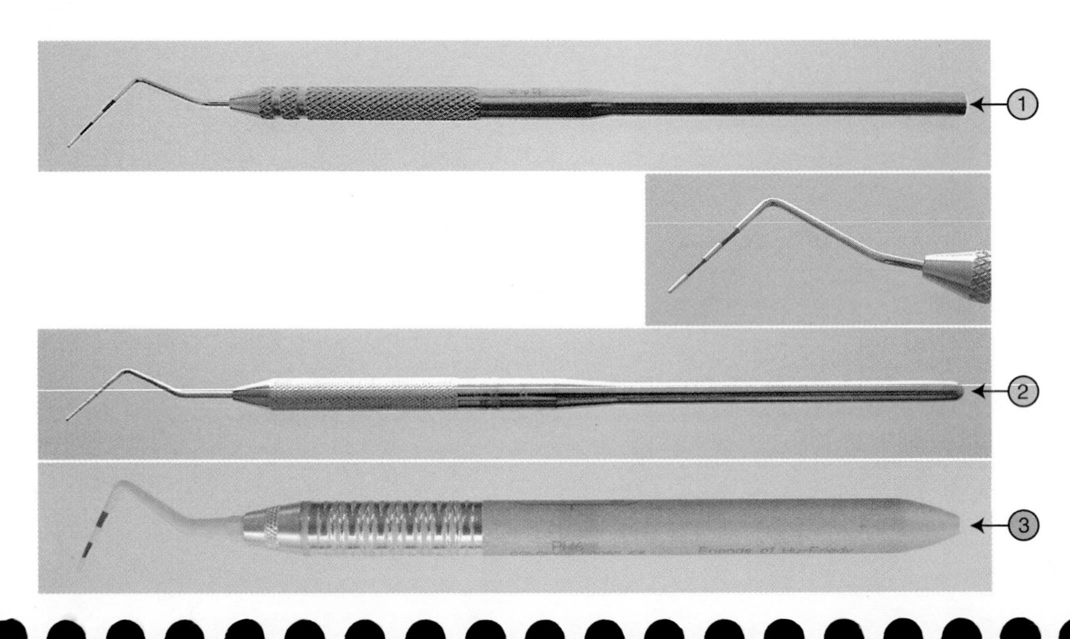
1
2
3

Periodontal Probes

FUNCTION To measure periodontal pocket depth in millimeter increments

CHARACTERISTICS Flat or rounded ends

Millimeter-increment markings vary for each style:

① Color coded—Black markings for millimeter measurements
② Other styles—Indentations in metal for millimeter measurement
③ Color-ended probe with black visible markings; replaceable tip, different tip designs, safe for implant probing

Double-ended style available with probe on one end, explorer on the other

Computerized probes available

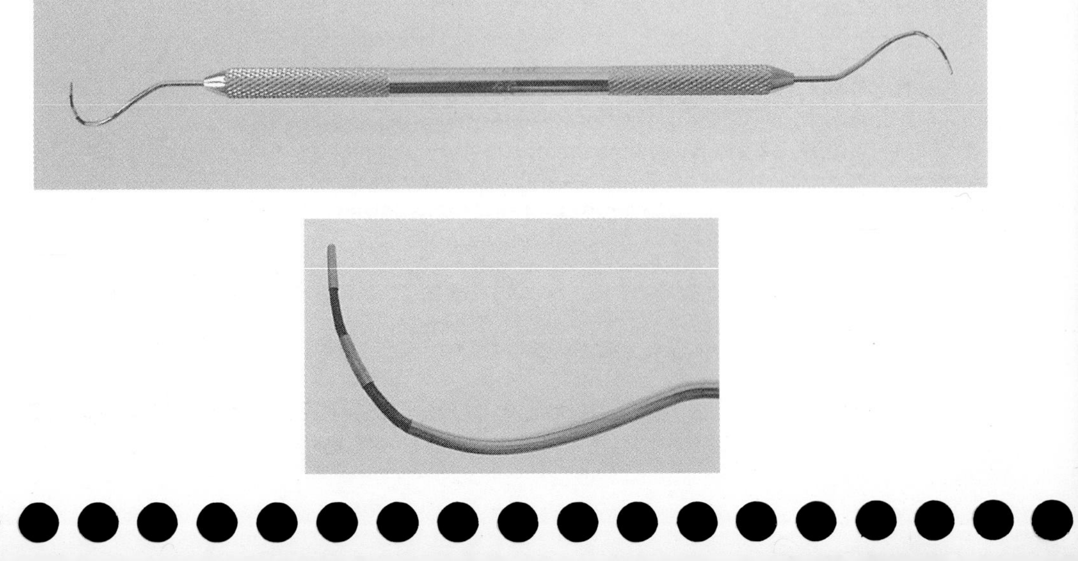

Furcation Probe

FUNCTION To measure horizontal and vertical pocket depth of multirooted teeth in furcation areas

CHARACTERISTICS Flat or rounded ends
Single or double ended
Millimeter-increment markings vary for each style:

- Color-coded—Black markings for millimeter measurements
- Other styles—Indentations in metal for millimeter measurements

Example: Nabors probe (color coded)

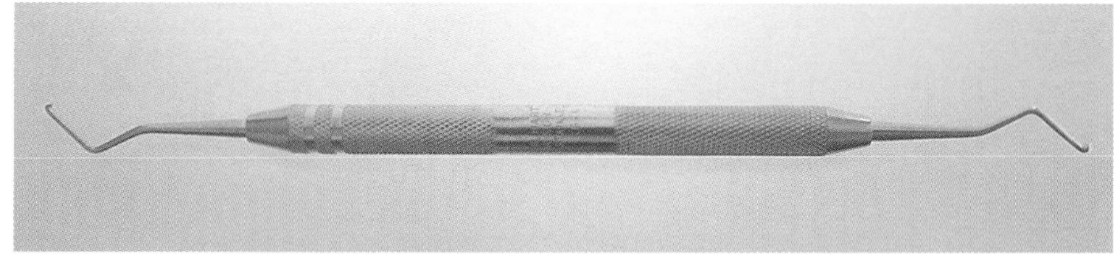

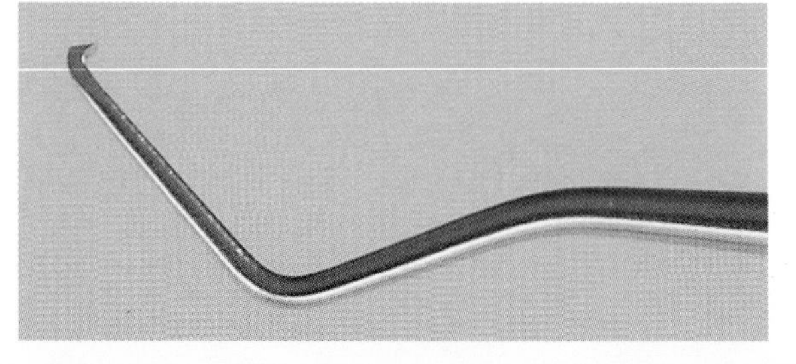

INSTRUMENT

Mesial/Distal Hoe

FUNCTION To remove subgingival and supragingival calculus

CHARACTERISTICS

Used with pulling motion
Straight cutting edge
Single or double ended
Designed to function in anterior or posterior locations

- Anterior hoe—Shorter, straighter shanks
- Posterior hoe—Longer, angled shanks

430

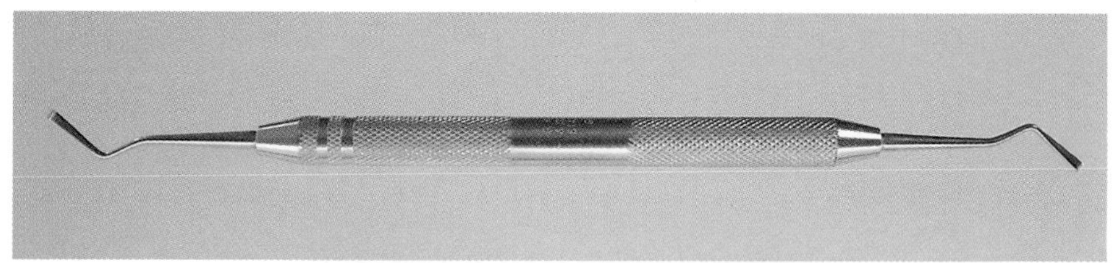

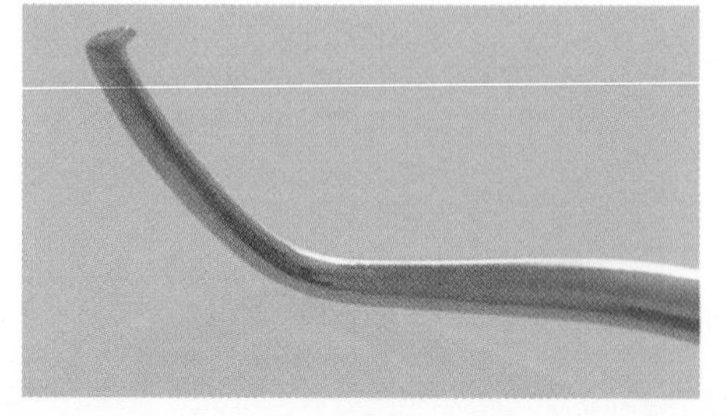

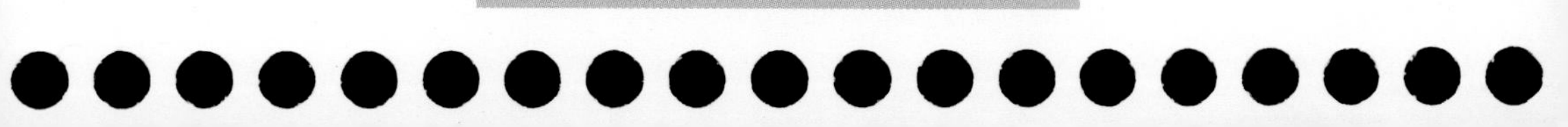

Buccal/Lingual Hoe

FUNCTION To remove subgingival and supragingival calculus

CHARACTERISTICS Used with pulling motion
Straight cutting edge
Single or double ended
Designed to function in anterior or posterior locations

- Anterior hoe—Shorter, straighter shanks
- Posterior hoe—Longer, angled shanks

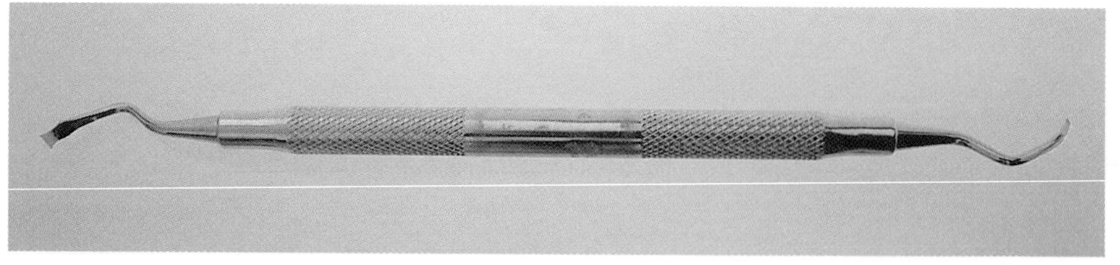

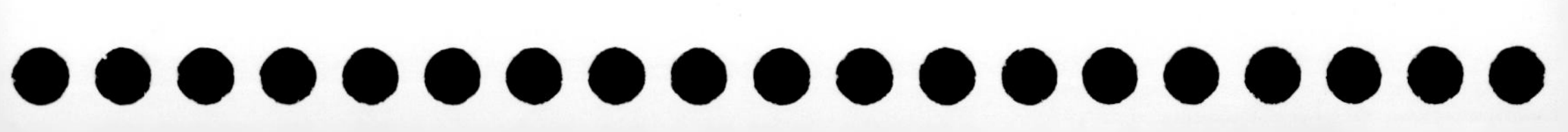

INSTRUMENT

Back-Action Hoe

FUNCTION To remove bone adjacent to teeth without causing trauma

CHARACTERISTICS Double ended
Variety of sizes and shapes

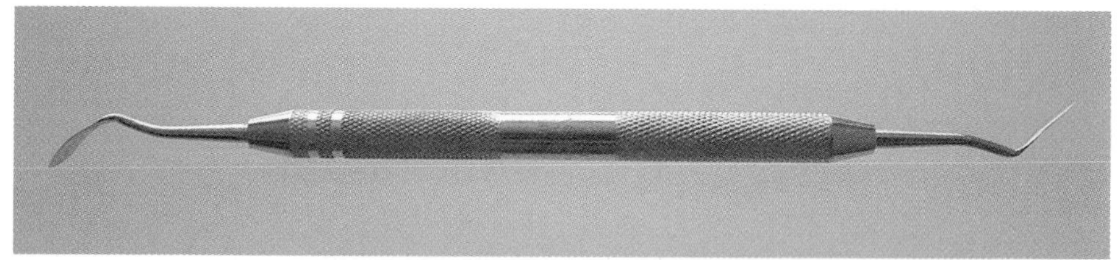

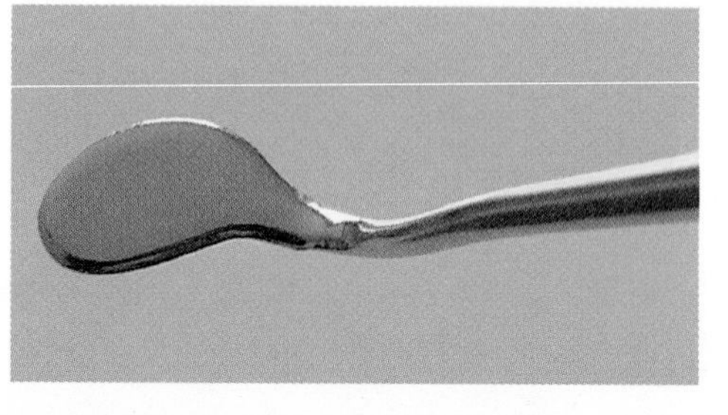

Periodontal Knife—Kidney Shaped

FUNCTION To use for bevel incision for gingivectomy
To use for gingivoplasty

CHARACTERISTICS Variety of sizes and shapes
Name by designer: Kirkland, Goldman-Fox, Buck, Solt
Example: Goldman-Fox 7

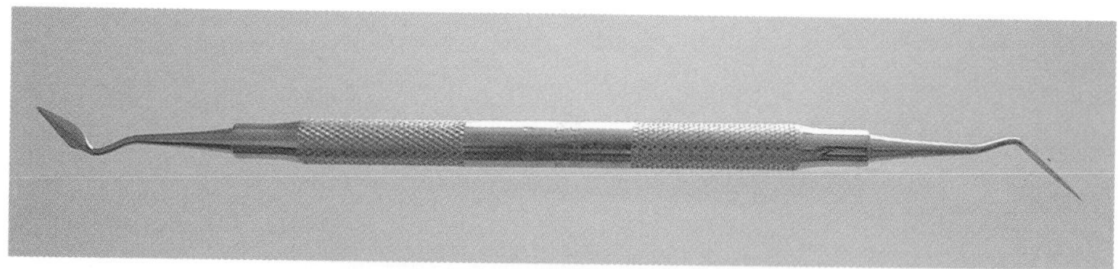

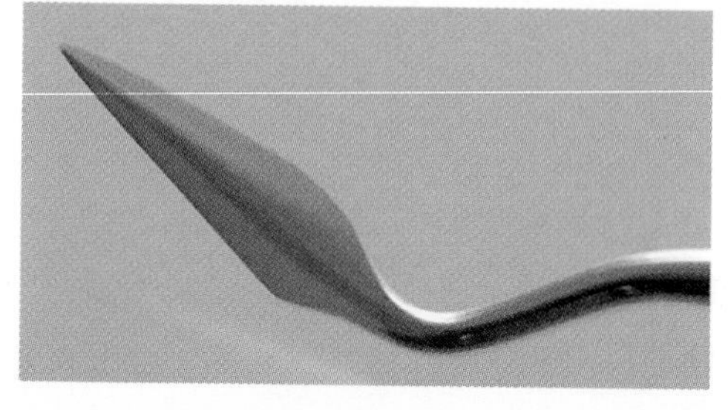

Interdental Knife—Spear Point

FUNCTION

To use for interdental cutting of gingiva
To remove tissue

CHARACTERISTICS

Blade angulated for easier use
Name by designer: Orban, Goldman-Fox, Buck, Sanders
Single or double ended
Range of sizes
Example: Buck 5/6

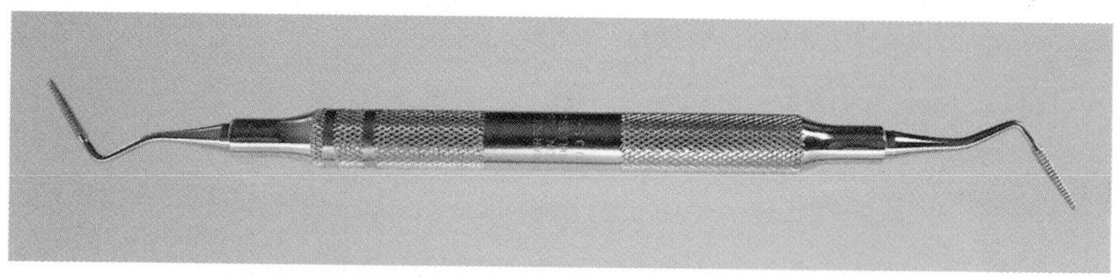

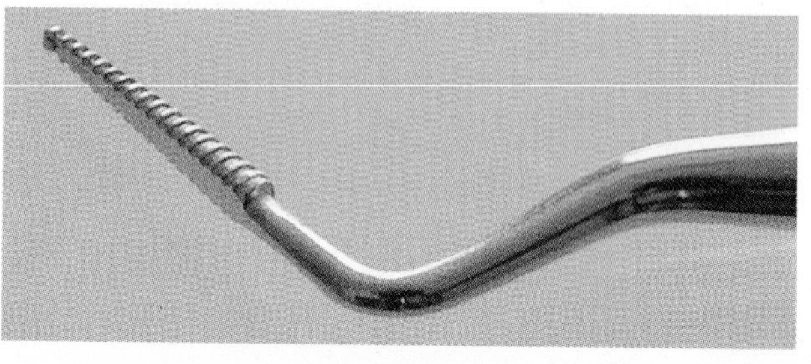

Interdental File

FUNCTION To crush and remove heavy deposits from subgingival and supragingival interproximal areas

CHARACTERISTICS Used with push or pull motion
Various angles—Curved, straight, mesial/distal, and buccal/lingual
Examples: Sugarman, Schluger, Buck
Range of sizes available

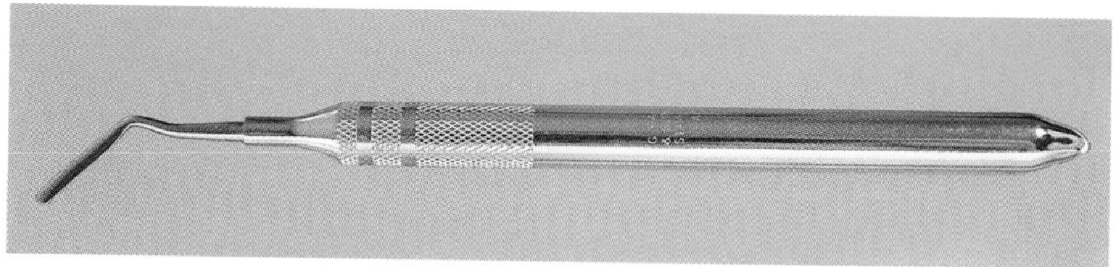

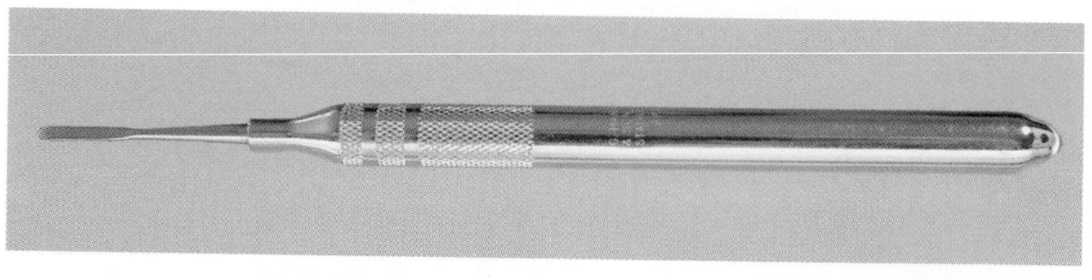

INSTRUMENT

Periotomes

FUNCTION

To cut periodontal ligaments for atraumatic tooth extraction
To use when dental implant placement is indicated

CHARACTERISTICS

Thin, sharp blades—Cause minimal damage to periodontal ligaments and surrounding alveolar bone
Straight or angled blades
Single or double ended
Range of sizes available
Some manufacturers make replaceable tip

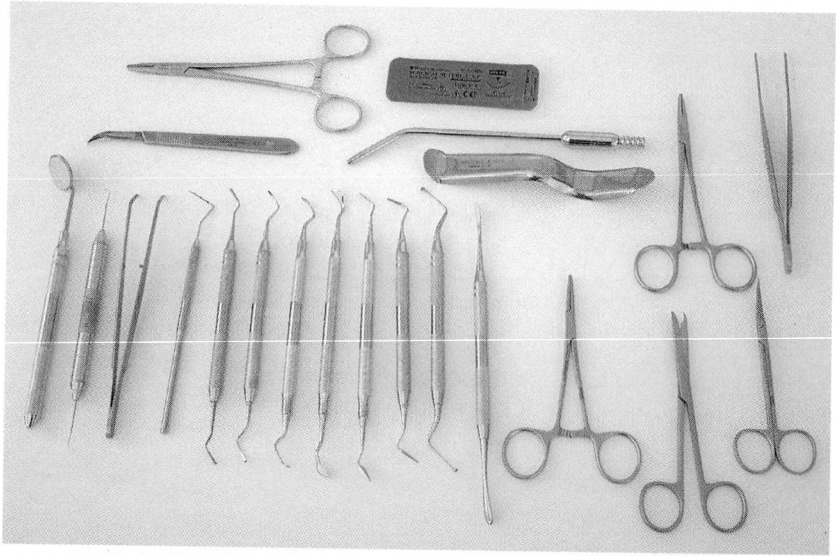

Periodontal Surgical Procedure

TOP ROW (FROM LEFT TO RIGHT)

Needle holder, sutures, scalpel with # 12 blade surgical aspirating tip, check and tongue retractor (Minnesota), hemostat, tissue forceps

BOTTOM ROW (FROM LEFT TO RIGHT)

Mouth mirror, explorer, cotton forceps (pliers), periodontal probe, mesial/distal periodontal hoe, buccal/lingual periodontal hoe, surgical curette, kidney-shape periodontal knife, interproximal knife, bone file, surgical curette (Molt), periosteal elevator, hemostat, suture scissors, tissue scissors.

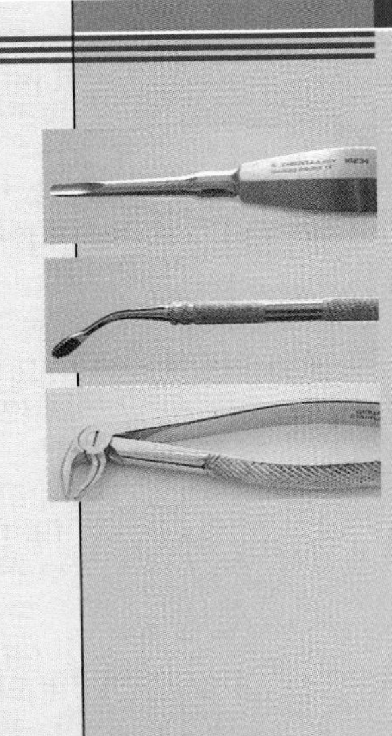

CHAPTER 16

Oral Surgery Instruments

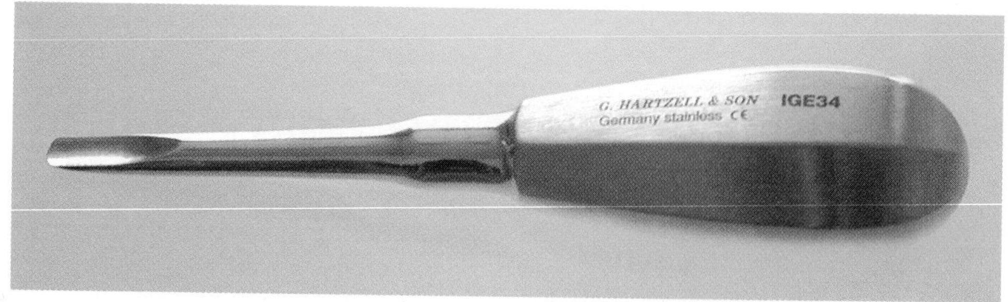
G. HARTZELL & SON IGE34
Germany stainless CE

INSTRUMENT

Straight Elevator

FUNCTION

To loosen tooth from periodontal ligaments before extraction
To separate and lift tooth from socket

CHARACTERISTICS

Single ended
Range of sizes available

Ours is thinner handle

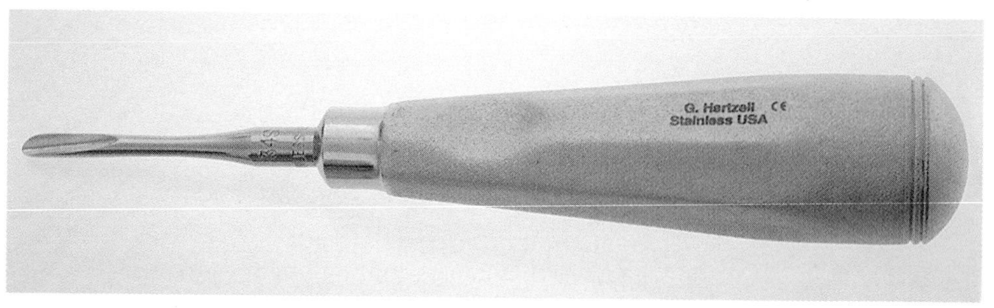

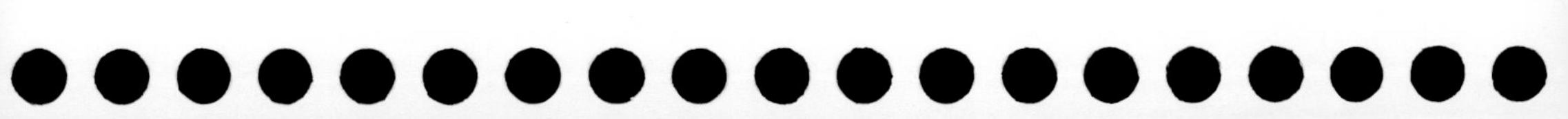

Luxating Elevator

FUNCTION

To cut periodontal ligaments before extraction
To rock tooth back and forth before extraction

CHARACTERISTICS

Single ended
Sharp blade on working end
Range of sizes available

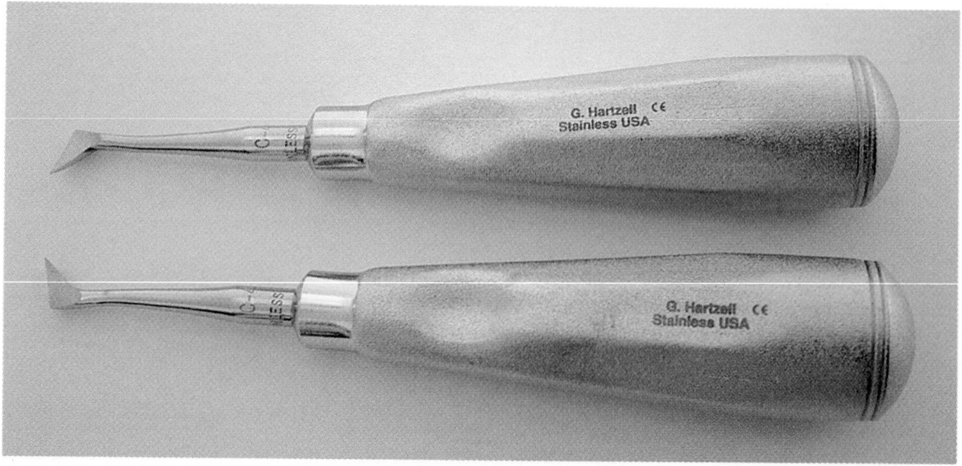
G. Hartzell
Stainless USA
G. Hartzell
Stainless USA

Root Elevators

FUNCTION

To loosen root
To separate and lift root from socket
To use on posterior teeth

CHARACTERISTICS

Single ended
Right and left pairs
Range of sizes available
Example: Commonly used type: Cryer

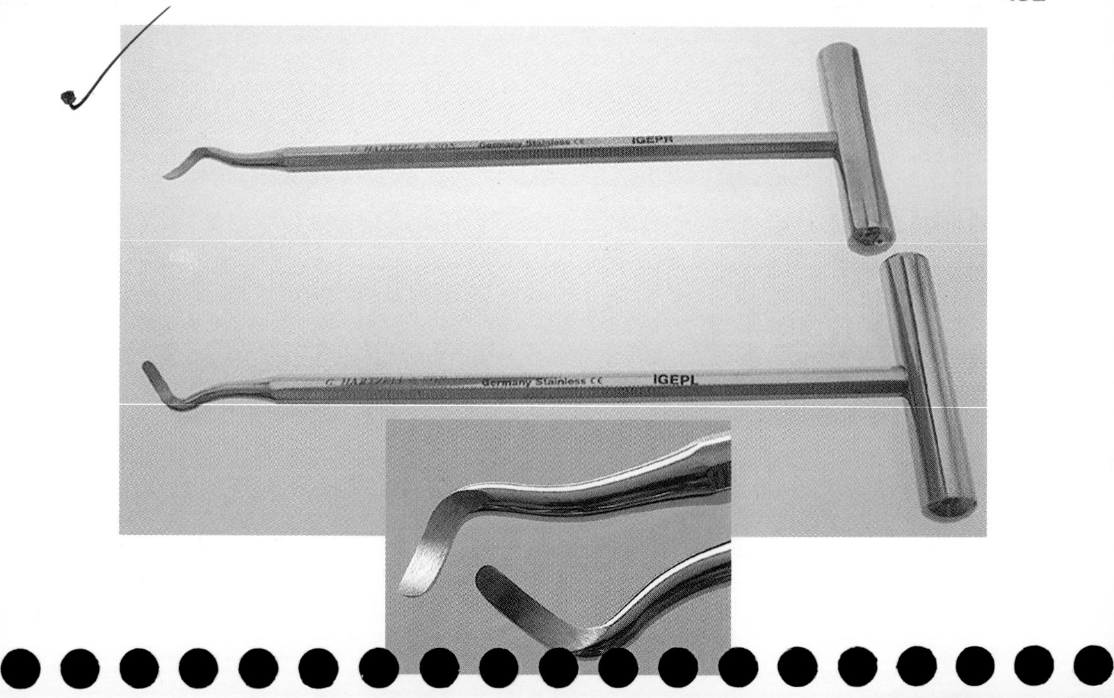
Germany Stainless CE
IGEPR
Germany Stainless CE
IGEPL

T-Bar Elevators

FUNCTION

To loosen tooth from periodontal ligaments before extraction
To separate tooth from alveolus
To use on posterior teeth

CHARACTERISTICS

Single ended
Rounded or pointed
Right or left pairs
Range of sizes available

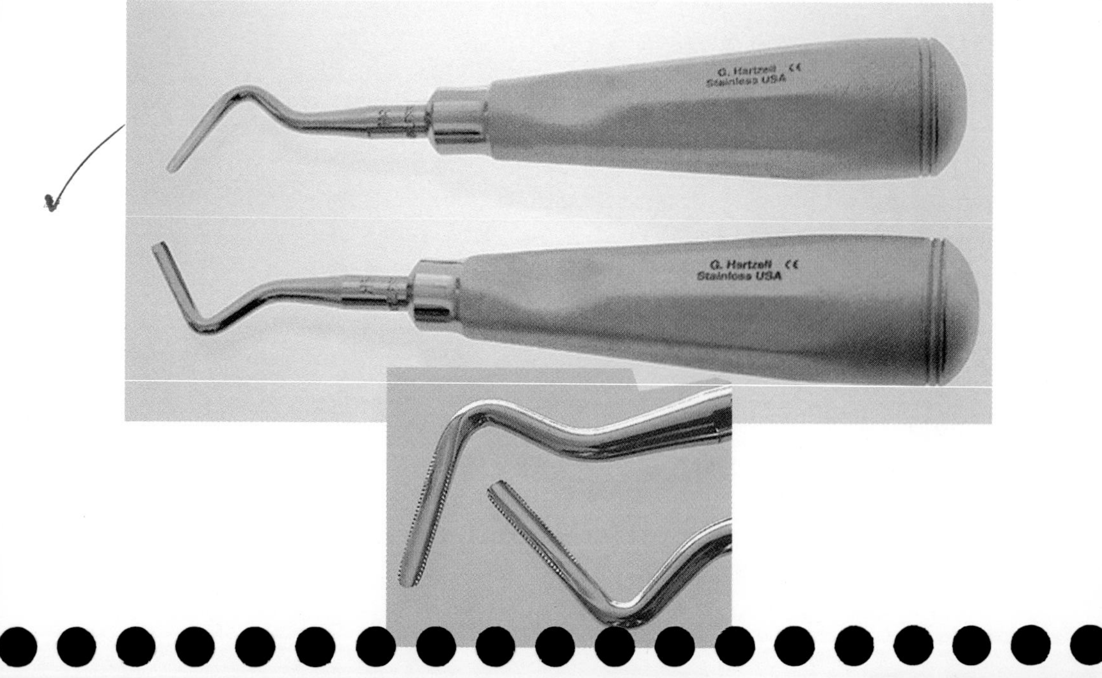

G. Hartzell CE
Stainless USA
G. Hartzell CE
Stainless USA

Root-Tip Elevators

FUNCTION To lift and remove fragments of root

CHARACTERISTICS
Single ended
Rounded or pointed
Straight or right-and-left pairs

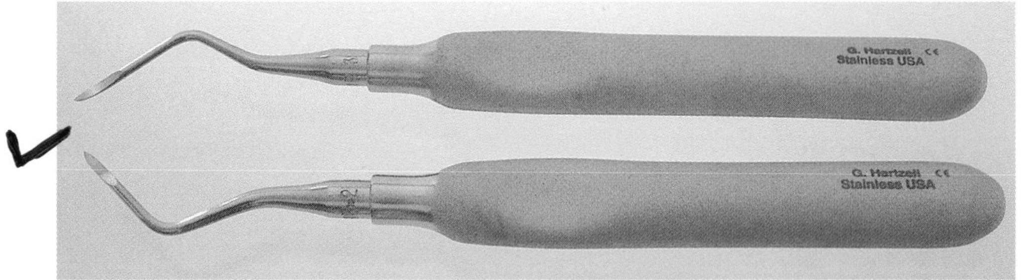
G. Hartzell
Stainless USA
G. Hartzell
Stainless USA

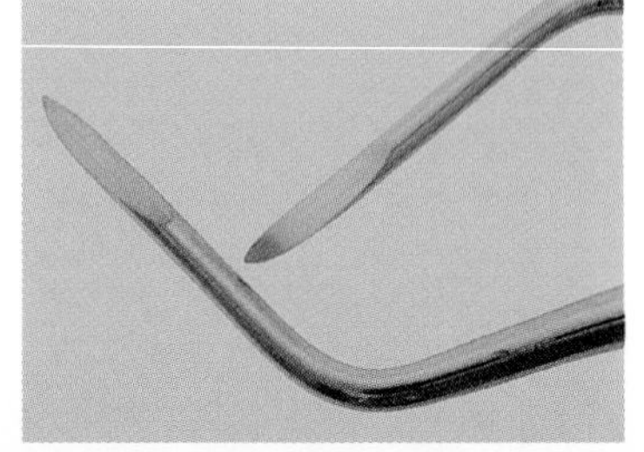

INSTRUMENT

Root-Tip Picks

FUNCTION To lift and remove small root tips in difficult areas

CHARACTERISTICS Pointed at working end
Straight or right-and-left pairs

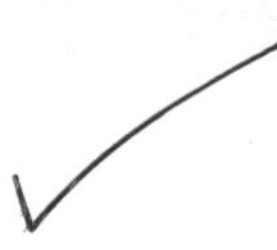

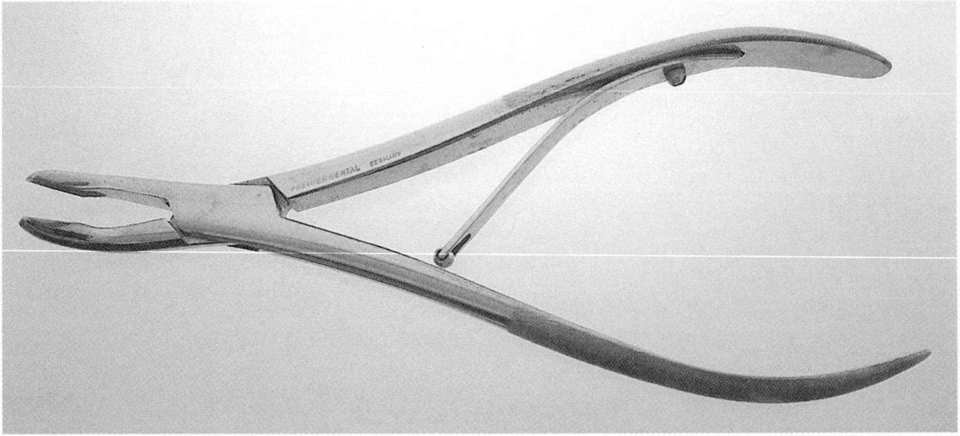

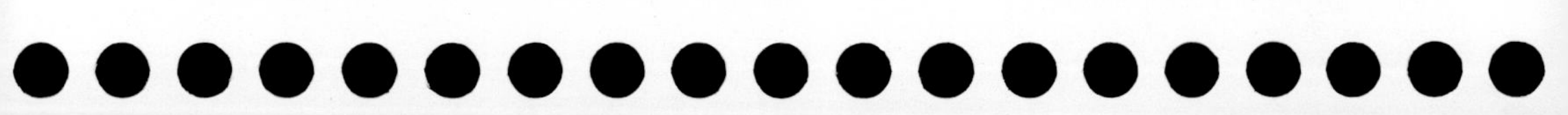

INSTRUMENT

Rongeur

FUNCTION To trim and remove excess alveolar bone after extraction of teeth
To contour alveolar bone after multiple extractions

CHARACTERISTICS Variety of sizes and angles

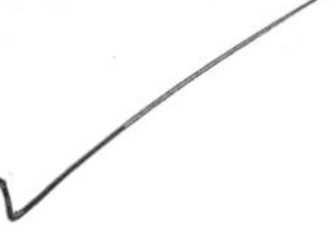

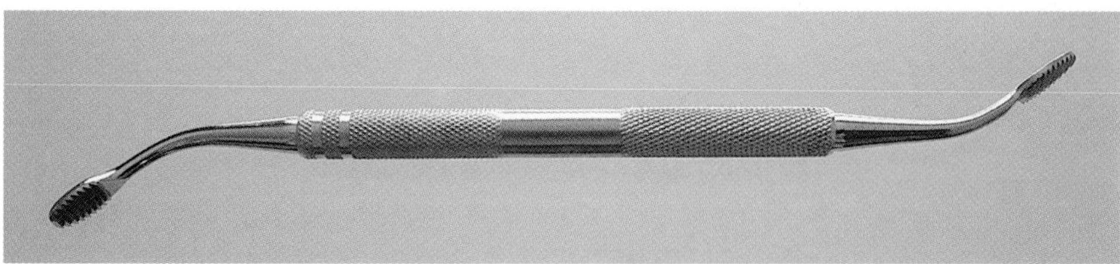

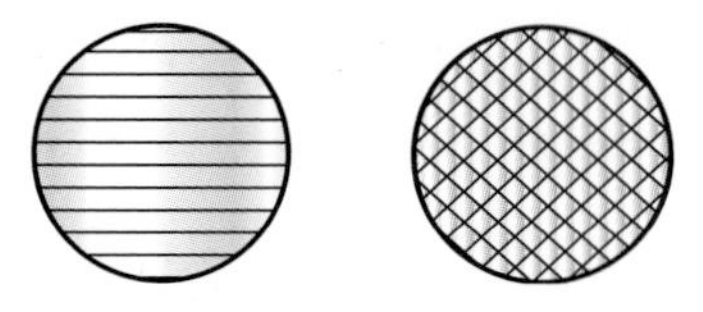

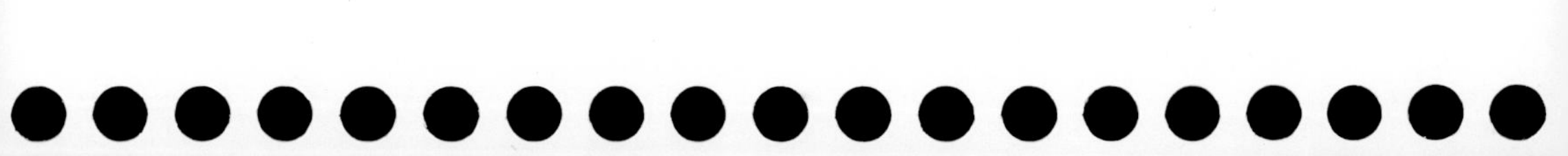

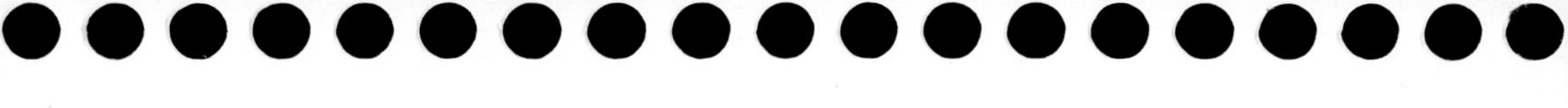

INSTRUMENT

Bone File

FUNCTION To remove or smooth rough edges of alveolar bone

CHARACTERISTICS Used with push-pull motion
Straight-cut or crosscut cutting end
Variety of sizes, angles, and shapes

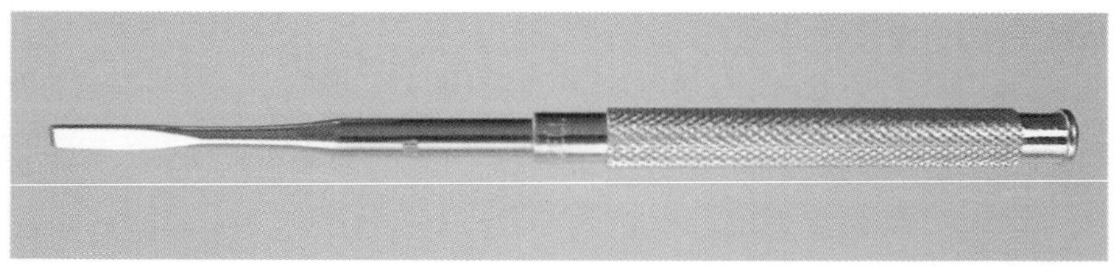

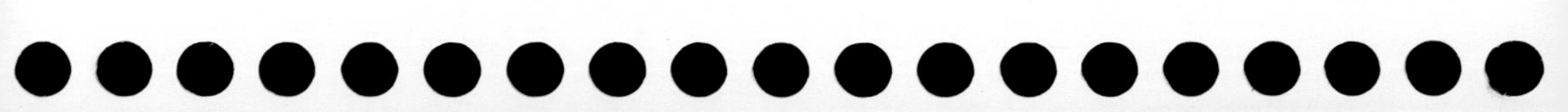

INSTRUMENT

Surgical Chisel

FUNCTION

To split or section a tooth for easier removal by tapping on chisel with mallet
To reshape or contour alveolar bone

CHARACTERISTICS

Single-bevel chisel—For contouring or removing alveolar bone
Bibevel chisel—For splitting teeth
Styles—Surgical chisels, bone splitter
Range of sizes available

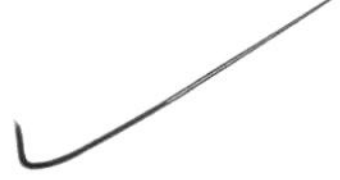

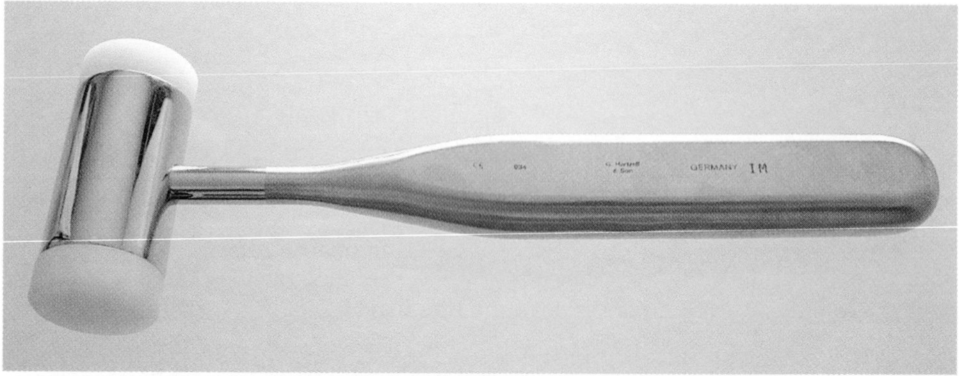

INSTRUMENT

Surgical Mallet

FUNCTION To use with bone chisel to section tooth for easier removal by tapping on chisel with surgical mallet

To use with bone chisel to reshape or contour alveolar bone

CHARACTERISTICS Range of sizes available

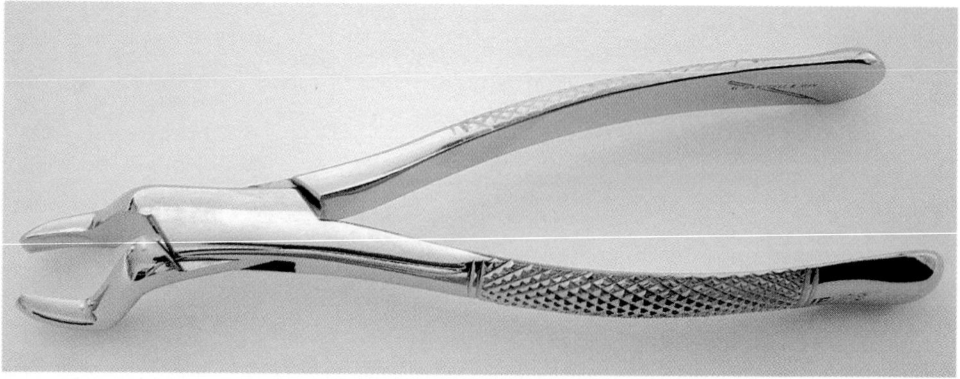

INSTRUMENT

Universal Maxillary Forceps No. 10S

FUNCTION To extract maxillary molars

CHARACTERISTICS Straight handle

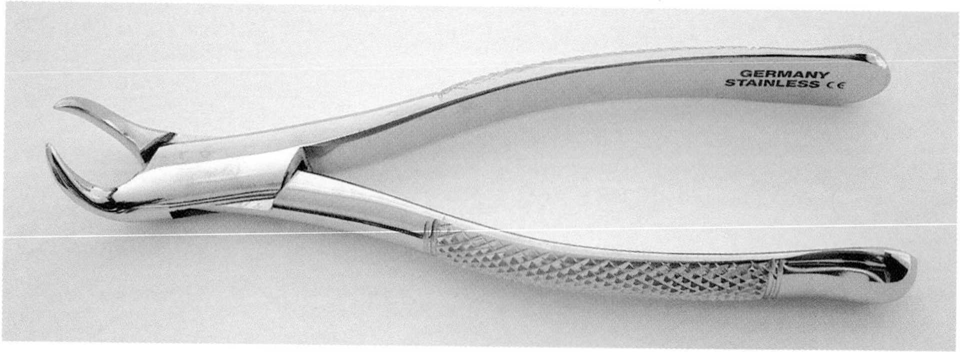

INSTRUMENT

Universal Mandibular Forceps No. 16

FUNCTION To extract mandibular first and second molars

CHARACTERISTICS Straight handles or one curved handle
Referred to as cowhorn forceps

470

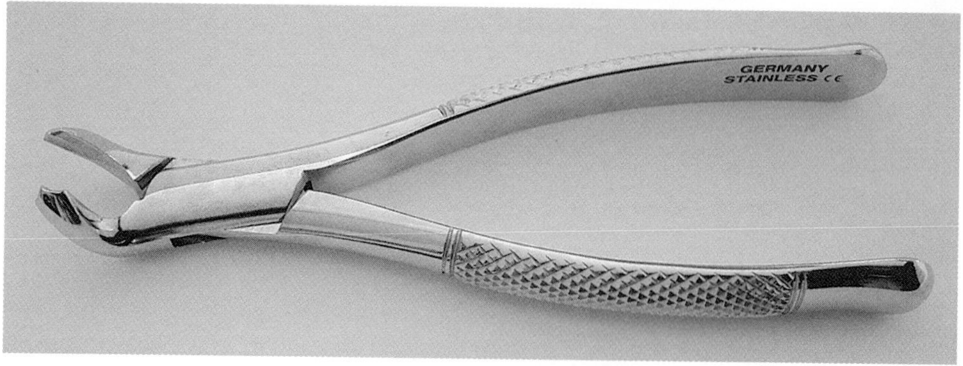

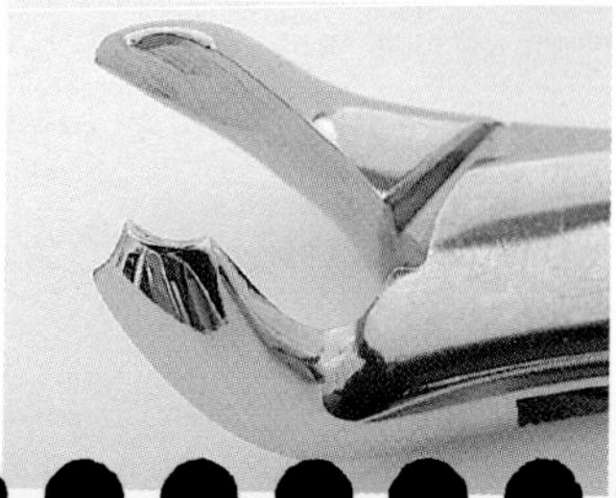

INSTRUMENT

Mandibular Forceps No. 17

FUNCTION To extract bifurcated mandibular right first or second molars

CHARACTERISTICS Straight handles

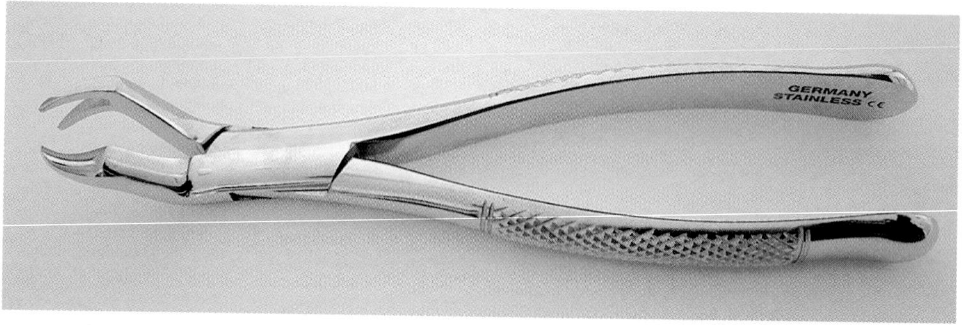

INSTRUMENT

Maxillary Right Forceps No. 88R

FUNCTION To extract trifurcated maxillary right first or second molars

CHARACTERISTICS Right-split beak—For engaging lingual root

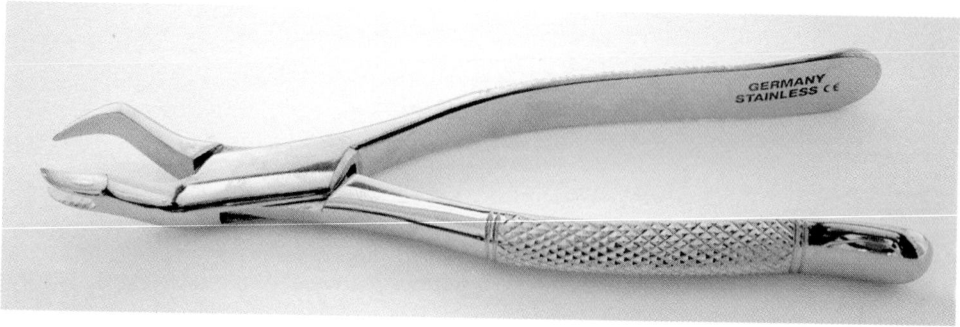

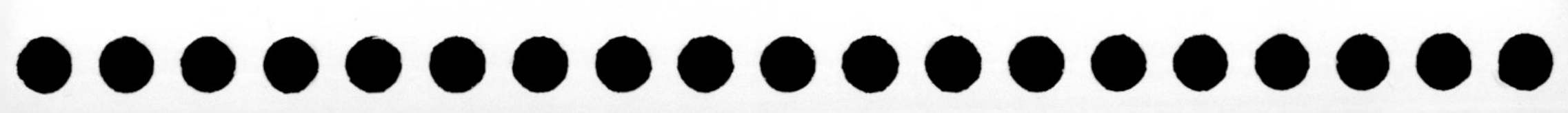

INSTRUMENT

Maxillary Left Forceps No. 88L

FUNCTION To extract trifurcated maxillary left first or second molars

CHARACTERISTICS Left-split beak—For engaging lingual root

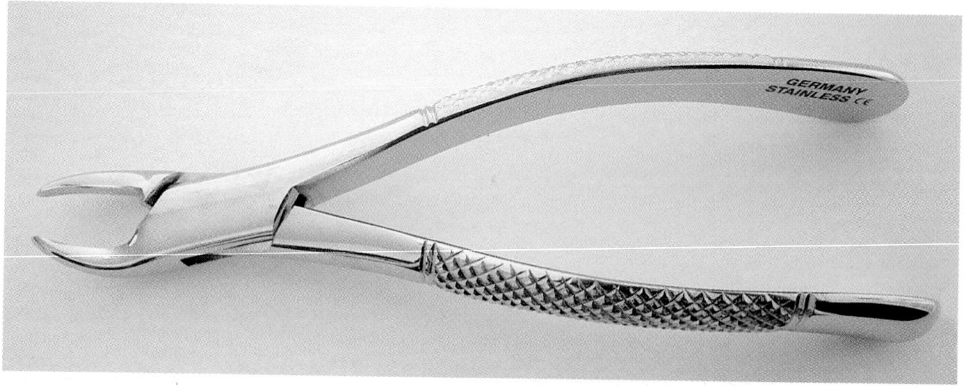

Maxillary Universal Forceps—Cryer 150

FUNCTION To extract maxillary centrals, laterals, cuspids, premolars, and roots

CHARACTERISTICS Straight handles or one curved handle

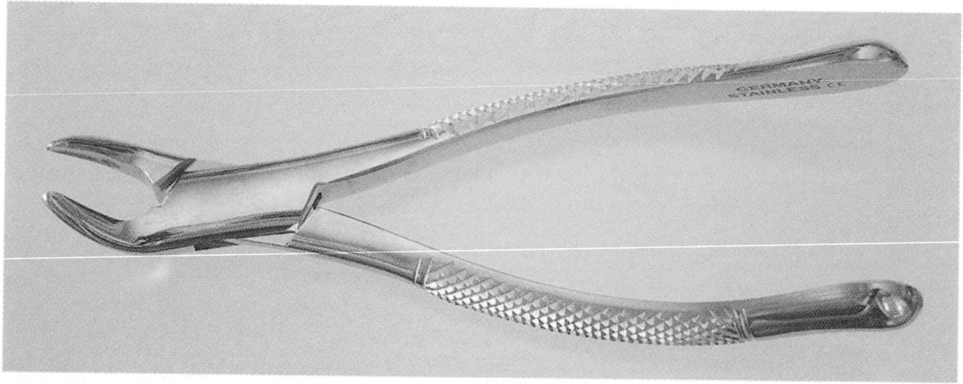

Mandibular Universal Forceps—Cryer 151

FUNCTION To extract mandibular centrals, laterals, cuspids, premolars, and roots

CHARACTERISTICS Straight handles or one curved handle

480

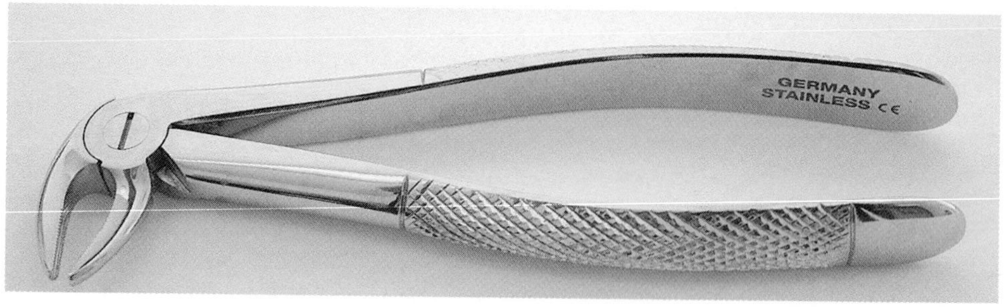

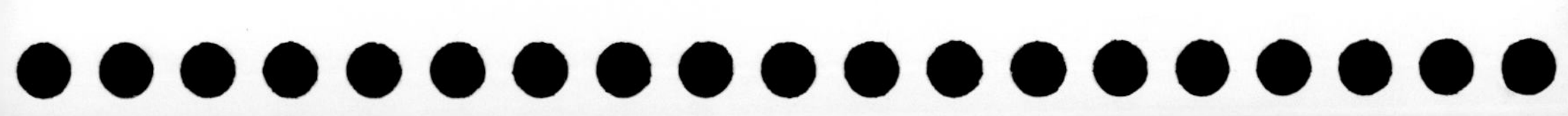

INSTRUMENT

Mandibular Anterior Forceps

FUNCTION To extract mandibular anterior teeth

CHARACTERISTICS Serrated beaks

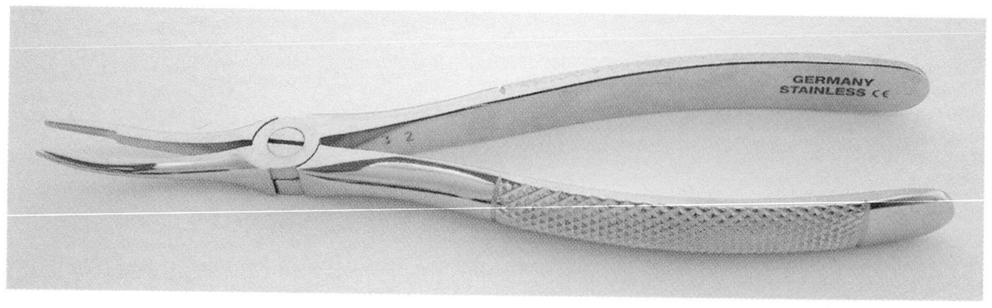
GERMANY
STAINLESS CE
1 2

INSTRUMENT

Maxillary Root Forceps

FUNCTION To extract maxillary roots

CHARACTERISTICS Narrow, serrated beaks
Straight handles

484

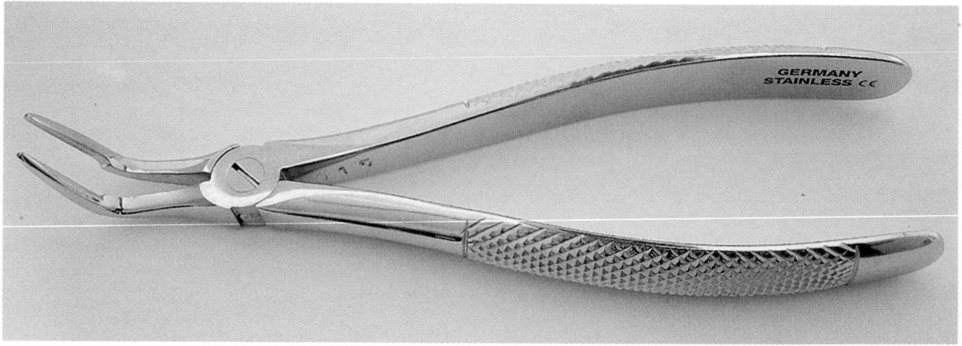

INSTRUMENT

Mandibular Root Forceps

FUNCTION To extract mandibular roots

CHARACTERISTICS Narrow, serrated beaks
Straight handles

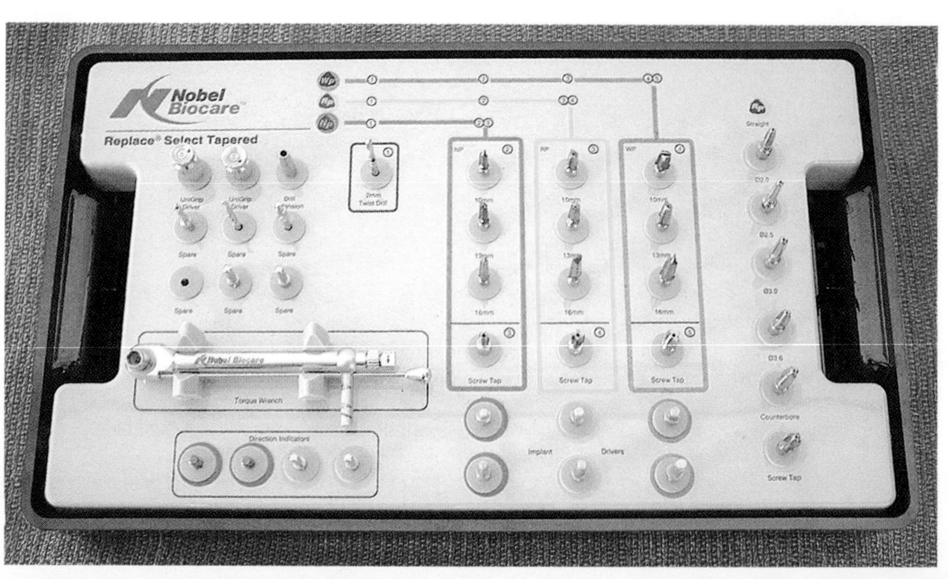
Nobel Biocare
Replace® Select Tapered
2mm Twist Drill
NP
RP
WP
10mm
13mm
16mm
Screw Tap
Spare
Torque Wrench
Direction Indicators
Implant
Drivers
Straight
Counterbore
Screw Tap

INSTRUMENT

Implant System

FUNCTION To use for implant surgery

CHARACTERISTICS Components—Depth drills, thread formers, hand wrench, ratchet, ratchet adapter, hex driver

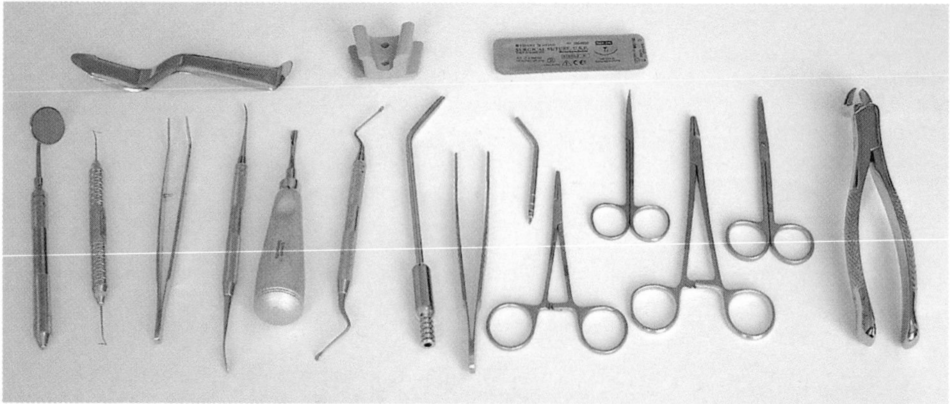

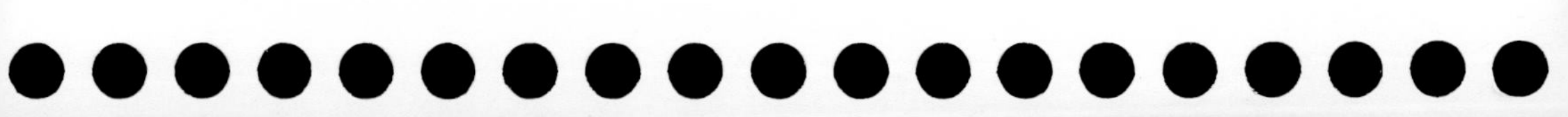

Extraction of Maxillary Right First Molar

TOP ROW

Tongue and cheek retractor (Minnesota), mouth prop, sutures

BOTTOM ROW (FROM LEFT TO RIGHT)

Mouth mirror, explorer, cotton forceps periosteal elevator, straight elevator, surgical curette tip, surgical aspirator tip, tissue forceps, A/W syringe tip, hemostat, tissue scissors, needle holder, suture scissors, and maxillary forceps No. 10S

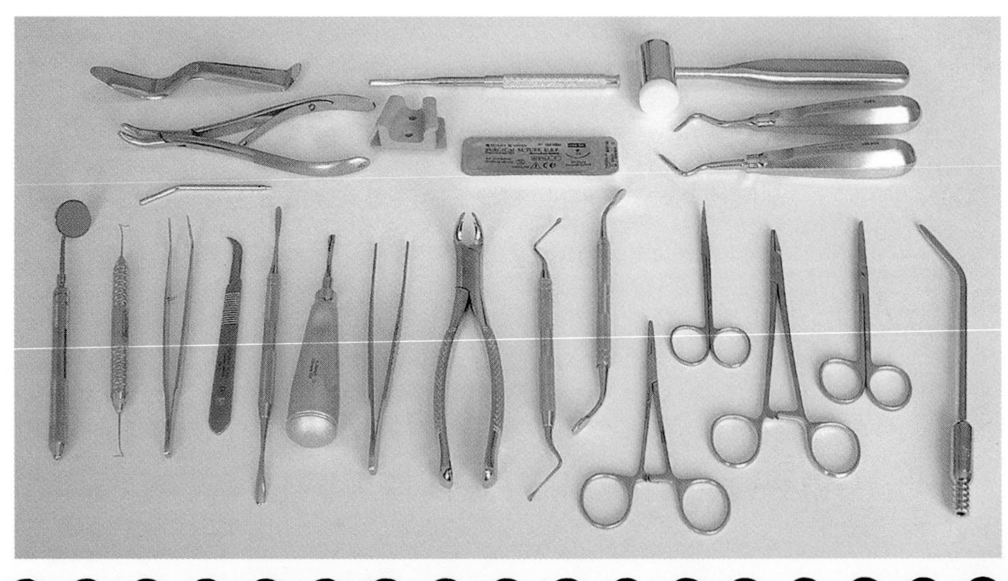

Extraction of Impacted Mandibular Molar

TOP ROW LEFT TO RIGHT

Tongue and cheek retractor (Minnesota), Rongeurs, air/water syringe tip, mouth prop, surgical chisel, sutures, surgical mallet, root elevators

BOTTOM ROW (FROM LEFT TO RIGHT)

Mouth mirror, explorer, cotton forceps (pliers), scalpel with # 12 blade, periosteal elevator, straight elevator, tissue forceps, surgical forceps # 16 (cowhorn forceps), surgical curette, bone file, hemostat, tissue scissors, needle holder, suture scissors, surgical aspirator tip

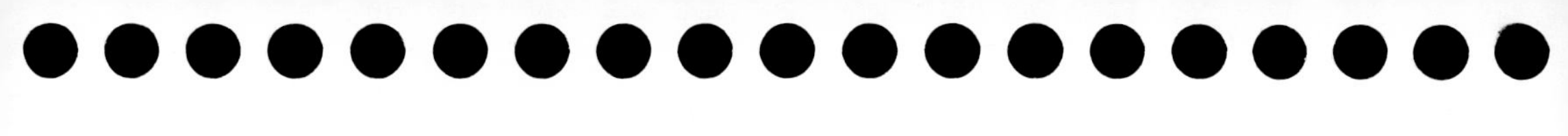

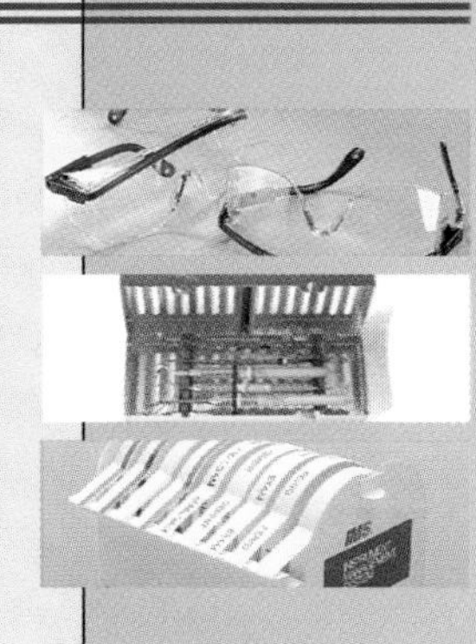

CHAPTER 17

Sterilization Equipment

INSTRUMENT

Laboratory Coat

FUNCTION To protect clothing or surgical scrubs during sterilization process

CHARACTERISTICS Disposable or cloth (cloth gown must be made of polyester and cotton in accordance with state and federal regulations)
Cuffed long sleeves
Closure at neckline
Moisture resistant (against contamination by liquids)

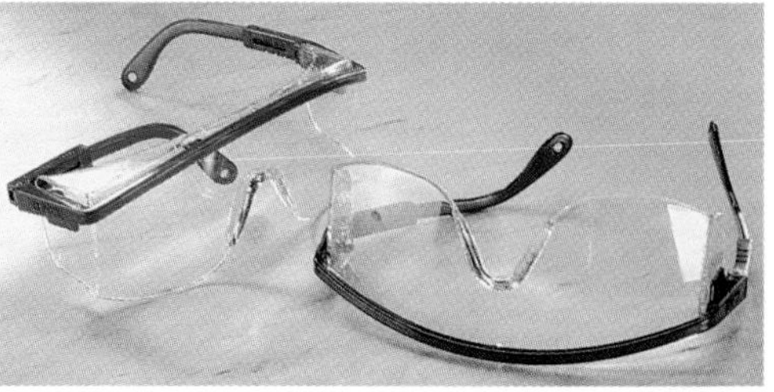

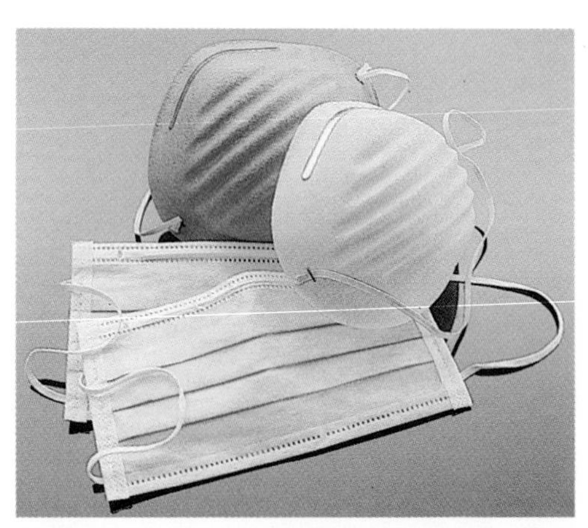

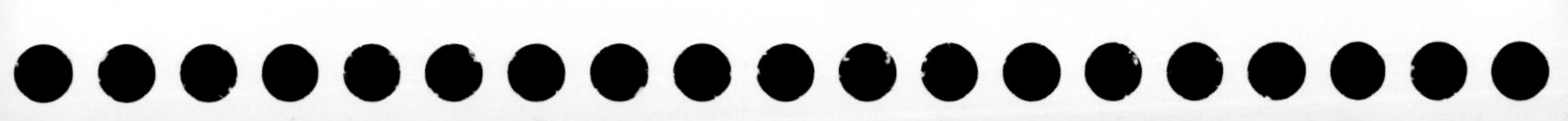

Protective Glasses (Eye Wear) and Protective Mask

FUNCTION To protect against chemicals, airborne pathogens, bacteria, and viruses during processing of instruments for sterilization

To protect against airborne pathogens, bacteria, and viruses during patient care and against scrap filling material during restorative and rinsing phases of patient treatment

CHARACTERISTICS Glasses:

- Extend to sides, top, and bottom of eyes for complete protection
- Variety of styles available (some styles are larger to fit over prescription glasses)
- Facial shields available for eye protection (mask must be worn)

Protective Glasses (Eye Wear) and Protective Mask (continued)

CHARACTERISTICS **(continued)**

Masks:

- Dome shaped or flat

PRACTICE NOTES

1. Glasses are disinfected between patients.
2. A new mask is used with each patient.

500

Nitrile Utility Gloves

FUNCTION
To protect hands during processing of instruments for sterilization procedures
To wear during treatment room disinfection
To wear for preparation and handling of chemicals

CHARACTERISTICS
Chemical resistant
Puncture resistant
Ribbed for nonslip grip
Sterilize according to manufacturer's recommendation
Range of sizes

PRACTICE NOTE

1. Gloves are disinfected after each use.

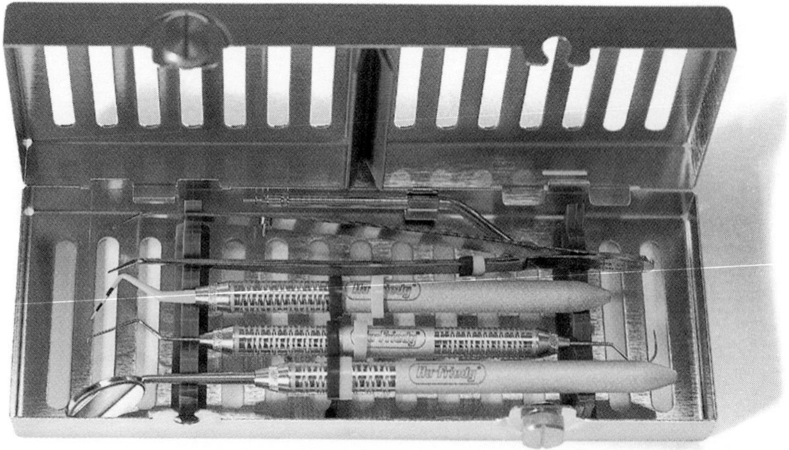

502

INSTRUMENT

Cassette

FUNCTION

To use for instruments as tray setup
To use for instrument sterilization

CHARACTERISTICS

Available in metal or resin
Color coded—To aid identification of tray setups
Range of sizes

PRACTICE NOTE

1. Instruments in the cassette may be cleaned in an ultrasonic cleaner and then wrapped and sterilized.

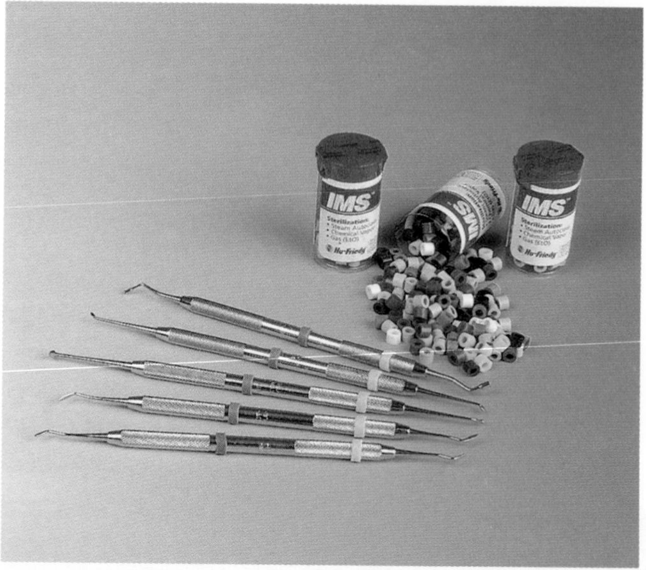
IMS
Sterilization:
Hu-Friedy
IMS
Sterilization:
Hu-Friedy

INSTRUMENT

Color Coding System for Instruments

FUNCTION To color code instruments for organization and identification of tray setups

CHARACTERISTICS Autoclavable
Variety of colors—Color coding coordinates with color cassettes

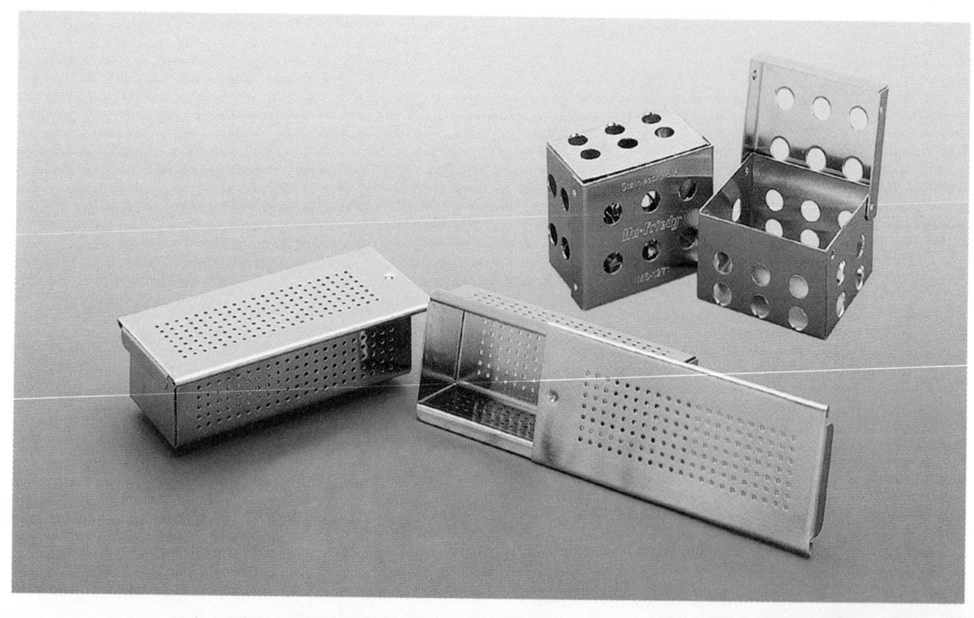

INSTRUMENT

Parts Box for Sterilization

FUNCTION To use for sterilization of small items (e.g., burs, dental dam clamps)

CHARACTERISTICS Range of sizes

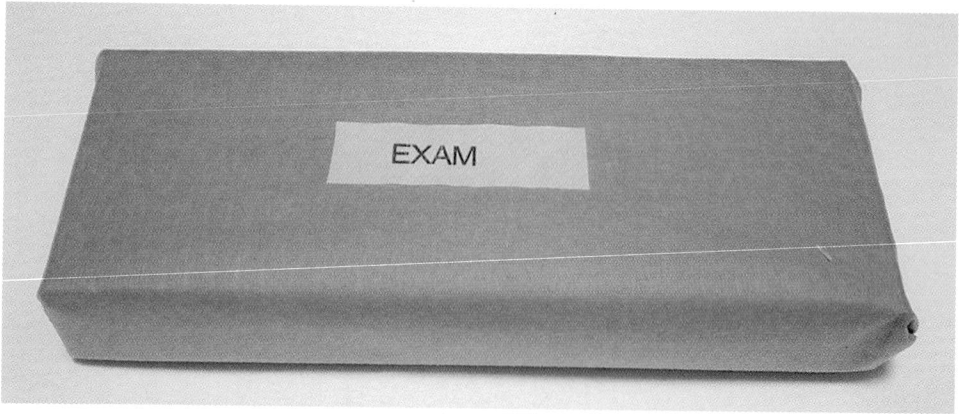

EXAM

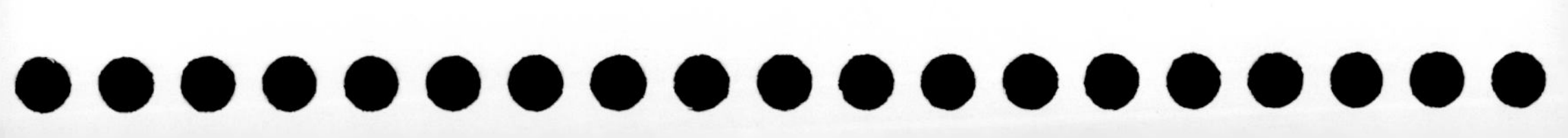

Cassette Wrap

FUNCTION

To use to wrap cassette during sterilization
To use to store cassette after sterilization
To use for tray cover during dental procedure

CHARACTERISTICS

Range of sizes—To accommodate cassettes

PRACTICE NOTE

1. Cassettes should be kept in sterile wrap until the procedure is ready to start.

STERILIZED
FOR YOUR
PROTECTION
By:
Date:

Sterilization Pouches

FUNCTION To be used for sterilization of instruments

CHARACTERISTICS Indicator strips (on outside of pouch)—Turn colors to verify sterilization
Range of sizes

PRACTICE NOTE

1. Instruments should be left in the pouches until the procedure is ready to begin.

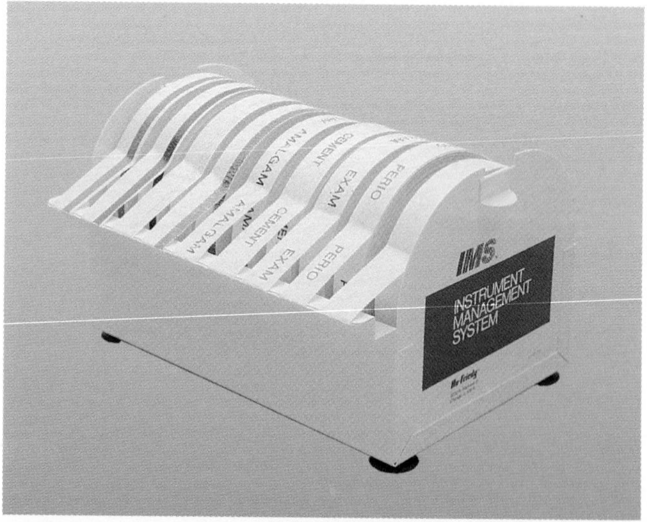

Process Monitor Tape and Dispensing Unit

FUNCTION

To secure wrap on outside of cassette

To use outside cassettes to indicate exposure of instruments to a certain temperature (by color change in strips on tape)

CHARACTERISTICS

Available in preprinted tray setup procedures

Available with color coding

Available blank for labeling tape with procedure and/or instrument content

PRACTICE NOTE

1. When monitor tape is placed outside a cassette, the strips change color with exposure to temperature.

BD Sharps Collector
BIOHAZARD
WARNING
PELIGRO

Sharps Container

FUNCTION To serve as storage receptacle for used needles, scalpel blades, orthodontic wires, endodontic files, and all other disposable sharp items used intraorally

CHARACTERISTICS Must be a puncture resistant
Must be labeled "Biohazard"
Must have a reclosable top

PRACTICE NOTE

1. Sharps containers must be disposed of according to state and federal regulations.

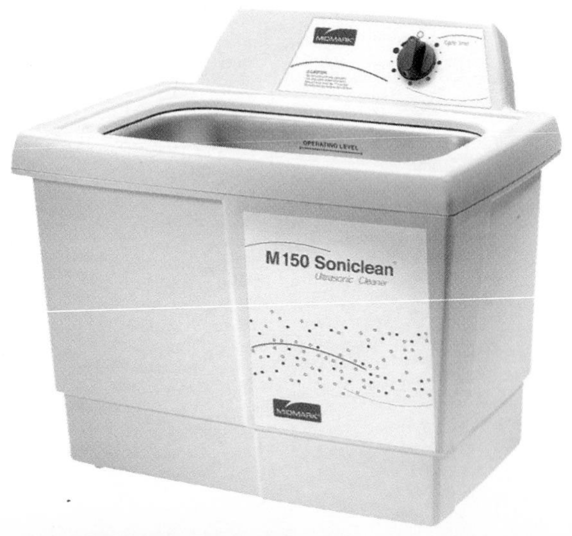
MIDMARK
M150 Soniclean
Ultrasonic Cleaner
OPERATING LEVEL
MIDMARK

Ultrasonic Cleaning Unit

FUNCTION To remove debris and bioburden from instruments

CHARACTERISTICS Reduces risk of exposure to pathogens during sterilization process

PRACTICE NOTES

1. Tank is filled with antimicrobial or general all-purpose solution especially designed for the ultrasonic unit.
2. Debris is removed by mechanical means; sound waves create tiny bubbles that cause inward collapse (implosion) and removal of material.

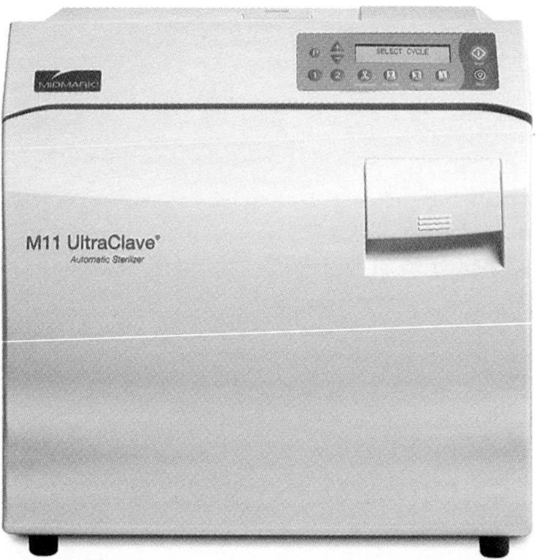
MIDMARK
SELECT CYCLE
M11 UltraClave®
Automatic Sterilizer

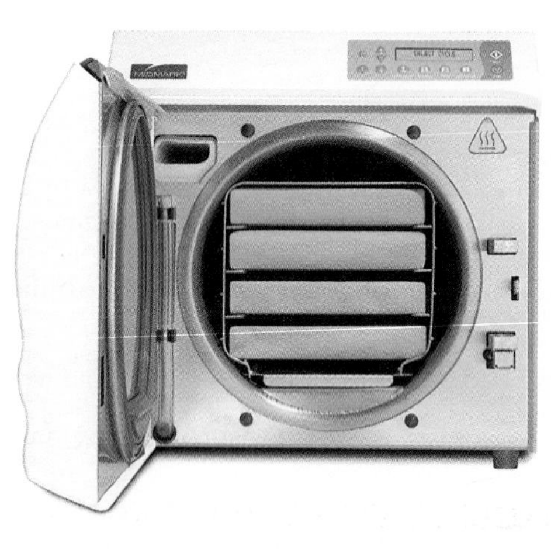
MIDMARK
SELECT CYCLE

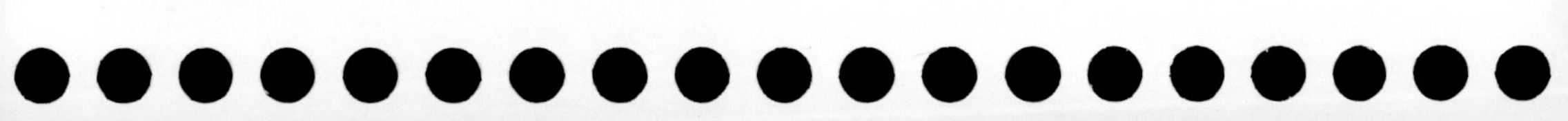

Sterilizer—Autoclave (Saturated Steam)

FUNCTION To kill all microbes, viruses, bacteria, and fungi, thereby sterilizing instruments

CHARACTERISTICS Uses steam under pressure—15 pounds per square inch (psi) at 250° F for 20 minutes
Shelves available for cassettes
Various styles and manufacturers
Range of sizes

STATIM

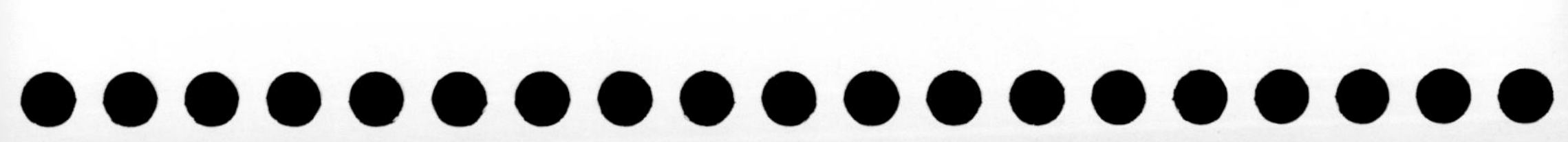

Sterilizer–Autoclave ("Flash")*

FUNCTION

To kill all microbes, viruses, bacteria, and fungi, thereby sterilizing instruments

To use for quick sterilization of instruments and handpieces

CHARACTERISTICS

Unwrapped instruments:

- Steam under pressure—15 psi at 270° F for 3 minutes

Wrapped instruments

- Steam under pressure—15 psi at 250° F for 15 minutes *or* 15 psi at 270° F for 11 minutes

Shelves available for cassettes

Various styles and manufacturers

Range of sizes

*This method is not recommended for use as a routine sterilization procedure.

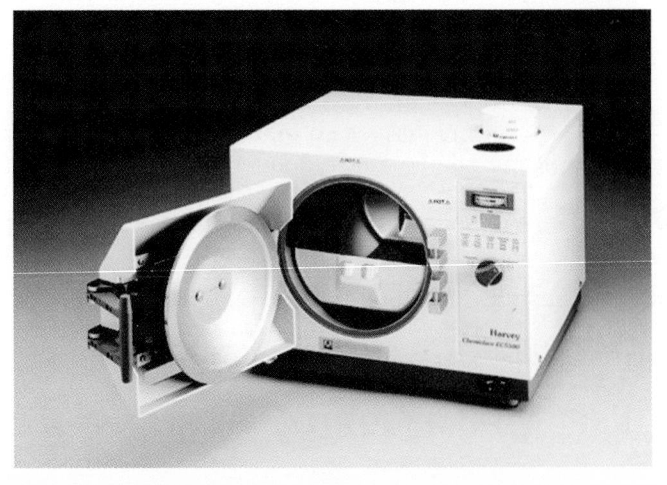
Harvey

Sterilizer—Chemiclave (Unsaturated Chemical Vapor)

FUNCTION To kill all microbes, viruses, bacteria, and fungi, thereby sterilizing instruments

CHARACTERISTICS Uses chemical solution (alcohol, 0.23% formaldehyde, ketone, acetone, water) in a pressurized chamber—20 to 40 psi at 270° F for 20 minutes
Shelves available for cassette
Various styles and manufacturers
Range of sizes

PRACTICE NOTE

1. State and local agencies require proper hazardous waste disposal. A Material Safety Data Sheet (MSDS) is required for the solution.

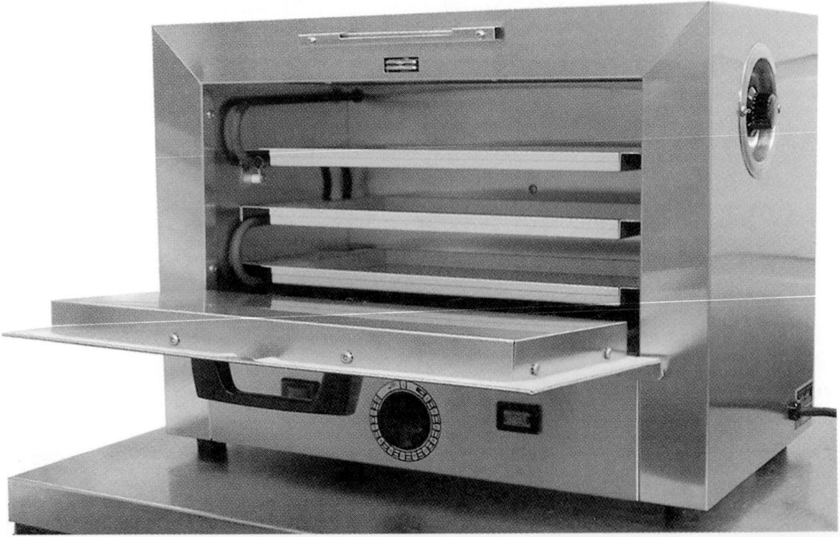

Sterilizer—Dry Heat (Static Air)

FUNCTION To kill all microbes, viruses, bacteria, and fungi, thereby sterilizing instruments

CHARACTERISTICS Oven-type sterilizer
320° F for 60 to 120 minutes
Shelves available for cassettes
Various styles and manufacturers
Range of sizes

PRACTICE NOTES

1. Packaging/wrapped material must be able to withstand high temperatures.
2. Door cannot be opened during sterilization cycle.
3. Items cannot be layered or stacked, but should be placed on their edges.

526

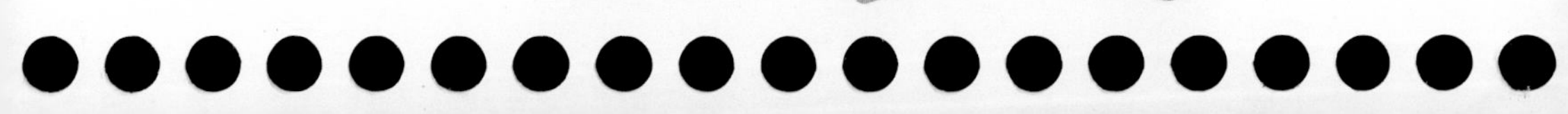

INSTRUMENT

Sterilizer—Dry Heat (Rapid Heat Transfer)

FUNCTION To kill all microbes, viruses, bacteria, and fungi, thereby sterilizing instruments.

CHARACTERISTICS Forced air type sterilizer
375° F for 12 minutes (wrapped)
375° F for 6 minutes (unwrapped)
Instruments placed in preheated chamber
Various styles and manufacturers
Range of sizes

PRACTICE NOTES

1. Packaging/wrapped material must be able to withstand high temperatures.
2. Door cannot be opened during sterilization cycle.

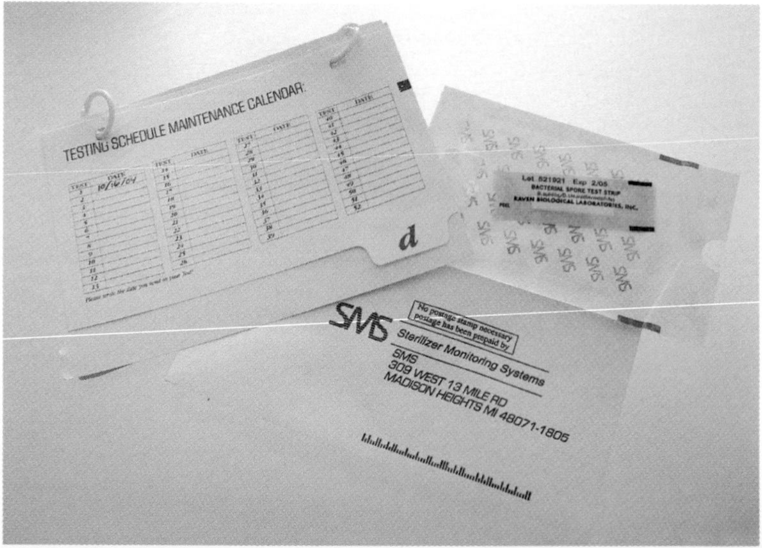
TESTING SCHEDULE MAINTENANCE CALENDAR:
d
Lot 521921 Exp 2/05
BACTERIAL SPORE TEST STRIP
RAVEN BIOLOGICAL LABORATORIES, INC.
SMS
No postage stamp necessary postage has been prepaid by
Sterilizer Monitoring Systems
SMS
309 WEST 13 MILE RD
MADISON HEIGHTS MI 48071-1805

Biological Monitors for Sterilizers

FUNCTION To confirm efficacy of sterilization, with documentation of results in office sterilization log

CHARACTERISTICS The device is placed in the sterilizer for one cycle of instruments. It is then mailed to the manufacturer, which mails back the findings. The results are logged in the office sterilization records.

PRACTICE NOTE

1. The Centers for Disease Control and Prevention (CDC), the American Dental Association (ADA), and the Office Safety and Asepsis Procedures Research Foundation (OSAP) recommend at least weekly testing of sterilizers. State requirements may be different.

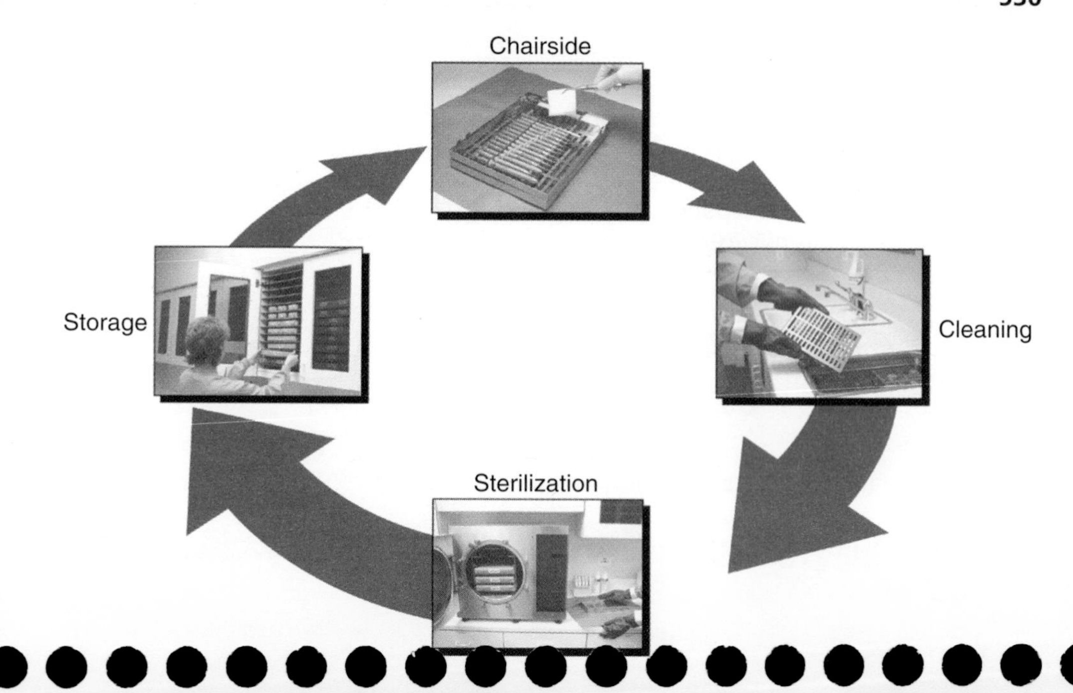
Chairside
Cleaning
Sterilization
Storage

Sterilization Management System

CHAIRSIDE Cassette with instruments used as a tray setup

CLEANING Nitrile utility gloves used to remove cassette from ultrasonic cleaning unit

STERILIZATION Wrapping of cassettes in preparation for sterilization

STORAGE Sterilized, wrapped cassette placed in storage

PRACTICE NOTES

1. Packaging/wrapped material must be able to withstand high temperatures.
2. Door cannot be opened during sterilization cycle.
3. Items cannot be layered or stacked but should be placed on their edges.

Index

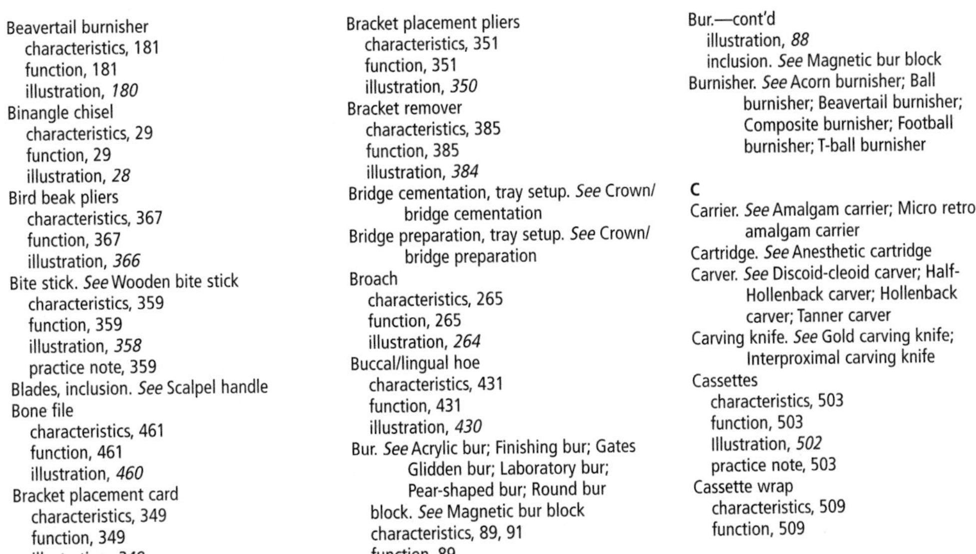

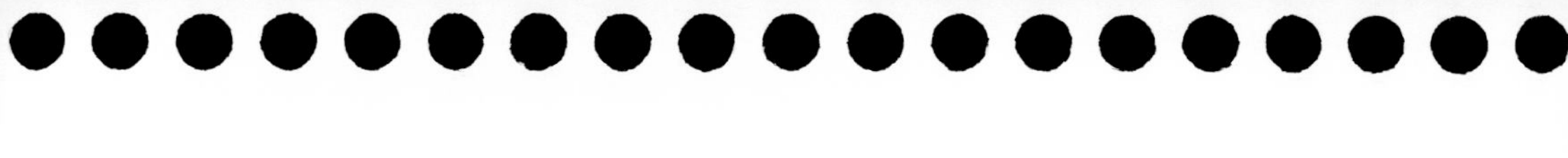

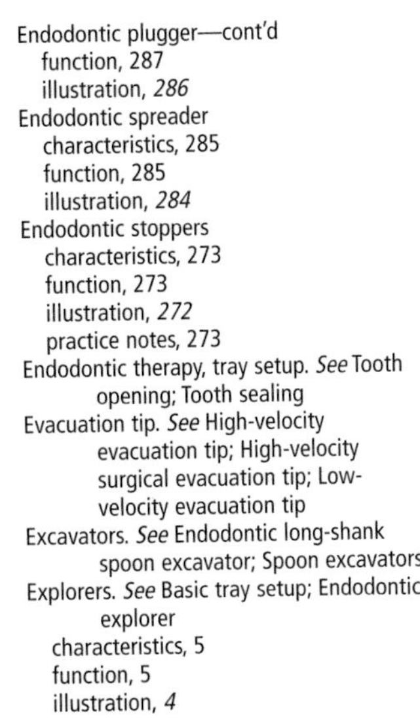

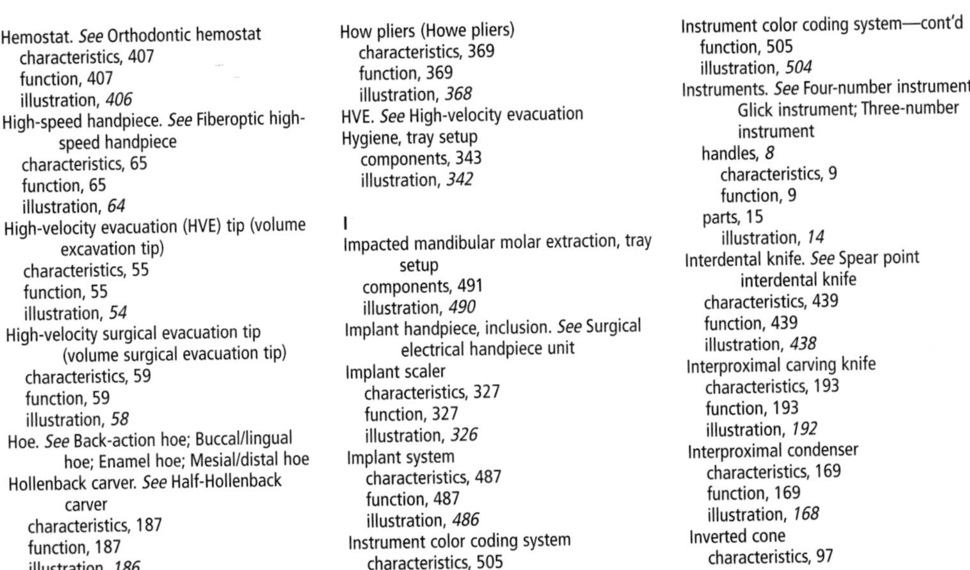

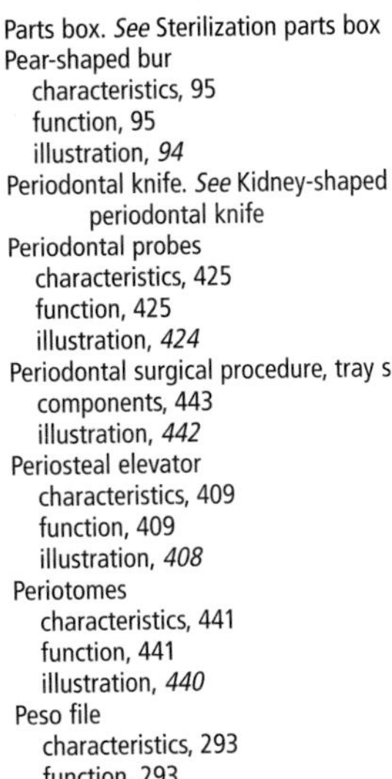

R

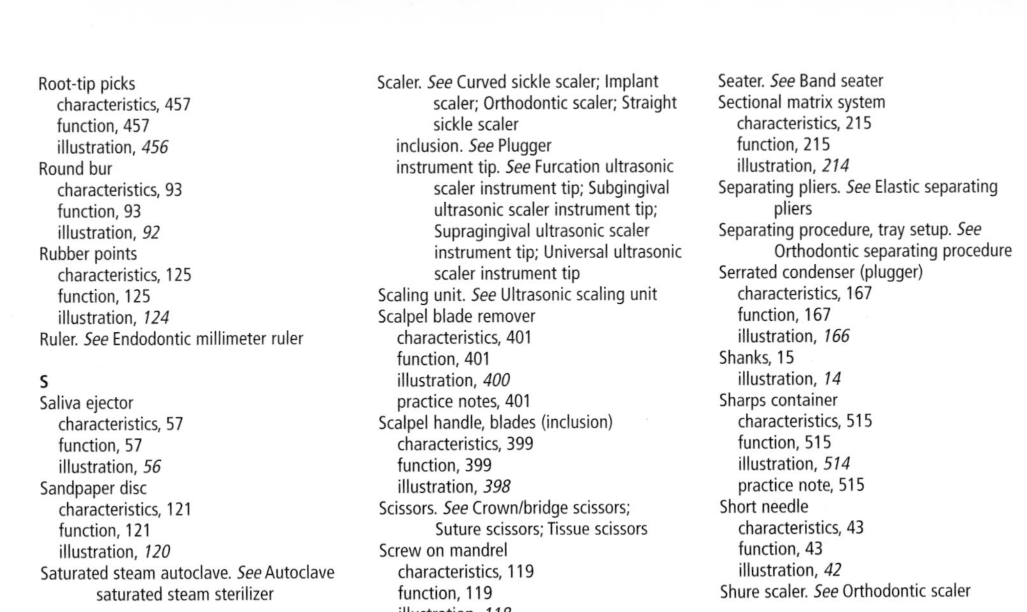

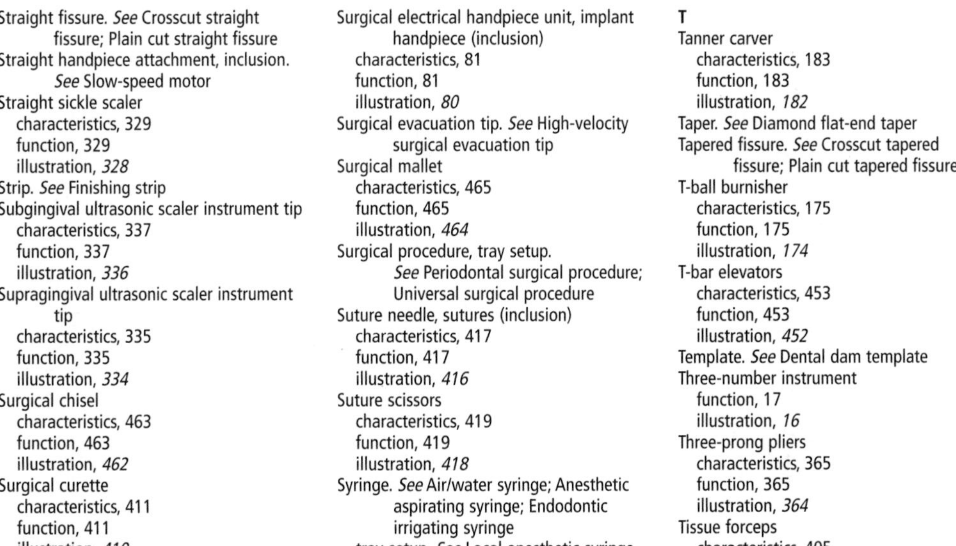